NEW MALADIES *of the* SOUL

EUROPEAN PERSPECTIVES

EUROPEAN PERSPECTIVES

A Series in Social Thought and Cultural Criticism

Lawrence D. Kritzman, Editor

European Perspectives presents English translations of books by leading European thinkers. With both classic and outstanding contemporary works, the series aims to shape the major intellectual controversies of our day and to facilitate the tasks of historical understanding.

NEW MALADIES *of the* SOUL

Julia Kristeva

Translated by Ross Guberman

New York   **COLUMBIA UNIVERSITY PRESS**

Columbia University Press wishes to express its appreciation for assistance given by the government of France through Le Ministère de la Culture in the preparation of this manuscript.

Columbia University Press
New York   Chichester, West Sussex

Copyright © 1995 Columbia University Press
All rights reserved

Les Nouvelles maladies de l'ame
Copyright © 1993 Librairie Artheme Fayard

Library of Congress Cataloging-in-Publication Data

Kristeva, Julia, 1941–
    [Nouvelles maladies de l'ame. English]
    New maladies of the soul / Julia Kristeva ; translated by Ross Mitchell Guberman.
        p.   cm.—(European perspectives)
    Includes bibliographical references and index.
    ISBN 0-231-09982-7
    1. Psychoanalysis and philosophy. 2. Semiotics. I. Title.
II. Series.
B2430.K7543N6813   1995   94-32204
150.19'5—dc20   CIP

Printed in the United States of America

c 10 9 8 7 6 5 4 3 2 1
p 10 9 8 7 6 5 4 3 2

CONTENTS

TRANSLATOR'S NOTE

I have attempted to make this translation as clear and readable as possible. As a result, I have occasionally sacrificed the author's syntactic or stylistic idiosyncrasies for the sake of lucidity and rhetorical ease. I have been obliged, however, to employ the same highly technical psychoanalytic and semiological terminology that the author uses throughout this text. Although this vocabulary should not pose a problem for those who are well versed in contemporary French literary and psychoanalytic theory, it may present an obstacle for other readers who wish to grasp the author's complex arguments but who are distracted by some of these technical concepts.

I would refer the latter group to J. Laplanche and J.-B. Pontalis' *The Language of Psychoanalysis,* Donald Nicholson-Smith, tr. (New York: Norton, 1973), especially the articles on acting out, affect, castration, cathexis (investment), countertransference, disavowal, ego-ideal, fantasy, imaginary, instinct (drive), phallus, primary identification, splitting of the ego, symbolic, and thing-presentation/word-presentation. One term that may be unfamiliar to many readers, but that is of great importance for the present text, is the psychoanalytic notion of *representative.* Laplanche and Pontalis inform us that Freud developed the concept of "representative" most notably in his Metapsychology papers of 1915 and in his theory of repression. They speak of "the notion of a representative—by which [Freud] means a kind of *delegation*—of the soma within the psyche" (p. 364). The articles on affect representative, instinctual (drive) representative, and psychic representative in *The Language of Psychoanalysis* offer more complete information. I would also like to caution readers that when Kristeva uses the word "symbolic," she is often referring less to Lacan's notion of the Imaginary, the Symbolic, and the Real than to her well-known distinction between the semiotic and the symbolic (see the first part of her *Revolution in Poetic Language,* Margaret Waller, tr. [New York: Columbia University Press, 1984]).

With three minor exceptions, I have been faithful to the translations of psychoanalytic terms that are given in the English edition of Laplanche and Pontalis' text. Following Margaret Waller's practice in her translation of *Revolution in Poetic Language,* I have retained the French term "investment" when speaking of cathexis and its compounds. Moreover, in the spirit of modern psychoanalytic theory, I have chosen "drive" over "instinct" and "instinctual." Finally, I have Americanized some British spellings of psychoanalytic terminology.

I have prepared my own translations of all quoted works that do not have published English translations.

I could not have translated this text without the help and encouragement of many people. I had the assistance of several bilingual scholars who aided me through many linguistic twists and turns, including Romain Blondel, Jean-Luc Collard, and Claudine Kahan. For specialized medical and scientific terminology I am indebted to Dr. Jeffrey Arenson. A number of people in the French, English, and Comparative Literature departments at Yale University graciously read portions of the manuscript, pointed out confusing passages, and made many invaluable suggestions. I would especially like to thank Nora Devine, Laura Dickinson, Jessie Hill, Brooke Jewett, Tanya Pollard, Arielle Saiber, Benjamin Simons, and Candace Skorupa. Finally, I am grateful for Julia Kristeva's continued support and encouragement. She read many of these chapters and answered pertinent queries.

NEW MALADIES *of the* SOUL

One. THE CLINIC

I. THE SOUL AND THE IMAGE

> *It is more important that men create the logos of the soul than of the body.*
> —DEMOCRITUS

Do you have a soul? This question, which may be philosophical, theological, or simply misguided in nature, has a particular relevance for our time. In the wake of psychiatric medicines, aerobics, and media zapping, does the soul still exist?

Medicine or Philosophy?

Fruitful debates between ancient Greek doctors and philosophers caused the "psyche" to undergo some delicate variations before becoming the "anima" of the Latin Stoics. Doctors of antiquity returned to the metaphysical distinction between the body and the soul and came up with a viable analogy that prefigured modern psychiatry: they spoke of "maladies of the soul" that were comparable to maladies of the body. These maladies of the soul included the passions, from sadness to joy and even delirium. Although some doctors used this parallelism to support a "monistic" conception of human beings, for most of them, the radical difference between the psychic and somatic realms was confirmed by their mutual presence, if not their isomorphy.

Dualisms have prevailed since antiquity, some thought to con-

3

sist of complementary dynamics of flux, and others of troublesome contradictions. Despite scientific efforts that have attempted to reduce it to soma, the psyche, which we have failed to locate (is it in the heart? the humors? the brain?), has remained an implacable enigma. As a structure of meaning, the psyche represents the bond between the speaking being and the other, a bond that endows it with a therapeutic and moral value. Furthermore, by rendering us responsible to our bodies, the psyche shields us from biological fatalism and constitutes us as speaking entities.[1]

Christ's incarnation, that is, the body-and-soul Passion of Man-God, gave momentum to the psychic dynamic that has been nurturing the inner life of Christian humanity for two thousand years. Passionate excesses directed toward the absolute subject—God or Jesus—ceased to be pathological. Instead, they were thought to map out the mystic itinerary of a soul aiming for the Ultimate. Before mental illness could be rethought, however, the dialectic of the Trinity had to be broken, anatomy had to adapt to the body, and the paroxysmal humors had to become objects of observation and surveillance. At that point, mental illness entrenched itself in the sacred space of the insane asylum. Michel Foucault has written a brilliant history of this clinic, which acknowledged the soul, but only as a sign of a sick body.[2] Let us recall, however, that this gesture began well before the Age of Reason, for its roots can be traced to Greek philosophy and medicine, which introduced the distinction and analogy between maladies of the body and maladies of the soul. Like the ancient Greeks, modern psychiatrists—notably Philippe Pinel[3]—have subscribed to physical and moral theories of the origins of mental illness.[4]

Freud can be placed in this tradition, for he explicitly promoted a philosophical dualism[5] that he developed through his conception of the "psychic apparatus"[6]—a theoretical construction that is irreducible to the body, subject to biological influences, yet primarily observable in linguistic structures. Fixed firmly in biology by the drives yet contingent upon an autonomous logic, the soul, as a "psychic apparatus," gives rise to psychological and somatic symptoms and is modified during transference.

By giving priority to the psyche, however, the inventions of the unconscious and of transference do more than resurrect the ancient Greek debate about the soul and the body. What is more important, the Freudian notion of the psyche challenges this formerly presumed dualism and goes beyond the hypertrophy of the psychological that many see as the defining feature of psychoanalysis. In this vein, several aspects of psychoanalysis cross the boundary between body and soul and explore various elements that transcend this dichotomy: for instance, the energy component of drives, the determination of meaning through sexual desire, and the inscription of the treatment within transference, which is understood to be a repetition of prior psychosensory traumas. Nevertheless, the linguistic mechanism remains at the core of treatment: as a signifying construct, the speech of both the analysand and the analyst incorporates different *series of representations*. We recognize the diversity of these series, yet we can rightfully claim that they are primarily "psychic" in origin, irreducible as they are to the biological substrata that contemporary science has more or less categorized for us.

By proposing *different* models of the soul, psychoanalysis expands our notion of the "psyche," acknowledges the peculiarities of our means of signification, and absorbs pathology into specific logical systems. Although the notion of psychological illness does not lose its specific validity, psychoanalysis tends to associate it with one of the logical possibilities inherent in any Freudian "psychic apparatus" or Lacanian "speakbeing" [*parlêtre*]. Although the notions of "norm" and "anomaly" are also challenged, the impact of psychoanalysis is not confined to the ensuing subversion—one that has attracted libertarian spirits for almost a century. The emphasis on *meaning* and the use of *eroticized speech* in transference remain the most important features of the singular adventure of Freud's discovery.

Loyal to the ethics of the person that the West has developed within the folds of its philosophy, religion, and science, psychoanalysis appeals to the life of speaking beings by reinforcing and exploring their *psychic life*. You are alive if and only if you have a psychic life. However distressing, unbearable, deadly, or exhilarating it may be, this psychic life—which combines different systems of representation that involve language—allows you access to your body and to other people. Because of the soul, you are capable of action. Your psychic life is a discourse that acts. Whether it harms you or saves you, you are its subject. Our purpose here is to analyze psychic life, that is, to break it down and to start over. The substantial effects of meaningful representations have never been recognized and put to use with so much precision and force. With Freud, the *psyche* is reborn. Enriched by the Judaic pluralism of its interpretations, the soul has evolved into a multifaceted and polyphonic psyche that is better equipped to serve the "transubstantiation" of the living body. Hence, we can appreciate the powerful synthesis Freud made of the traditions preceding his own, for by assigning a new value to the soul, Freud was able to elaborate a course of action that is at once therapeutic and moral.

Progress in the natural sciences, notably in biology and neurobiology, has enabled us to envision the death of the soul. Since we are continually decoding the secrets of neurons, their tendencies and their electrical dynamics, do we still have a need for this age-old chimera? Have we not come up with cognitive constructs that can account for cellular as well as human behavior?

However that may be, one cannot help noticing that the subject, whose soul was considered banished from the "pure" sciences, is making a triumphant comeback in the most sophisticated biological theories that make up cognitive science. "The image is present in the brain before the object,"[7] claim biologists. "Cognitive architecture is not limited by the nervous system; on the contrary, the nervous system is penetrated by the cognitive architecture that takes place there."[8] "We cannot dispense with a teleonomy here."[9] "I cannot see how we might conceive of mental functioning that did not include a representation of the goal, that is, that did not imply a subject that attempts to represent both itself and its expected goal."[10]

Image before object, subject, teleonomy, representation: where is the soul to be found? If cognitive science is not to lead biology toward a spiritualist rebirth, we must ask how a soul is made. What kinds of representations and which logical varieties constitute the soul? Psychoanalysis does not necessarily have the answers to these questions, but it is the one discipline that is searching for them.

Can We Speak of New Patients?

At the same time, everyday experience points to a spectacular reduction of private life. These days, who still has a soul? We are all too familiar with the sort of emotional blackmail that reminds us of television serials, but this coercion is merely a by-product of the hysterical failure of psychic life that romantic dissatisfaction and middle-class domestic comedy have already depicted for us. As for the renewed interest in religion, we have reason to wonder if it stems from a legitimate quest, or from a psychological poverty that requests that faith give it an artificial soul that might replace an amputated subjectivity. For an affirmation emerges: today's men and women—who are stress-ridden and eager to achieve, to spend money, have fun, and die—dispense with the representation of their experience that we call psychic life. Actions and their imminent abandonment have replaced the interpretation of meaning.

We have neither the time nor the space needed to create a soul for ourselves, and the mere hint of such activity seems frivolous and ill-advised. Held back by his aloofness, modern man is a narcissist—a narcissist who may suffer, but who feels no remorse. He manifests his suffering in his body and he is afflicted with somatic symptoms. His problems serve to justify his refuge in the very problems that his own desire paradoxically solicits. When he is not depressed, he becomes swept away by insignificant and valueless objects that offer a perverse pleasure, but no satisfaction. Living in a piecemeal and accelerated space and time, he often has trouble acknowledging his own physiognomy; left without a sexual, subjective, or moral identity, this amphibian is a being of boundaries, a borderline, or a "false self"—a body that acts, often

7

without even the joys of such performative drunkenness. Modern man is losing his soul, but he does not know it, for the psychic apparatus is what registers representations and their meaningful values for the subject. Unfortunately, that darkroom needs repair.

Of course, the society that shapes modern individuals does not leave them stranded. They can find one possibly effective solution for their problems in neurochemistry, whose methods can often treat insomnia, anxieties, certain psychotic states, and some forms of depression. And who could find fault with that? The body conquers the invisible territory of the soul. Let it stand for the record. There is nothing you can do about it. You are overwhelmed with images. They carry you away, they replace you, you are dreaming. The rapture of the hallucination originates in the absence of boundaries between pleasure and reality, between truth and falsehood. The spectacle is life as a dream—we all want this. Do this "you" and this "we" exist? Your expression is standardized, your discourse becomes normalized. For that matter, do you really have a discourse of your own?

If drugs do not take over your life, your wounds are "healed" with images, and before you can speak about your states of the soul, you drown them in the world of mass media. The image has an extraordinary power to harness your anxieties and desires, to take on their intensity and to suspend their meaning. It works by itself. As a result, the psychic life of modern individuals wavers between somatic symptoms (getting sick and going to the hospital) and the visual depiction of their desires (daydreaming in front of the TV). In such a situation, psychic life is blocked, inhibited, and destroyed.

We see all too easily, however, that this mutation may be beneficial. More than just a commodity or a new variant of the "opium of the people," the current transformation of psychic life may foreshadow a new humanity, one whose psychological conveniences will be able to overcome metaphysical anxiety and the need for meaning. Wouldn't it be great to be satisfied with just a pill and a television screen?

The problem is that the path of such a superman is strewn with traps. A wide variety of troubles can bring new patients to the analyst's couch: sexual and relationship difficulties, somatic symptoms, a difficulty in expressing oneself, and a general malaise caused by a language experienced as "artificial," "empty," or "mechanical." These patients often resemble "traditional" analysands, but "maladies of the soul" soon break through their hysterical and obsessional allure—"maladies of the soul" that are not necessarily psychoses, but that evoke the psychotic patient's inability to symbolize his unbearable traumas.

As a result, analysts must come up with new classification systems that take into account wounded "narcissisms," "false personalities," "borderline states," and "psychosomatic conditions."[11] Whatever their differences, all these symptomatologies share a common denominator—the inability to represent. Whether it takes the form of psychic mutism or adopts various signs experienced as "empty" or "artificial," such a deficiency of psychic representation hinders sensory, sexual, and intellectual life. Moreover, it may strike a blow to biological functioning itself. In a roundabout manner, the psychoanalyst is then asked to restore psychic life and to enable the speaking entity to live life to its fullest.

Are these new patients a product of contemporary life, which exacerbates our familial situations and infantile difficulties and makes them into symptoms of a particular era? If not, are dependence on medicines and refuge in the image merely modern renditions of the narcissistic inadequacies common to all times? Finally, have patients changed or has analytic practice changed, such that analysts have sharpened their interpretations of previously neglected symptomatologies? These questions as well as others will be asked by the readers of this book, just as they are asked by its author. The fact remains, however, that analysts who do not discover a *new malady of the soul* in each of their patients do not fully appreciate the uniqueness of each individual. Similarly, we can place ourselves at the heart of the analytic project by realizing that these new maladies of the soul go beyond traditional classification systems and their inevitable overhaul. What is more important, they embody difficulties or obstacles in psychic representation, difficulties that end up destroying psychic life. Revitalizing grammar and rhetoric, and enriching the style of those who wish to speak with us because they can no longer remain silent and brushed aside: do such projects not mirror the new life and new psyche that psychoanalysis wishes to unearth?

The Phantasmatic Operative Composition

The following analytic fragment will offer us a concrete example of one of these new maladies of the soul: phantasmatic inhibition. Didier, who lived off of the images of his paintings, was nevertheless unable to tell a story, that is, to construct a pictorial tale of his passions. Since his desire lacked narrative, it canceled itself out. Didier could thus be considered a symbolic emblem of contemporary man—an actor or consumer of the society of the spectacle who has run out of imagination.

The paradox of Diderot's actor portrayed a seasoned professional who could imitate other people's feelings extremely well, but who was unable to feel anything himself. The Enlightenment philosopher exalted this capability, which has since been transformed into something disturbing, for in our world, both the producer and the consumer of images suffer from lack of imagination. Their helplessness results in impairment. What do they want from their analyst? A new psychic apparatus. But before opening itself to the language of phantasmatic narrative, the development of this new psychic apparatus must recreate the image within transference.

Didier had written me a letter that said he admired my books on art and literature. An amateur painter, he told me that his "relationship problems" were what had persuaded him to enter into analysis. He believed I was the only person able to guide him in "such a venture." The letter revealed a reader of psychoanalytic and literary texts as well as a well-informed art lover.

For several years, I was witness to Didier's discourse, which he formed with learned and guarded words and delivered in a monotone. At times, I found the paradox of the situation laughable or even absurd. I had a hard time remembering that Didier was "my patient," since I was completely convinced that he spoke for the sole purpose of ignoring me. Even when I was able to break through to this "impenetrable scuba diver," this "invisible Walkman" (metaphors I used when reflecting upon his mental and libidinous automatism), Didier managed to neutralize what I said right away: "That's true, I was about to say so myself, absolutely, I already thought of it . . ." And he would remain in a state of "submersion" without ever being affected by my interpretations.

From the first sessions, I was struck by Didier's laconic speech, which I might have seen as a sign that treatment was impossible. I felt, however, that the frugality of his discourse was perfectly appropriate for someone who complained of so much suffering. He spoke of his suffering by confiding various "stories" to me in the "operative" and "technical" fashion typical of those afflicted with psychosomatic illnesses. He disposed of these stories as if they were lifeless objects or sterilized waste products. Didier described himself as lonely, unable to love, neutral, detached from his colleagues and his wife, even indifferent to his mother's death. Only masturbation and painting were able to sustain his interest.

Born after a girl, Didier was adored by his mother, who dressed him as a girl and gave him a feminine hairdo until he started school. She dominated her little boy's life while making him into the locus of her inverted desire, for by transforming her son into a daughter, she could love herself as a little girl. Didier did not say "my" mother or "our" mother, but "the" mother. I was to realize that the definite article was a party to a defensive system—that of Didier's *perverse combinative*—which could protect him from the suppressed, exciting, and devastating intimacy he shared with "his" mother. I use the term *perverse combinative* because his exclusive sexual activity of masturbation coincided with somatic symptoms and sublimations (his paintings). This kept his discourse in the abstract (the Mother), and kept his selfhood in glorious isolation. If "the Mother" is not someone, there is no one.

On several occasions, I realized how much Didier, like many patients, challenged traditional systems of psychiatric classification. Didier's psychic organization did not really correspond to any standard diagnostic grouping, despite his obsessive isolation, his psychosomatic tendencies, and an immaturity that caused his masturbation fixation. I chose to focus on his *most pronounced perverse traits* because I sought to make his drives come forth through his discourse, and then to analyze them within the context of a lively and complex transference. Although this was just what my patient feared most, I found it necessary to focus on Didier's obsessional character and narcissistic personality. Caught between a polite, listless discourse and his solitary intellectual and artistic activities, Didier wished to convince himself (and his analyst) that he had no soul, as if he were nothing but a robot who occasionally got sick.

Before marrying "the Mother," Didier's father had married a foreign woman. A romantic aura thus gave some substance to an absent father and served as a protective device against the intrusive presence of "the Mother." I considered this trait to be a component of Didier's sexual identity, despite the dubious desire of his mother—a desire that might have guided him toward homosexuality, if not psychosis. Didier had no clear memory, however, of the heavenly times he had spent fused with his mother. In fact, his mother's death had made only a small impact on him. Didier's regret was that his mother had been the only person allowed to look at his paintings. Their means of communication consisted of displaying themselves, inducing the pleasure of the female onlooker, becoming aroused, and exhibiting themselves once more. They communicated without words—from hand to eyes, and vice versa, or by blending different substances into a new painting that he would show her.

Yet this ploy came to a halt, and from that point on, Didier found masturbation to be less pleasurable. His loyalty to the dead one had taken another form—as a vacuum to be avoided or as a condemned cave. Didier kept his mother's apartment the way she had left it. Since it was *forbidden,* the apartment was a space Didier needed to own. Was his mother untouchable because of a paternal condemnation that was still removed from Didier's discourse?

Along with this prohibition of a relationship that was simply *too crowded,* the apartment was henceforth *emptied* of the mother's stimulating presence.

That was how I visualized this maternal space to which Didier had often referred, determined as he was to allow the closed-off apartment to guard wholeheartedly yet secretly a passion that he thought did not exist ("empty"?)—although he wanted me to make him aware of it. There I was, appealed to and rejected, at once called on and closed out, just as the analytic process itself would prove to be.

I would first like to mention the way my patient often manipulated me. Though he seemed cooperative, we had to play the game according to his rules.[12] Similarly, he outlined his personal plan to restrict the analysis to the mere pursuit of *knowledge:* "I'm not interested in feelings, I just want to know."

According to Freud, the pervert solders the drive and the object (this mechanism could be the basis of the relationship between *closeness* and *command*). But the pervert primarily idealizes drives, since "a piece of mental work" sets in once the perverse structure begins to take shape.[13] Indeed, for the pervert, the psychic activity of idealization is essential (we shall see this in the case of Didier), though this activity has a dual nature. On the one hand, very young children are aware of their mother's desire for them—a desire to which they react by building up a defensive fantasy that is in *symbiosis* with that of the mother. On the other hand, a defensive psychic activity like idealization could be contrasted with the chaotic drives that the young ego is still unable to work out. By *denying* this chaos, the young ego covers it up.

Produced as they are by denial, the psychic activity of idealization and the display of knowledge take on ingenious yet static traits comparable to Winnicott's "false self" or Marty's "operative thinking."[14] I realized that Didier's discourse, like his pictorial output, had this ingenious quality: it was elaborate, well-informed, and technically perfect, yet intended to prevent the recognition of drives, especially aggressive ones.

Denial and Impairment of Language

Didier steered me toward a particularly perverse organization that was constantly threatened—or stabilized—by his somatic symptoms, obsessions, and "false self." This economy, which based itself upon the denial of maternal castration, maintained the omnipotence of the mother and of the child identified with her. A similar narcissistic omnipotence reinforced the patient's bisexual fantasies and made him impervious to any relationships, which could have only occurred through the experience of a lack. Hence, absolutely nothing was missing from the fusional symbiosis between the phallic mother and her son-daughter. The quadruple couple had it all.

This autoerotic omnipotence, however, struck all the components of this closed system with denial, and phantasmatic omnipotence was converted into impairment. There was an impairment of the mother, since she was not an object of desire, but merely a passive support or a fetishist decoration of her son's autoerotic pleasure, and an impairment of the son, who, like his mother, had evaded the oedipal ordeal that would have enabled him to face castration and phallic identity. Finally, this erotic impairment—which had neither subject nor object—had found a parallel in Didier's thought processes. Although Didier's display of symbolic competence was appropriately organized according to grammatical, logical, and social norms, it was nevertheless a "false self," an artificial discourse that had no bearing on his affects and drives. Without becoming an actual splitting of the ego, denial led to a conflict between the patient's symbolic functioning and the secret zone of his unspeakable drives.

Didier had indeed failed to create a veritable perverse *structure*. Yet because of his denial and his objectless sexualization, his perverse economy contained preoedipal conflicts, which we can assume to be all the more violent since they seemed so frozen. They were so frozen that the patient's symbolic formations could not assume a protective role against the threat of his drives. He thus displayed somatic symptoms: the thin autoerotic layer gave way to a metaphor, the symptom of dermatitis. Was he guilty about masturbating, or did this symptom depict the fragility of his narcissistic identity, an identity that his skin had once protected? In any event, his skin disease worsened after his mother's death.

It seems to me, then, that Didier's perversion separated drives and their psychic representatives from language and symbolic functioning. This separation brought the body out into the open and exposed it to somatic symptoms. Autoeroticism and artificial discourse were attempts to get around these break-ins by creating not an identity, but an enclosed, self-directed, and contained totality, an anal-sadistic, independent, and self-sufficient totality that lacked nothing and needed nobody.

In order for us to find a linguistic access to *drives* and the *other* (which were denied and absorbed like the rest), this defensive function would have to be disturbed. Only then could we embark on an anamnesis of the Oedipus complex, first by restructuring it from a preoedipal latency that remained fragmented and encysted, and then by carrying out an analysis of these phenomena.

The "Operative" Dream of a Catastrophic Identity

Even Didier's accounts of his dreams seemed defensive, neutralizing, and "operative."[15] The dream in question, like so many others, came across as a fragmented tale filled with associations that resisted analysis:

Didier is leaning out of a window in his family home. He feels ill, or someone pushes him. He falls into an open space. He experiences a moment of intense anxiety that makes him scream, though he is unsure about this. In any event, the dream is a silent one. He suddenly finds himself in front of mirror and sees a reflection of his sister's face. This agitates him quite a bit and makes him wake up.

Didier spoke of his "scream" and his "agitation" with characteristic neutrality. He gave no details of the house, the window, or the mirror. The dream "mirrored" the empty space—it was a frozen dream. I think of his anxiety when faced with an abyss, that is, his anxiety when faced with castration of women, of his sister. Perhaps there was also an anxiety-ridden fantasy of his birth or lack thereof: would being born around these people have rekindled his fear of nonbeing? If his father had stayed with the foreign woman, or if his mother had rid herself of (and not simply rejected) the boy that disappointed her so much that she disguised him as a girl, Didier could have missed being born. The gaping window represented the inconsolable anguish of nonbeing—a black hole of narcissism and a murder of the self that guided me toward some undeveloped areas of Didier's psyche. Since his intense and chaotic drives were neither sublimated nor worked out, they inscribed *emptiness* into the patient's libido and spirit.

If my hypothesis of a "narcissistic black hole" was correct, then Didier's seeing himself as his sister, as a woman, or as his mother's double could have sealed off this "black hole" for good. But Didier did not mistake himself for his sister—he had "frozen" this possible transvestism, just as he had frozen the anguish of his annihilation.

He had "thought quite a bit" about these people. Neither his father nor his mother was interested in his sister—thus womanhood was not a very enticing proposition. He saw no solution; there was nothing for him to do but remain impaired. The fear of being nothing but a woman indicates that this man ran the risk of aphanisis. When faced with the abyss under the window and the mirror with its reflection of his sister, Didier chose—the mirror. This means that he transferred the combination of his conflictive drives and their inaccessible, frozen object onto his *ego*. He coolly remained his mother's fetish object, the boy-girl of maternal masturbation. Through an autoerotic, almost autistic withdrawal, this woman had compensated, I imagine, for the jealousy that must have resulted from her memory of the foreign woman, as well as from her thinly disguised nostalgia for the father.

I was able to interpret Didier's fear of losing his sexual identity, but I also suggested that his fear might conceal a catastrophic anxiety about the *total undoing of the ego*. "I don't think so," he denied apathetically. Then silence—the curtain fell—refusal. No more progress was forthcoming. Indeed, Didier admitted to me that he would never throw himself "into that window" and that he "would never give birth to anyone." Perhaps he also hoped that nothing would arise from our work together. I tried to associate his opacity with his mother's padlocked apartment: Didier did not wish to let me in on his private life because his mother had taken everything with her. He was afraid that his mother would discover his passions, his fears, his hatreds. He reassured himself by remarking that "she was no specialist." Was he afraid that if he opened up to me, I would let him fall out of the window? Or rather that I would hold up a mirror that failed to reflect his masculine face?

Theory in the Countertransference

After all, resorting to a "wavering" theoretical activity is the "third ear"—removed yet implicit and indispensable—that inflects the phenomenon of countertransference with a relevant analytical interpretation. As I listened to Didier and came up with appropriate "constructions," I was reminded of W. H. Gillepsie's observations of the pervert's omnipotence. According to Gillepsie, the perverse economy can be linked to psychosis, since the pervert stands between repressed defenses and a schizoid or split character.[16] In a similar vein, Edward Glover had already considered perversion to be a neutralization of infantile aggression as well as a compromise that preserves the reality sense.[17] Influenced by Winnicott's work on the mother-nursing infant relationship and the transitional object,[18] most modern writers on the subject emphasize the psychotic potential of perversion. Joyce McDougall has established a relationship between the perverse personality and the archaic preoedipal disorganization of the ego.[19] These problems, for which perversion provides a defensive screen and the "false self" a crystallization, point to the narcissistic symptomatology that André Green has analyzed.[20] Furthermore, my work with Didier takes into account some of Lacan's propositions concerning perversion:[21] perverse fetishism does not obliterate the paternal function. By preserving the disavowed value of the paternal function, fetishism gives rise to it [*père-version*].[22] Lacan's reflection on language and psychic functioning led me to investigate the pervert's particular use of language as well as his imaginary productions (dreams and fantasies).

In this clinical and theoretical context, I noticed that Didier only gave up his "neutrality"—which was hardly a benevolent one—when he would speak to me about his paintings. The highly "specialized" and "technical" *content* of what he said kept me from imagining what his paintings might look like. During such moments, however, his *voice* would become animated, his face would redden, and his emotions would rise to the surface.

It seemed that painting was the hidden portion of the iceberg that Didier was constructing with his discourse. Saying "to see" said nothing to him. His passions were kept from infiltrating his speech. Didier "meant" *in another way*. In order to maintain a psychological identity that his narcissistic ego had failed to create, substitutions of his thing-presentations (his paintings) replaced the relationship between thing-presentation and word-presentation. He diminished the impact of his fantasies by interweaving action and meaning, and he increased his self-referential pleasures, including masturbation. In exchange, linguistic signs were cut off from meaning, cut out from his actions, and cut away from affect—they became ritualistic, empty, abstract signs.

Painting and Exhibition: To Name Is Not to Act

I thus formed a "countertransferential conviction" that the *direct* language of Didier's affect and desire was to be found in his *painting* more than in his speech. I also felt that we had perhaps been mistaken in restricting the treatment to a consideration of Didier's defensive speech, instead of *also spending time on* the means of expression by which I believe he had encoded his traumas and desires. He brought me some pictures of his artwork—a combination of collages and paintings—and described them to me one at a time. I was struck by the violence of this pictorial "discourse," a violence that sharply contrasted with the neutrality, extreme politeness, and abstract discourse that had characterized his previous dealings with me. The artist worked with various entities—docile objects that were fractured, cracked, and broken up as if slaughtered—and thereby created a new identity. And not a single face espoused the fragments of these mutilated persons, who were primarily female, and who were shown to have a derisive nature and an unsuspected ugliness.

Hence, the "black hole" of the identity trauma had discovered a language in painting. Left without the isolating recourse to obsessional speech, Didier's sadistic drive was given free reign. A jouissance came forth, one that required fragments of other people's bodies in order to foster a perverse phantasmatic that was not even accessible during the masturbatory act.

I had replaced the dead mother, who was kind enough to accept her son's artwork even though she never showed any reaction to it. Yet there was one important difference: by *giving a name* to the sadistic fantasies, I dissociated myself from the maternal position and performed a veritable "phantasmatic graft" on this patient. Indeed, when the erotic content of an audacious visual representation is not recognized or when it is denied through aesthetic abstractions, can we really speak of a fantasy? In Didier's case, I thought that this question was a legitimate one, since the "images" (which, *for me,* represented his fantasies), seemed *isolated* from his conscious discourse, resistant as he was to any associative work that might have led us to his unconscious fantasy.

I thus set out to *give a name* to the buried fantasies (whether isolated or genuinely split) as well as to their sexual meaning. In this way, I offered a strange interpretation if there ever was, an interpretation that bore witness to an unmistakable countertransferential element. I offered Didier *my own* fantasies, which his paintings elicited in *me.* While we were pursuing this path, however, an imaginary and symbolic contract was established between us. Even though he found my discourse "reductive" and "oversimplified," Didier began to accept, adjust, change, or reject my interpretations of his collages. From that point on, he could give his own name to the phantasmatic that lay behind his cool technique. Three psychic events followed that appear to have been turning points in Didier's analysis.

To Smash Her Face In

He mentioned that he had fought with his wife, who was born in and had lived in a foreign country. I emphasized that he wanted to "smash a foreign woman's face in." Didier rejected my interpretation, assuring me that in his view, *I* was the foreign woman. It was difficult to imagine that Didier's wife was the object of a pervert, since his sexual activities were so solitary. Nevertheless, in the form of a permissive, if not indulgent, superego, she "participated" in his masturbatory pleasure. She incited less her husband's aggression than his marked disregard for her. He could thus discount the sexual act with the other (she is not worth it, so "it" is not worth it) and split [*clive*] the denigrated erotic act of masturbatory pleasure.

His wife's "foreignness" acted as insurance against the fear of being swallowed up and devoured by the satisfaction his mother gave and received: *she* came from somewhere else; *she* could not be seductive and destructive like "the Mother." Didier could thus make her into a victim of an omnipotence that was eventually acted-out, most likely wished-for, and, as opposed to the case of his mother, never put into action.

This session was followed by some extremely violent interactions between Didier and his wife. Following these altercations, he spoke more freely and in more detail about his sexuality as well as his genital-anal masturbation. The ensuing mixture of intense jubilation and shame was in marked contrast with his habitual modesty. As a memory of an absolute experience and a polymorphous excitement, masturbation acted out a boundless sadomasochistic body, a complete body that had become a sex organ that was eager to get rid of any strong tensions since it was unable to split up tensions into words or into contact with another person.[23]

Even Didier's mouth had remained locked up with "the Mother," who was untouchable in his memory—a condition that the "condemned" apartment symbolized very well. Weaned very late, Didier had guarded the secret of such an unspeakable orality, as sexual tension had settled on anal and genital zones that were developed later. This "condemnation" of the mouth can be related to a precocious and adept use of language that remained neutralized and mechanical for a long time, as did Didier's orality.

The Dream of Bifocal Symbiosis

While we were trying to "defrost" Didier's drives and speech, he described to me a second dream:

> Didier is in his parents' bed. They are making love. But he is not simply between them—he is both of them, at once vagina and penis. He is both the man and the woman, the father and mother who are indiscernible in the sexual act until they experience the sensation of vaginal jouissance.

Philip Greenacre has noted that the pervert combines the child's need with the parent's sensitivity.[24] In Didier's case, the union seems to have occurred through the sensitivity of *both* parents, which leads me to speak of a *bifocal symbiosis*. During the masturbatory act, his ego treated his body not as a "lost object," but as a primal scene that included a simultaneous symbiosis of both parents, fostered by the fantasy of an absolute sexuality (which was experienced in a different way from alternative bisexuality). Did this sort of sexuality not create a barrier to detailed, expressible representations? The bisexual fantasy can be interpreted as a hindrance to verbal communication with another person, communication that assumes sexualization, thus division. In Didier's case, it would be more accurate to speak of excitability than of sexuality, insofar as he dismissed his contact with others— which is the essence of eros itself.

In such an economy, self-satisfaction and disillusionment replace eroticism and depression, and they expose the body to either a corporeal *acting-out* or to a somatic symptom. While rediscovering his fantasies and feelings, Didier spoke *to me*. As time went on, a certain mutual affinity as well as a search for answers replaced his monologues. When he returned from his vacation, Didier told me that his dermatitis had disappeared.

"Collages" and "De-Collages" of Phantasmatic Operative Compositions

We can now have a fuller understanding of the function of the fantasy in Didier's psyche. After analyzing his artwork, I analyzed the dream-"collage"[25] he made of *both parents'* sex organs. The presence of the father, who is definitely not a minor character in this story, was restricted to adorning, tormenting, exciting, or exalting female figures. We can assume that by participating in an act of sexual intercourse between his parents, Didier could replicate his mother's fantasy as well as her dual desire—at once homosexual (for her rival) and heterosexual (for her husband). Since these elements are difficult to integrate, the pervert retains them in all their disparity—and this serves to excite him. By juxtaposing these elements, the pervert tends to neutralize them. As a result of this compromise, the analyst sees the pervert's fantasy as a dramatization, a staging, or an artifact. In Didier's case, a *phantasmatic operative composition* (paper collages, dream collages) thus intervened between *drives* and *discourse,* which he kept detached from each other.

I suggested he do some interpretive work on his various collages, and his reflections resulted in some changes in the realm of erotic representation. A new type of *dream,* which was followed by an important series of associations, indicated that progress was being made toward the elaboration of a subjective unity.[26] The dreamer responded to the child's need to experience the unity of his composite body, a unity that hinged on an illusory fusion of disparate components (father, mother, idealized first wife). This dreamlike unification followed the path of verbal signification, was inflected by primary processes and the experience of drives and the senses, and mirrored the phantasmatic activity. From then on, the enunciation of actions in the first person ("I" + verbs) replaced the fabrication of the acted (the collages) whose sublimating movement lowered the threshold of anxiety and facilitated phantasmatic construction.

From Anality to the Father: Punishment and Symbolization

The "primarily positive" transference shifted toward the paternal pole of the Oedipus complex. Hence, the patient reported to me a series of dreams that depicted an exceptional violence against his father. Analyzing them in terms of anal drives led to an increased understanding of the patient's perverse character. The desire to attack anally his father was interpreted as a desire for revenge against this father, who had allowed Didier to be his mother's passive object. At that point in the analysis, I became this negligent father, and the attacks were directed toward me (Didier had come to feel threatened by anal drives that had previously been unconscious). Through the same dreamlike images, however, he continued to avenge the fear that my interpretations induced—the fear of being reduced again to passivity. Didier's treatment brought forth repressed anal conflicts, but perhaps it did not eliminate them.

Even if such an objective were possible, I believe it would be a questionable, if not dangerous, one for a patient like Didier. His perversion provided a thin shield for a narcissistic deficiency that was locked-in through the help of anality (through an anal excitability that creates a barrier to genitality and through different productions like painting that idealize anality). In such an economy, an anality that is capable of development remains vital—in a "broken down" form—to maintaining psychic identity. Given these precautions, two perspectives are foreseeable: either the liquidation of the anal shield can lead to a psychotic collapse, or this liquidation can be transformed into a long-term analyst of anal occurrences. The latter alternative is clearly the secret of many analytical callings, but Didier was not ready to assume such a role. Nevertheless, it became possible to analyze Didier's oedipal conflicts with his father.

Didier's attempt to define himself as a man required him to confront his oedipal rivalry with his father. Before this oedipal fury, disavowal had brought about the fantasy of a total sexual experience. Sexualization had come to insinuate a paternal threat of castration that caused Didier to put his father to death. I am convinced, however, that oedipal guilt (toward an analyst presumed to disapprove of the "total jouissance" her patient desired, imagined, and offered her) had partaken in multiple causes of a minor malady to which Didier was subject. As minor as this illness may have been, it worried Didier a great deal, since he already had been required to undergo surgery.

Didier's somatic symptoms show that psychic representation can continue without taking complete control of conflictive drives. In what way was this patient's perverse economy responsible for somatic resolution of the Oedipus complex? By exposing himself to this "punishment," did Didier not wish to punish *me*—a woman and an analyst—because he was unable to resolve his sexual conflicts without the intervention of a masculine third party? Even if that were the case, I continue to believe that the surgeon's pivotal intervention was intentionally chosen in the physiological register of *acting-out,* even of "collage" and "de-collage." In this sense, it bore witness to the pervert's irreducible and inaccessible erotic intimacy. On the other hand, by reporting these events within the transference, the patient preserved a privileged place for the treatment: a place for the imaginary and the symbolic, a place where the drama of his individuation process could be played out.

The Gift of the Portrait: A Psychic Metamorphosis

At the end of his treatment, Didier handed me a portrait of myself. It was not a collage, but a painting he had made from a photograph in which I was holding a cigarette. In the portrait, however, my fingers surround nothing at all.

All the signifiers from the first dream can be found in the portrait. Nevertheless, each element was articulated in a different way—as an ironic smile, an Indian statue hand, the wheel of the mandala. The foreign woman reconstructed in a mirror, without fault or falter, the gaze harmlessly endured, and the presence of nothing. "Nothing between the hands, no penis, no fetish. I did well, didn't I," he said while smiling "knowingly," though he had become freer and more dynamic.

We began with a defensive idealization of the analyst. We then engaged in a consideration of semiotic productions,[27] that is, of the collages that could be seen as facsimiles of primary processes and thing-presentations, in which idealizations shift to sublimations. Interpreting these collages fostered the implementation of the fantasy by putting it into words. At the same time, taking into account the senses (touch, sight), which are considered a sign of drives (oral, anal, urethral), encouraged him to work through drives that had been repressed or sublimated.

Interpreting polymorphous pregenital fantasies, which uncovered a significant sadomasochistic element, led the patient to the final stage of psychic development: the rediscovery and reconstruction of his Oedipus complex. Hence, a portion of our analytical work was less an anamnesis than a reconstruction of the missing or wounded components of the subject, before these elements could be dismantled ("analysis"). Resorting to a restructuring and "sublimating" language may prove indispensable when treating "narcissistic personalities" in general.

The analyst may be struck by the interminable nature of this sort of treatment. Why and when should it end? The answer is more complicated in the case of perverts than it is for other patients because the pervert's psychic apparatus is incomplete, though such incompleteness can also be a source of erotic and existential mobility for the treatment. One question remains: what does it mean to "analyze a perversion?" At the end of our work together, I had the impression that Didier's "perverse organization" had merely turned itself around.[28] If at first the partial pleasures, actings-out, and collages seemed to be an absolute that would tolerate no needs, at the end of the treatment they were endowed with a "negative"—an indefinitely analyzable neurosis. Without disappearing, this perverse shell fit into a structure in which the other person counts (thanks to transference and countertransference). This also allows for the testing of partial pleasures and fantasies that will be formulated. Is this not inevitable, if we agree with Freud that all sexuality is perverse?

Nevertheless, the "perversion" that brushes the autistic avoidance of sexuality with an excessive growth of autoerotic pleasures is different from a sexuality that includes an element of perversion. The latter can be characterized by the work of representation, which opens the subject to its psychic space—the advent of a negative and of its procession of castration, difference, and the other. Yet this negative is just a thin layer, an imaginary and symbolic graft—a psychic graft—that we have implemented. The surge of perversion feeds it, the vulnerability of narcissism threatens it. But is there anything harder for the pervert than to admit not only his own castration, but also that of his wife and his analyst?

I remain a figure, but one that Didier enjoys without immuring it in the tomb of inexpressible excitement, and without massacring it, either. By painting my portrait and accompanying it with his own commentary, Didier gave me what I had given him. Everything was more complicated than it had been in the beginning. Analytic work was made possible, and it gave Didier access to his own psyche. By giving a name within transference to his stratified, isolated, and resistant representations, analysis restored drives and language to the phantasmatic operative constructions that Didier's collages had been. His lifeless, neutralized "act" and his suffering body were transferred into a new dynamic space—a psychic life with and for another person. Now Didier has to keep going.

By creating the "logos of the soul," Didier was able to provide himself with a new body. This was Democritus' project, as well as Freud's. We are only at the beginning; it's just a beginning. We recognize the breadth, the modesty, and the humbleness of analysis. But these days, what else is bringing intimacy back to life?

2. IN TIMES LIKE THESE, WHO NEEDS PSYCHOANALYSTS?

I am picturing a sprawling metropolis with glass and steel buildings that reach to the sky, reflect it, reflect each other, and reflect you—a city filled with people steeped in their own image who rush about with overdone make-up on and who are cloaked in gold, pearls, and fine leather, while in the next street over, heaps of filth abound and drugs accompany the sleep or the fury of the social outcasts.

This city could be New York; it could be any future metropolis, even your own.

What might one do in such a city? Nothing but buy and sell goods and images, which amounts to the same thing, since they both are dull, shallow symbols. Those who can or wish to preserve a lifestyle that downplays opulence as well as misery will need to create a space for an "inner zone"—a secret garden, an intimate quarter, or more simply and ambitiously, a psychic life.

Yet that is where the story gets complicated. The West has been crafting this inner life since the beginning of the Christian era, when Plotinus transformed a Janus-faced Narcissus into two hands joined in prayer. Inner life has been reinforced by the spiritual path and carnival of the Middle Ages, and it has been shaped by Montaigne's fragile ego, Diderot's passions, and the meditations of Hegel and Kant. It has since become a psychic drama, a psychodrama.

Plotinus has degenerated into . . . Dallas. Indeed, the residents of this steel city are not in want of inner drama—in fact, they are as anxious, depressed, neurotic, and psychotic as the Freudian unconscious would wish them to be. If we believe, however, that we can escape from the surface value of our actions, we fall into the trap of psychology. Therefore, psychoanalysis has some work ahead of it, since Freud's doctrine seeks precisely to free us from this suppressed space of psychological ill-being.

The city that I chose as an image of contemporary life encourages us to include *social history* as one of the elements of organization and permanency that constitute psychic life. Using the terminology of our industrial society, one could say that psychoanalysis turns money into time and joins painful affect with language—language that may be listless or indecipherable, but that is always directed toward other people. Such an extraordinary metamorphosis, which goes against the tide of the market economy as well as the neurosis that it patterns, may also shed light on psychosis. Two thousand years of inner experience have built this prison of the soul, a prison that offers psychoanalysis an innocent vulnerability in which it can pierce a hole that will serve to resound the polyphony of our motives.

Proust has accorded us the finest summary of what is becoming (or will soon become) the Freudian psyche: "Those who suffer feel closer to their soul."[1] Or perhaps:

> *For even if we have the sensation of being always enveloped in, surrounded by our own soul, still it does not seem a fixed and immovable prison; rather do we seem to be borne away with it, and perpetually struggling to transcend it, to break out into the world, with a perpetual discouragement as we hear endlessly all around us that unvarying sound which is not an echo from without, but the resonance of a vibration from within.*[2]

Here, Proust evokes the permanency of the psyche and offers a glimpse of its limits. Freud has provided us with a preliminary method for achieving this sort of listening, but we still need to elaborate our approach. Our empathy and familiarity with the malady of the soul will enable us to transcend the psyche—forever.

The psychic realm may be the place where somatic symptoms and delirious fantasies can be worked through and thus eliminated: as long as we avoid becoming trapped inside it, the psychic realm protects us. Yet we must transform it through *linguistic activity* into a form of sublimation or into an intellectual, interpretive, or transformational activity. At the same time, we must conceive of the "psychic realm" as a *speech act,* that is, neither an acting-out nor a psychological rumination within an imaginary crypt, but the link between this inevitable and necessary rumination and its potential for verbal expression.

For this reason, the current onslaught of psychological illness, which takes the form of "soap operas" that inevitably cater to the other side of the society of performance and stress, seems to call out to psychoanalysis. "Tell us the meaning of our inner turmoil, show us a way out of it."—such is the cry of psychological helplessness, of the *alter ego* of the society of the spectacle. As a result, psychoanalysis wagers to modify the prison of the soul that the West has made into a means of survival and protection, although this prison has recently been revealing our failings. This wager is therapeutic as well as ethical, and incidentally, political. Yet although we may seek the acceptance and even expansion of psychoanalysis, our wish is coming up against some substantial barriers.

I am not referring to the ever-present danger of transforming psychoanalysis into a normalization that would guide patients toward social success. Such a deterioration of psychoanalytic treatment, traditionally American, is widely known and denounced, and even if it remains a threat, resisting it was primarily a matter for the past that we still must keep in mind.

In my view, psychoanalysis will soon be confronted with two major issues that concern the problem of the organization and permanency of the psyche. The first issue pertains to its competition with the neurosciences. From now on, "take a pill or talk" may replace "to be or not to be." The second issue regards the challenge to which psychoanalysis is subject as a result of our desire to *remain in ignorance,* a desire that is in harmony with the apparent simplicity that pharmacology offers, and that also reflects the negative narcissism of modern man.[3]

Biology and Language: Freudian Drives and the Imaginary

The analytic position could be briefly outlined as follows: an unconscious psychic life is governed by determinants and restrictions that can be described and modified through an interpretation of the transference relation.

Some of these determinants and restrictions are *biological* in nature: recent advances in neurobiology and pharmacology have had an impact on our *behavior* and have enabled us to modify certain *fragments* of psychic life. The connection between analytic treatment and these interventions is more topical than ever, and this link is attracting the attention of analysts—who consider each concrete situation to be a singular experience.

The "attack" of the neurosciences is not making psychoanalysis defunct, but it is encouraging us to reconsider the Freudian concept of the *drive.* The drive is a pivot between "soma" and "psyche," between biology and representation—the highest level of organization and permanency to which Freudian listening and theory can aspire—that is, to which analytic construction (or imagination) can aspire. For what we understand by biology is—drives and energy, if you wish, but always already a "carrier of meaning" and a "relation" to another person, even though this person may be yourself.

Owing to its dual nature (biological and energetic/semiotic), the drive is also a structure. Within the space between its source (an organ) and its aim (satisfaction), its strength or weakness governs the restrictions placed on each subject. These restrictions circumscribe relationships that are among the most stubborn, because they are the most archaic (onto- and phylogenetically speaking), and the most discordant in terms of linguistic expression. In addition, the ego and its object relation are shaped within this drive framework.

The structure of the subject bases itself upon the different positions of the ego with respect to the different modalities of the object, and we must underscore that egos as well as the types of objects formed within the space between drives and language are *diverse in nature*. Nevertheless, any Freudian analyst would know that these subjective structures are charged with both the fate of drives and their dual nature (one that stems from biology and *non*linguistic representation).

For example, the fantasy, which could be considered a result of the eruption of the drive into the dispassionate logic of judgment— a logic that consequently finds itself transformed into a hallucination or a fit of delirium, reminds us that drives (and by implication, affects) form not only a myth, but also an element of organization and permanency that incites changes in the activity of thinking (as well as of judging and speaking). We also need to analyze the intermingling of drives and language with respect to the dulling of affects, to the disavowal of the object, and to the lifeless speech that characterizes those who suffer from depression.

That depression denies the meaning of discourse—which is to escort eros to the object—implies that the aggressive (or death) drive prevents a separation between the ego and the object. In its place, the death drive ushers in a melancholic subject—a negative Narcissus, an absolute master not of an object, but of a deadly *Thing* that must never be lost.[4]

In short, if we take the "myth" of the drive seriously, we must realize that an *imaginary deployment* reconstructs the logic of the drive in order to free up the linguistic restrictions that ultimately govern our capacities as speaking beings. It does so to show that this element of organization and permanency (discourse) consists not only of myriad significations and logical implications or presuppositions, but also of an interruption of the ability to produce speech (which can be schizophrenic or depressive—the figures vary). This imaginary deployment thereby reveals itself as a privileged witness to the *meaning* of the drive that joins the *signification* of speech.

Once fascinated by linguistics, contemporary psychoanalysis has a growing interest in drives, an interest that stems from Freud's legacy as well as from the daunting impact of the neurosciences. As a result, contemporary psychoanalysis has been attempting to decode the drama of drives while going beyond the *signification of language* that conceals the *meaning of drives*.

Traces of the meaning of drives can be translinguistic. Let us take the example of the voice: vocal stresses and rhythms often harbor the secret eroticism of depressed people who have severed the bond between language and the other, but who have nevertheless buried their affects in the hidden code of their vocalizations— in which the analyst may discover a desire that is not as dead as it may seem.

This brings me to the elements of organization and permanency that are the immediate object of analytic interpretation, insofar as they stem from our relation with others and are manifested through language. In light of what I have said concerning the primacy of drive destiny, these restrictions on signification would appear to constitute a complex, *heterogeneous* structure that is formed from the first years of our lives, grows and develops alongside us, and ultimately determines our symbolic destiny.

As a result of the growth of linguistics and of the other "human sciences" during the 1960s, the notion of *structure* in psychoanalysis (for which we are primarily indebted to Jacques Lacan) has enabled us to surmise more accurately than ever the organization of this *symbolic destiny,* this "being of language" that governs psychic life. Freudian analysts will agree that a discourse or symptom with which someone entrusts us can be taken as a whole, whose parts can only acquire meaning through the relationship between speaking subjects and their addressee, notably their analyst.

What is more, Freudian analyses have already noted that while this network of signifying relations that characterize symptoms, discourses, transference, and subjects is a *theoretical construction,* it is nevertheless the only *reality* in which psychic life can be manifested and developed. *A fortiori,* it constitutes the sole reality that offers the analyst—to whom someone has made a direct request— the possibility of intervening and modifying it. This aspect of analysis brings up three pressing questions:

1. Can we reduce the fate of speaking beings to *language* and *speech,* or do other *systems of representation* have a bearing on their logical features and on the actual psychic level that encompasses meaning for the subject?
2. Which characteristics of *interpretive language* are able to echo the symbolic fate of subjects, and thus affect and modify their biological substratum?
3. If analytic treatment is capable of such modifications, how might we define its boundaries and its *ethics?*

• The growth of semiology, which has encouraged us to contemplate various signifying systems (the iconic code, the musical code, and so forth) that are irreducible to language (whether language is considered as a specific language or a discourse, a structure or a grammar, an utterance or an enunciation), has shattered "linguistic imperialism." In like manner, the return to Freud, and more specifically to his conception of *representation,* has acknowledged the diversity of psychic representatives: thing-presentation, word-presentation, drive representative, affect representation. This has resulted in a "multilayered" model of psychic *signifiance,* one that incorporates heterogeneous *marks* and *signs.* Analysts must be aware of this polyphony if they wish to approach the discourse that is addressed to them from different linguistic and translinguistic levels (the voice, movement, and so forth) as well as to identify the levels that reveal the significance that discourse has for transference.

• In an ideal situation, interpretive silence would make these different structures of meaning, which shelter the subject's symptom, reverberate into his conscious. More directly and more frequently, however, analytic *interpretation* is what reveals the diverse linguistic and translinguistic expressions of ill-being and restores them to the subject. How does it do this? By giving a name to the familial determinants that have tainted sexual development with a given symptom or structure. What is more important, though, is that interpretation offers an *appropriate formulation* that is expressed in elliptical, metaphorical, or condensed terms, and has a bearing on both the analyst's affects and its own series of psychic representatives (of words, things, and drives).

A veritable poiesis comes into play here, one that includes the musical qualities of the voice as well as tropes and the rhetorical analysis of mental functioning. As the ultimate reality of transference and countertransference, this poiesis has an effect on conscious listening and exerts an influence on the patient's unconscious psychic representatives, which can be assumed to be closely related to the flux of the neurons that make up subcortical, "electrical," or "humoral" systems. Perhaps there is nothing that would form links between unconscious psychic representatives or separate them from the realm of neurobiology. Yet, while theoreticians and scientists are pondering the relationship between psychoanalysis and neurobiology, interpretive language is producing its own psychosomatic effects.

• If we take this to be true, we cannot help being struck by the violence of analytic interpretation. The mere fact that patients ask us to fulfill their request does not seem to justify such violence. Does their request not constitute an integral part of the symptom as well as the onset of its excess? Consequently, the ethics of psychoanalysis might base itself on two requirements that are characteristic of the Western rationalism from which it stems:

• On the one hand, there is a need to uphold a *single* meaning, a *single* truth that is valid and demonstrable in a given situation. This is the "normative" side of psychoanalysis. Indeed, the norm is dictated by the state of psychoanalytic theory and by any given analyst's position within it.

• On the other hand, there is a need to preserve respect (by way of freedom) for the patient's desire and jouissance, which are what determine his ability to accept our interpretation (since the structure of the patient emerges out of his particular resistance to our interpretation). At the same time, the validity of interpretation itself is challenged, for the analyst's jouissance is revealed, although it is clouded by the "truth" of his interpretive construction.

No other discourse in the history of Western rationalism has wagered to counterbalance truth and jouissance, authority and transgression. The ensuing equilibrium preserves the vitality of this discourse, a vitality that grows out of the immanence of death (the discourse of knowledge) and resurrection (the discourse of desire). As a result, psychoanalysis upsets the social contract, which is founded, according to Freud, on an act of murder. Analysts do not shy away from being dead fathers of knowledge, but they are also subjects of affect, desire, and jouissance. Consequently, they are distanced from schools and institutions and concentrate instead on restructuring other people's psyches.

Each Treatment Is Unique

Two phenomena prompt us to consider each analytic situation to be a specific microcosm: first, the various forms of psychic representation that turn toward language even though they are irreducible to its grammatical and logical structures, and second, the bipolarity of transference and countertransference that cloaks interpretive discourse.

To put it another way, although the psychiatric notions of "structure" (hysterical, obsessional, schizophrenic, paranoid, etc.) can offer an initial and rudimentary outline that the analyst may find useful, these notions are unable to withstand a microanalysis that is attentive to the diversity and polyvalence of psychic representatives. We have an growing interest in structural interferences as well as "borderline states" that go beyond their status as new clinical occurrences indicating the growth of subjectivity and psychic states, for they also have the advantage of challenging the foundation of traditional classification systems.

Hence, although the interest that psychoanalysts have in the linguistic and translinguistic expression of psychic determinants can sometimes make analysis appear abstract, this abstraction ends up personalizing each treatment as much as possible. Each treatment becomes an ideolect, a work of art, as well as a temporary installation of a new theoretical creation within the Freudian world. As a result, we would like to know which features of this discourse can be identified with Freudian thought, as well as where we can draw the line between loyalty, innovation, and dissension.

The history of the analytic movement combined with the current ecumenism of its tenets (Freudian, Kleinian, Winnicottian, Lacanian, and so forth) shows that despite various misunderstandings and impasses, Freud has staked out a path that all innovators must respect if they lay claims to psychoanalysis. It is admittedly a narrow path, one in which sexual experience resists language. This leads to repression and to the related necessity that we use language in order to interpret hidden unconscious signs. But it is also the path through which the eroticization of language within transference allows us to convey sexual experience and to relieve symptoms, which in turn endows us with a greater capacity for signification. Need I emphasize that in proposing that this be the goal of analysis, I am in no way advocating the normalization of the patient?

Two Obstacles to Analytic Speech

I shall briefly outline two examples of analytic treatment, examples that will serve to underscore my remarks and to point out two often-met obstacles to analytic speech.

DEPRESSION

Florence, a thirty-year-old woman who suffered from intense bouts of manic-depression, came to see me. She had previously attempted analysis with one of my colleagues, but she stopped going because she felt it was aggravating the intensity and frequency of her cycles. Florence had consulted a psychiatrist before coming to me. He put her on imipramine, but her previous analyst was unwilling to pursue treatment under such conditions.

At first we engaged in psychotherapy. After a while, though, Florence chose to lie down on the couch. She was still taking imipramine at the time. A few months later, she went off antidepressants and continued her analysis without taking any medication. Florence believed that imipramine had diminished her excessive anxiety and had allowed her to speak about the tragic events of her childhood and her life without falling back into the states of serious depression that she had often experienced. Her anxiety threshold seemed rather low, and its stabilization during treatment encouraged drives and their representatives to bond with verbal representations.

It seemed to me, however, that a certain distancing resulted from these chemical interventions—which seemed necessary though provisional. Nevertheless, I believed that in addition to the bonds they supported between drives and words, they offered another advantage. The introduction of a third party (medication, psychiatry) tempered Florence's manic elation—for she was not omnipotent and neither was I; a third party and an alternate reality were involved.

This also enabled us to tackle her narcissism, on the one hand, and its projection onto the exaggerated idealization with which she adorned me, on the other. Hence, a modified anxiety threshold made it possible to confront the manic-depressive devices that Florence had put into place in order to deal with loss and separation. A new object relation was established between us, one that was less catastrophic and less threatened by the unbearable danger of the annihilation she feared might follow a real or imaginary separation. Once this new object relation—which was also a new subjective structure—became stronger, Florence stopped taking imipramine. From that point on, she tried to rely solely on the symbolic and imaginary network that we had built up through the "regional" help of imipramine. She did so without resorting to chemical products, but to the psychic representatives we had restructured and whose disorganization was much less threatening to her than before.

During the portion of the analysis during which she was taking imipramine, I had the impression that the intensity of her drives was in check, but that her discourse was "numbed." My feeling arose primarily from the fact that while taking imipramine, Florence was able to have dreams pertaining to anxiety states that she had previously been unable to represent—the anxiety of being swallowed up and devoured by her mother, and inversely, the anxiety of swallowing up and devouring her mother. Yet even though Florence was able to have and report these dreams (which already was a substantial psychic development as compared to the depressive silence and "blank death" of the depressed signifier that had once characterized her), she approached her dreams with a sense of distance and a defensive lack of understanding. Then, in the second phase of the analysis, we were able to return to these dreams and analyze them.

FIRST DREAM: A dream about a cannibalistic wedding. The wedding resembles her parents' wedding photo. In this dream, the guests eat each other's body parts and heads. The scene takes place in the staircase of my building.

SECOND DREAM: Florence vomits after the sex act, and her mother's head falls into the basin. She has this dream just before becoming pregnant.

In what way were we able to return to these dreams? Florence, who became a mother during her analysis and who continued treatment without the use of medication, had nevertheless developed another symptom. She had become very frightened by her relentless and exhausting fantasies of assassinating her daughter, and she never tired of telling me how preoccupied she was with these obsessions. Florence specified that she did not really feel capable of acting out her fantasies, although she was quite worn out by her phantasmatic ruminations.

I said, "assassin—basin—assimilate." By way of this interpretation—which was highly condensed and which bore witness to a tragic, grotesque poetics—Florence was able to ascertain the meaning of her drives as well as the symbolic signification of her two previous dreams. Then, she could relate them to her current anxieties. Her desire to assassinate her daughter was a by-product of her desire to assimilate (devour) imipramine, and more important, to absorb the head and body parts (breast, basin [*sein, bassin*]) of her mother (the cannibal dream) that she chose to spit up into a basin (the vomiting dream) in order to make a place for her own child (to become pregnant, to occupy her own basin).

The meaning of drives in her dreams had already taken effect in her psyche by pushing aside her depressive symptoms, if only because her effort to report her dreams came to replace a melancholic silence. Nevertheless, the meaning of her drives failed to attain the signification of speech, and my interpretations spurred no associations. Eventually, however, the meaning of her drives was able to attain a symbolic signification, a working-out.

Assassin—basin—assimilate. I considered my interpretation to be a "vibration from within" (as Proust would say) that resounded between inexpressible, anxiety-ridden, or depressive drive representatives and an explanation that the patient, with the help of certain aspects of my interpretation, came up with herself—an explanation of her depressive side as well as her manic one. Florence did not wish to assassinate her daughter. She merely wished to reject the image of the daughter who she herself was, the assassin-cannibal daughter that constituted her self-image, a daughter who assimilated, devoured, and "vomited" her mother in order to avenge her infantile paralysis (her immobility from the basin) that had seriously handicapped her when she was very young and had separated her from her mother (orality is often overinvested in order to encompass an object that has eluded a failing motivity).

Like the explanatory, rhetorical work we subsequently engaged in, my transferential word-play resulted from my empathy with my patient's drive economy. I identified with her narcissistic wound and her oral voracity, as well as with her manic attempts to use devouring and evacuation to avenge the depressive *Thing* for which there were no linguistic signs, but only echolalia that bore the intensities of her drives. My interpretation reintroduced this drive economy into the assassin's divested language (Florence wanted to kill, but she felt detached and distanced from her otherwise obsessive desire). What may have appeared to be "word-play" served to revitalize language and transference, on the one hand, and the analysand, on the other. My interpretation accomplished this by recalling infantile time and the history of the archaic fantasy, and by compensating for a narcissistic wound.

I would like to emphasize a few aspects of this analytic fragment that I consider to be of paramount importance for psychoanalysis today and, why not, tomorrow.

• The role that pharmacology played in this treatment leads me to believe that the dialogue between neuroscience and psychoanalysis will follow two basic trends. First, there will be an increasing number of patients who undergo joint treatments (pharmacological and psychoanalytic), and this alliance will require an accurate assessment of the effects of medication as well as of their interaction with transference. Second, the public will need to be made aware of the vast array of psychological illnesses that are not targeted by pharmacology—illnesses that reaffirm the need for traditional psychoanalytic treatment. We require a more precise analysis of the relationship between the psychic apparatus and transference. In other words, our analyses will have to be attentive to the "translatability" of drives into words.

• The "signifier of death" is readily apparent to analysts who are aware of the depressive speech that results from the patient's *disavowal of the signifier* ("lifeless" speech that is painstaking, void, monotonous, accelerated yet self-effacing, "nonexistent"), and from the devalorization of language as an aspect of transference.

• Desire and the determinants of the symptom that are not signified within speech, however, seem to have deposited or coded their meaning in the preverbal register (of voice and intonation) or in a homophony that leads to the play of signifiers, or to an echolalia.

• Analytic interpretation may become a temporary party to regression and stagnation by making itself an echo of such meaning while serving as a bridge to intellectualization and to conscious formations not only of trauma, but also of desire that works within a language directed toward the other.

• Depression appears to stem from a relation to the other that is not separated from depressed subjects, but that remains under their grasp in the form of their *Thing,* which is unnameable and deadly (we discovered this symbiotic reunion in the "paradise not lost" of the "suicide wedding"). This particular object relation is clearly embedded in the "form" as well as the "content" of depressive discourse: both object relations and the structure of discourse function at the same level as the determinants of depression. Consequently, the intervention of analysis depends, or should depend (by way of its form and signification), on these two permanent factors of the subject's psyche—the *object* and *discourse.*

PERVERSION

The following factors have led to my interest in perversion, a disorder that is quite widespread these days and particularly resistant to analysis:

• Narcissistic satisfaction by a part object is supplemented by a fetishist and exhibitionist discourse of someone who is all-knowing and has no desire to learn.

• The overestimation of speech becomes a resistance to analysis: *affects* are split from the *discourse* that recounts the perverse fantasy. This sort of isolation persists even when a fantasy is reported to the analyst with the unconscious intention of including him in the patient's sadomasochistic economy.

• As a result, it may prove necessary to verify that *the image* and *the representations of the perverse act* are *possible* within transference. This sort of actualization of the perverse *scenario* within the treatment mobilizes the intensities of the preverbal affect or drive representatives, and constitutes a precondition for their "translation" into interpretive speech.

Didier entered into analysis with the complaint that he was unable to have any satisfying sexual relations.[5] It soon become apparent that his sexuality was voyeuristic and exhibitionist, masturbatory, and one in which sadomasochistic scenarios gave him the most pleasure. Didier was an amateur painter, though he never showed his paintings to anyone except his mother, while she was still living. Ever since his "audience" had died, his mother's apartment was closed off, and Didier dared not lay a finger on it or sell it.

Didier's discourse remained very fluent throughout his analysis. He knew everything and needed nothing from me. By way of his masturbatory speech, which bore witness to an exorbitant infantile power, Didier described his rituals as if he were reading a film script, coldly exposing the actions of actors whom he directed from afar. I had a feeling—or a countertransferential conviction—that Didier's secret resided in his mother's apartment, as well as in a *secret discourse* that entombed his drives and affects and prevented them from coming forth in his speech. This patient's speech was cut off from his affects; his affects were not to be found in his speech.

As a result, I agreed to look at Didier's artwork, which consisted of collages made of cut-up posters drenched or daubed with colors, of blank pages, and so forth. Didier's voice became increasingly animated. He would explain his paintings to me from the couch, or he would show me a photograph that allowed me to follow his remarks. Nevertheless, his discourse remained neutral, technical, and aesthetic. It was I who had to come up with the perverse signification of his exposition—of the cut-up organs, of the fecal substances. During the treatment, I allotted Didier a certain perverse acting-out—that is, the display of his paintings—and I transplanted onto this demonstration the discourse of the anti-perversion that he lacked.

He accepted this perverse fantasy—his or mine?—and his phantasmatic potential was thereby unleashed. Fantasies grew to replace his periods of acting-out without completely eliminating them. Nevertheless, since Didier was able to integrate them and to work them out by way of his discourse, he lost his relentless need to act out. Thus, he was able to create a new and more complex psychic structure.

In the pervert's case, the other is reduced to being the agent of the subject's sadomasochistic pleasure—which also ensures the subject's omnipotence. Although the ensuing discourse displays the logical and grammatical features of normative speech, it holds no heuristic or commutative value. Indeed, the unconscious meaning that it actually conveys resides in the neutralization of the other (the analyst) and in the reduction of a perverse megalomania into an object-fetish. If we wish to be privy to the workings of this unconscious determination, the speech-fetish must be dismantled. The analyst can use words to enrich the scenario-*image,* as well as the *act* that is in fact the pervert's "real language." And it will then become possible to endow speech with the multifaceted, heuristic, and commutative dimension it once had—the dimension in which the subject's complexity will be played out, and not the pervert's repudiation.

Insofar as the onset of transference is contingent upon the desire to know, to know *oneself,* and to transform *oneself* and grow, we have reason to wonder if this subjective pose is not historically determined. This subjective desire can appear in various guises, ranging from the ethical demands of a Jewish God to the Trinitarian mystery of Christian subjectivity and even to the "what do I know?" put forth by Montaigne, whose split ego prefigures in many ways the one that Freud has described. These different forms can be seen as foundations of Western history as well as of psychoanalysis (in the sense of an infinite appropriation of memory into a new history of subjects made ill by their symptoms). On the other hand, satisfying the narcissistic discontent that accompanies the modern crisis of values seems to be at odds with this sort of psychic inquiry, an inquiry that seems necessary for any transformation of subjectivity.

Psychoanalysis goes against the grain of the modern convenience that calls attention not to the end of the Story of Civilization, but to end of the possibility of *telling a story.* Nevertheless, this end and this convenience are beginning to overwhelm us, and we have been led to criticize and to reject them.

Be that as it may, psychoanalytic technique cannot ignore this narcissistic withdrawal and decline of desire. Psychoanalysis will need to acknowledge and assimilate these conditions before it can attempt to go further and to strive for a new form of self-knowledge, one that Freud has already outlined by placing the "malady" at the very essence of the psyche and by making psychic life into an interminable construction-destruction. The psychoanalytic approach to depression and perversion, among other "modern" symptoms, shows that the analytic field is reaching out to the very boundaries that offer it the most resistance.

In my view, contemporary psychoanalysis, and especially that of the future, is an art—I admit, an artifice—that may allow the men and women of our modern, sleek, lofty, costly, and profit-bearing cities to preserve a life for themselves. Why? Because the speaking being's life begins and ends with psychic life, a life for which speech is one axis of a heterogeneous dynamic. Freudian psychoanalysis has more to offer than a simple refuge for a society of spectacle and consumption. While acknowledging and assimilating the logic of monetary exchange, it also overthrows our alienating metropolises and incites real change. If it fails to do this, what else will inspire change, faced as we are with the glow of our silver high-rises, the implacable banality of banks, and the fact that destiny is being programmed into the genetic code itself?

Therefore, I suggest that in the future, psychoanalysis may be one of the few remaining endeavors that will allow change and surprise, that is, that will allow life. It will remain cognizant of the elements of psychic permanency (from biology to drives and language), but it will also provide support for those who wish to alter these elements. For by remaining loyal to Freud's skepticism while recognizing the resiliency of psychic discourse, we contend that such a modification is possible.

3. THE OBSESSIONAL NEUROTIC
AND HIS MOTHER

Although obsessional neurosis is not readily linked with a real or psychic trauma, the obsessional neurotic exhibits an excess of stimulation that is suppressed or explosive, impulsive and compulsive, and relentless and resistant to his defensive discourse. Obsessional speech is essentially an impenetrable protective device that prevents the return of affects or drives. For this reason, obsessional speech, which acts as a shield from some censured trauma, impairs the necessary associative process within transference; or worse, it exiles the associations to the workings of an artificial intellectualization and thereby diminishes the possibilities of analytic treatment.

We could base our search for the logic of this *excess* of stimulation as well as its *dissociation* from obsessional discourse upon the object relation, which parallels the "economic" conception that is sustained throughout the evolution of Freud's theories on trauma.[1] A given subject will find different occurrences to be more or less traumatic according to the type of relation to the other that has marked his life since his early years. *The structure can thus be a traumatic one.* Yet the obsessional neurotic spends his mortifying and confusing time dissociating himself from the bond with the other that molded him, a dissociation that serves to make the coldness of his defenses and the explosion of his sadomasochistic passion *seem natural.* Let us call to mind the object relations of this historian of accidents, this recorder of experienced or wished-for traumas.

From "Acts (−1)" to Dissociation

I shall focus on two notions that I believe have recently increased our understanding of obsessional neurosis:[2]

1. The obsessional neurotic may be characterized by a privileging of *doing* over *saying,* of the "procedural" over the "declarative," as Anderson puts it (of "If A then do B" rather than "A means B").[3] This formula offers a succinct description of obsessional thought's propensity for being *magical.* At the same time, it brings our attention to the fact that the obsessional neurotic experiences a *shortage of signs.* In a word, this stubborn thinker denies the *arbitrary nature* of the sign, which he transforms into an *act:* clearly not a pensive type, might he be a wild-eyed craftsman? D. Widlöcher,[4] A. Braconnier, and B. Brusset have emphasized that the obsessional neurotic bears witness to a breakdown of the *arbitrary nature* of the signifier, which is instantly *implemented, magically* and compulsively set in place, and incarnated as a form of *acting.*

Freud seems to distinguish between this *thought-action* that characterizes the obsessional neurotic and *the act itself.* He speaks of a "thought preliminary" to the "substitutive act" that "asserts itself with all the force of compulsion in place of the substitutive act." Freud finds this in the sort of "regression" that he describes as "preparatory acts [that] become substituted for the final decision" (RM, p. 244).[5]

For this reason, the absence of the arbitrary nature of the sign (or of the symbolic value of thought) leads to "preparatory," "preliminary" acts, i.e., acts minus 1, expressed as acts (−1). These acts hinder the logical links of thought as well as the specific acts that such a logic would require. Under the influence of the regression that is characteristic of such "acts (-1)," all of the obsessional neurotic's acts become compulsive, tentative, and subject to change.

2. Freud has stressed the importance that the senses of "sight" and "touch" have for the obsessional neurotic, for whether these senses are favored or avoided, they are persistent and intense. Pierre Fédida[6] and F.-D. Villa have drawn attention to this observation and have increased its scope: they assert that the hallucinosis of obsessional thought and behavior reach a hallucinatory motivity that presents itself "like a dream." The narrative of this dream sets itself up, however, as a barrier to regression, to the unconscious, and to analytic work itself.

In light of these two points, I should like to return to one of Freud's observations that I believe must be brought into question: "*The trauma, instead of being forgotten, is deprived* [through repression] *of its affective cathexis;* so that what remains in consciousness is nothing but its ideational content, which is perfectly colourless and is judged to be unimportant" (RM, p. 196, italics mine). Freud's remark suggests that the obsessional neurotic's trauma is deprived of its affective cathexis (investment). More specifically, he believes that it is the "*conscious memory* [that is] deprived of its affective cathexis." It is nevertheless a fact that the *idea* often falls under a certain "freezing" of the affective cathexis of the obsessional neurotic's trauma.

Now, the preponderance of both *paradoxical doing* (a *doing minus 1*) and *hallucinosis,* among other obsessional traits, would suggest that this is not the case. The affective investment is there—present, active, and intense; it lures the content of thought toward *acting-out* and *affect* by inscribing them with the compulsive logic of repetition and the regressive logic of inversion that leads to doubt and to the inability to make decisions.

I believe that obsessional repression dissociates the *psychic representative of affect* from *verbal representation.* This *dissociation* functions within the ever-forming system of signs. Obsessional repression causes "abstract" and "defensive" language and thought—which are split from psychic representatives of affect—to be separated from those psychic representatives of affect that are transplanted onto other semiotic phenomena (the gaze, the voice, movement) and transformed into a magical acting-out.

This acting-out eludes conscious defenses and allows for an immediate gratification of desire (like a fantasy that is "enacted" and that is no longer seen as a fantasy, but as "magic."). Anyone who observes the obsessional neurotic can sense the domination of acting-out over the psyche. In reality, it is a manifestation of an *immediately satisfied demand* that occurs before the *mediation of language* and *the other* even begin.

I would like to draw attention to this obsessional dissociation between *affect representation* and *verbal representation,* a dissociation that allows affect to be mobile, as well as free from the repression that governs language. Indeed, if repression had a bearing on *affect* itself, affect would return via the hysterical form of the symptom. Even though this possibility may not be outside the obsessional neurotic's grasp, the *psychic representative* of affect is what overcomes his *repression*—or rather, his dissociation.

The psychic representative of affect erupts into the domain of language and thought, and it produces not a somatic symptom, but a "symbolic monstrosity," a symptom of thinking—magical thinking—where "doing" is confused with "meaning," "hallucinosis," and so forth. The return of the affect representative within linguistic representation or thought endows it with semiological attributes related to the image, to sound, and to the sense of touch—attributes that are perceived as more active, direct, and effective.

As for affect, it is there—it is not repressed. It is merely deprived of its affective investment *for* verbal expression. Yet in the gaze, the voice, and the "acts (-1)," affect is far from divested: *it is powerful, lethal, and deadly.* This has an effect on the obsessional neurotic's dual character: he communicates through shadows, ghosts, and the deceased; his speech and thought are firmly implanted, yet his libidinal, dreamlike, and "procedural" actions are those of a murderous, greedy, and unbridled tyrant.

Thus, the obsessional symptom is rooted in language; it is centered on a language in which the verbal signifier is dissociated from the psychic representative of affect. Such dissociation impels the affect representative to search for other semiotic phenomena (gestural, visual, mobile), including *acts* that are *paradoxical*, "minus 1," and "procedural."

I shall attempt to compare this dual semiology (a divested language accompanied with other heavily invested semiotic materials and compulsive actions) to the obsessional neurotic's relationship to the *maternal object*.

The "Rat Man" Between Anal and Oral

In Freud's published case history of the "Rat Man" (a Dr. Lehrs) as well as in the original record of the analysis, little attention is paid to the mother of the patient. The French editors inform us that "the mother remains anonymous, and we do not know her age. We do know that she was adopted by the Speransky family." [7]

In the Rat Man case, Freud states that the patient told him about a "dream which represented the same conflict in relation to his transference onto the physician. He dreamed that my mother [Freud's] was dead; he was anxious to offer me his condolences, but was afraid that in doing so he might break into an *impertinent laugh,* as he had repeatedly done on similar occasions in the past. He preferred, therefore, to leave a card on me with the initials "p.c." [*pour condoler*-to offer condolences] written on it; but as he was writing the letters turned into "p.f." [*pour féliciter*-to congratulate]" (RM, p. 193).

When Freud deciphered this dream of the "dead mother," he interpreted it as a revival of the patient's dead mother, who was implicitly remembered by way of a transference onto the analyst (the desire to make the analyst's mother and the analyst himself die, just as the patient's mother had died). The mother was neither "put to death" nor "murdered," but she is a dead woman—a corpse—someone who no longer exists. This explains the "impertinent laugh," the nervous laughter that overtook this person who, when faced with the collapse of an absolute prohibition, lost his means of defense and symbolization, and quite literally negated himself in a spastic, demented, and aphasic jouissance.

This sort of submersion of the subject by an inexpressible affect (the "nervous laughter") is often considered to be a form of hysterical conversion. In this case, however, I see it as a trace of the challenge put forth to an archaic and maternal (the "impertinent laugh") authority figure. Moreover, it appears to be a trace of the motor satisfaction of putting the other (the mother) to death, the other that becomes merged with the self, both of them engaging in a single series of innumerable disturbances. The subject delighted in putting himself to death alongside the dead woman while defying her—devouring her, "screwing" her—through an obscene act of immediate gratification, that is, his spastic, masturbatory laughter.

In the original record of the case, Freud notes that he "gave his patient a modest meal" as well as some theoretical "fragments." *(Stück, ein neues Stückchen).*[8] The French editors note that "he played a maternal role."[9]

In the OR (p. 282), Freud recalls that the patient reported a "whole series of *representations.*"[10] (The word is missing from the manuscript. The French translators added it because of the verb *machen* at the end of the sentence.) This "representation" (a fantasy? a hallucination? an "act (-1)"?) depicts the "naked body of my mother. Two swords sticking into her breast from the side" ("like a decoration, he said later—following the Lucrece motif").

Lucrece, Collatinus' wife, who was raped by Sextus Tarquinius, stabbed herself to death. The dream notably transforms the daggers with which Lucrece kills herself into a decoration—a "still life." In Shakespeare's *The Rape of Lucrece,* Brutus, the son, is the first person to remove the dagger and to kiss his mother, fascinated as he is by the blood that flows from the wound—in her breast. Yet, the patient's "representation" travels from the breast to the lower body (note the shift from orality to genitality): "The lower part of her body and especially her genitals had been entirely eaten up by me and the children." In Freud's interpretation, the patient "had allowed himself to be led astray by a metaphor. Was not the content the [ascetic] idea that a woman's beauty was *consumed*— eaten up—by sexual intercourse and child-birth?" (OR, p. 283).

Nevertheless, this metaphor makes Freud forget two things. First, the mother was devoured by the son; an intense orality served as a link for both the archaic couple and the one formed by the patient and the analyst. Second, an analogy was set up between the female genitals, which were devoured by her children, and the patient's fear of seeing his own lower body devoured through the anus, in this case by rats.

The rats caused Freud to neglect orality as well as the fact that the Rat Man displaced his orality onto his anality. Although Freud makes a great deal of both the "rat" symptom and of anality when he describes his own role in the transference as being intrusive or "forceful," he lets silence rule over the oral eroticism in which he participated, if nothing else, by serving ritualistic meals to his patient.

The theme of devouring suggests that the patient is indistinguishable from his mother, and it imposes a logic of inversion (the subject becomes object and vice versa) that is manifested at other levels of his psychic functioning, which is exemplified by the onslaught of associations produced by this very episode. In this sense, a disgusting person, who eventually proves to be the patient himself, engages in oral sex with the analyst's daughter.

According to the *Original Record,* it was at the next day's session that the Rat Man reported the dream to which I have already referred: "My mother just died." Is it the same "dead mother" dream that is mentioned in the Rat Man case? If so, there has been a bizarre reversal: whereas in the Rat Man case, the dead woman is the analyst's mother, in the OR, the patient conjures up the death of his own mother. Although Freud was right to believe that this is a transference dream, by discounting the cannibal theme as well as the two-sided and reversible character of object identification, he chooses to limit his interpretation to the issue of aggressiveness:

"Hasn't it ever occurred to you that if your mother died you would be freed of all conflicts, since you would be able to marry?" "You are taking revenge on me" he said. "You are forcing me into this, because you want to revenge yourself on me."

Freud concluded that "he was afraid of being beaten by me." He also noted that the patient "kept hitting himself while he was making these admissions which he still found so difficult" (OR, p. 283–84).

The following session pursued the transferential and maternal themes, which are neglected in Freud's published study: "The next session was filled with the most frightful transferences, which he found the most tremendous difficulty in reporting. My mother *was standing in despair* while all her children were being hanged." The mother is no longer dead; she is desperate. It is Freud's mother who is in question, and the analyst interprets his patient's aggressive desire to have his analyst hanged.

I am drawn to this image of a desperate mother, as well as to the impossibility of speaking about her if not by displacing her into another realm, that of aggressiveness. The Rat Man could only speak about his mother if he eroticized their deadly and depressed relationship by way of the aggressiveness that both the other man (Freud) and his mother were to provoke. Thus, there were two ways in which he avoided having a relationship with his depressed mother: on the one hand, he thought that she was Freud's mother; on the other, it was easier for him to think about hanged children than about his mother's sorrow.

When he spoke, the patient consistently avoided the maternal figure. For example, whenever he mentioned his mother's naked body, he would quickly bury it (so to speak) and refer instead to his grandmother's body. In like manner, after talking about devouring or about young girls, he pictured Freud's son, who was licking his lips—which were surrounded by something brown (one thinks of excrement), as if it were tasty—and he remarked again: "it is I, and I'm doing it to my mother." The obsessional neurotic's mother is dead, anonymous, depressed, or that [mother] of another person.

That is all I shall say about the bond between Dr. Lehrs and his mother, such as it is described by these two Freudian texts. My reading, which is far from exhaustive, was motivated not by a desire to examine Freud from this specific perspective, but by some observations I have made of my own obsessional neurotic patients.

On the one hand, I have noticed that such patients rarely speak about their infantile relationship with their mothers. Although they are always willing to describe their conflicts with their fathers or brothers and do not shy away from obscenity when discussing their current or former experiences with women, *a veritable "buried mother" resides at the core of their psyche.*

On the other hand, this "buried mother" appears to be a magnet for a violent libido that is permanently satisfied and consequently unavailable for any symbolization that is not aural, visual, or tactile—that is, any symbolization that is not dramatically cut off from speech. It is as if the obsessional neurotic had *two languages:* the first one, secretive and nonverbal "speech," a tomb or a screen of the satisfaction that he had received following a precocious demand that he directed toward his mother, who was all the more accommodating because her feminine desires had been left unsatisfied. The other language appears to be a neutralized language and thought that are "dead," freed from the chains of this voracious demand, though consequently divested, superfluous, reversible, unconvincing, and uncreative.

This "buried mother" is not necessarily what André Green has called the "dead mother," who is dissociated or quasi-psychotic, a borderline case.[11] The "buried mother" is often a women who is simply depressive, sometimes depressed, but who masks her malady in an exaggerated activity level. The impression she inscribes in her son's consciousness is not that of a deadly object. On the contrary, it is often that of a stern mother. She comes across, however, as someone who has broken off two bonds: the erotic bond with the father, and the bond with language.

She is not an object of the father's desire, and she does not desire him either. She only experiences desire for her son and for a mirage—the sublime figure of a parent or a social figure to whom she dedicates her dreams. She fails to express herself—she is taciturn, "anonymous," voiceless. Her son does not retain any of her words, except perhaps a certain refusal to talk or play with him.

Nevertheless, the obsessional neurotic retains the intense impressions of exchanged looks, of being touched, of being cared for—an "anonymous" envelope that was not given to him by his mother, but that is always already there, an integral part of him, ineluctably destined for him, and inevitably devoured by him. It is as if a precocious amorous bond had attached itself to the *disavowal of the signifier* that characterizes the mother's depression (which is supported by a painful affect that cannot be represented).[12]

The son's demand fulfills his mother's frustrated desire, and it goes on to become a satisfied desire. There is no delay of symbolization, and there is no sign. On the one hand, there is depression, and on the other, the demand is transformed into a satisfied desire: all the conditions are met for the path of language toward the affect representative to be obstructed. Thus, language is formed in another world, split from the worlds of depression and demand. It develops into a second language—a secondary one associated with expulsion and penetration. If (and only if) this language can find an analyst who is strong enough, it can turn anal sadomasochism into the ultimate defense against the inaccessible repression represented by the fusion-devouring of the obsessional neurotic and his buried mother.

These observations had left me unsure of my ability as an analyst to occupy this space of the buried object, to bring it back to life, and then to attempt to revive my patients' amorous relationships—which tend to be consistently disappointing, divested as soon as they begin to take shape, and inevitably doomed to failure.

At that point, my rereadings of Freud enabled me to pinpoint this anonymity, this reversible orality, this nonverbal, impossible-to-represent necrophilia that is *acted out* and that, *like an inaccessible trauma,* characterized the bond between the Rat Man and his mother. These aspects had eluded me during my first readings.

Far from being as spectacular as certain obsessional disorders that harbor inaccessible traumas, the following two analytic fragments depict obsessional characteristics that are quite common. The semiology of these obsessional disorders consists of a predisposition to fail, the impossibility to choose, the reversal of desires, and of relationships that are disappointing, repetitive, and destined to failure. Such obsessional traits might have been rather ordinary, were it not for some tragic events that revealed that they stemmed from a sort of death disguised as satisfaction.

A Precocious Satisfaction

Pierre's father was an actor who had had his moment of glory during the postwar years; his mother was an unassuming office worker for whom the father apparently had so much disdain that he referred to his three boys—Pierre and his younger brothers—as the "maid's children." Pierre came into analysis with the complaint that he suffered from "chronic indecision"—which was how he described his inability to choose between two thoughts or two courses of action. His chronic indecision prevented him from engaging in any professional endeavors. He complained, moreover, of repeated disappointments in love: although "career women" earned his respect, he was physically attracted to "good-looking, vacuous girls—to tramps or drug addicts." Such women lost his interest once they satisfied him sexually, and they incited an intense hostility in him if they showed any sign of depth, desire, predilection, or character.

The first phase of Pierre's analysis centered on his relationship with his father. Pierre's discreet, unadorned, and guarded speech was accompanied by a flushing of the face that spread to his balding head, as if a sort of congestion were depicting a sexual excitement that his speech would render into a cool commentary. He informed me that between the ages of twelve and twenty, he had experienced frequent fainting spells that could be neither diagnosed nor treated. The ones he could recall had occurred after the representation of an aggressive act in which an older man attacked him from behind. During his analysis, Pierre had some dreams that represented his father as a thief breaking into his apartment, accompanied by a gang of drunken rabble-rousers who tried to rape him after leaving a nightclub.

Although we were not able to consider this portion of the analysis exhaustively, it did become subject to some working-through, once Pierre found the courage to interview his father—with a microphone, a tape recorder, and a transcription—about his "wild" days as an "actor." From that point on, possessing the cassette enabled Pierre to possess his father. His father's discourse had become his object; or rather, it had become a precious, harnessed, and acquired waste product.

Nevertheless, there was no change in Pierre's relationships with women. A compelling frenzy would drive him to win over a buxom young woman, who would quickly find herself "burned up," reduced to nothing, and "a real pain"—she herself a waste product, though a despised one. It was as if the sexual act had killed off the young woman's attractiveness and entailed a series of vengeful acts and mental cruelty against his victim—that is, until another woman could take her place.

Pierre did not like to speak about his mother, and he believed that his father's remarks concerning the "maid's children" had turned him against her for good: "I have no interest in her, she doesn't talk much, she has nothing to say." Yet, he nonchalantly informed me that they still lived in the same house, "on either end of the hallway," and that they "practically" lived together, even though they "did not notice each other's presence." It was an archaic symbiosis that was slightly embarrassing, a sort of complicity in a shameful fusion of waste products (that is, the maid and her son).

A memory surfaced:

Pierre shows his mother a wonderful boat he had made while dreaming about one of his father's journeys. She looks at him with empty, sad eyes that he thinks are "admiring," even though she does not say anything. He keeps trying: "What do you think of it?" She answers, "Absolutely nothing" and withdraws back into her sorrow.

What was "nothing"? Maman, the boat, or Pierre? There was no communication, just the feeling of being possessed. She truly possessed him, which offered him no serenity. Nothing but a feeling of being "rejected," "satisfied," but in the dark— "unacknowledged."

I linked this *satisfaction with being in the dark* and *with being unacknowledged* to Pierre's attempts to back off from the analysis and to engage in psychodrama. In his own words, "We cry out, we touch each other, we look at each other, something happens, it's not purely intellectual like psychoanalysis, where only speech matters." Nevertheless, Pierre remained unsatisfied by his experiences with psychodrama. He told me that the sort of rapport he experienced was a crude one, and that the other people were stupid and inferior to him. I said, "The people may be stupid and inferior, but they offer you a sensual satisfaction that is somewhat removed, as if it were on the other end of the hallway." Pierre, who was usually either exceptionally polite or simply sardonic, exploded at me and addressed me using the familiar *tu* form: "What the hell do you care—That really pisses you off, doesn't it?"

I will limit my remarks to this one episode of Pierre's analysis in order to emphasize the dissociation between speech and affect as well as the shrouding of the "archaic" object relation in affect and in preverbal representatives: movement, touch, and the gaze. While fleeing from analytic speech, Pierre sought these representatives through psychodrama. For this reason, I thought that my interpretation had *to verbalize,* and thus acknowledge, this affect, one that Pierre experienced not only as erotic (eroticism being anal and coming from the father), but also (and primarily) narcissistic—which would explain the wound that my interpretation rekindled in the patient, as well as its intensity.

By introducing a third party (that is, myself) into this necrophiliac and depressive relationship between mother and son, I abruptly switched off the defensive humming of Pierre's associative discourse, which had previously been broken down but was now giving way, due to the impact of the trauma that the patient had experienced from being identified with his abandoned mother—a depressed sexual object. To push this trauma aside, Pierre subjected his mistresses to it, and then subjected himself to the bitterness of his amorous disappointments.

The analysis continued not only by interpreting whenever possible the *theme* of the mother/son relationship, but also by "translating" into words Pierre's corporeal states and sensations that pertained to the senses of sight, touch, and hearing—senses to which he occasionally made elliptical references. I felt as if I were building a bridge between a body (whose *affects* were masked by maternal depreciation or depression) and a sociosymbolic *scene.*

The little boy had become fused with his mother's depression, a depression that also served as the locus of their silent, yet shared, satisfaction. Suppressed pleasure *acts* within this mutism by attaining an intense jouissance. Nevertheless, it is experienced as a total failure with respect to the "front of the stage," which is dominated by success, masks, and the pretense of paternal *discourse,* that is, "authoritative" discourse. The obsessional neurotic grieves for this jouissance, which is incessantly averted by his behavior, apprehensions, and rituals.

Accomplice and Traitor of the Depressed Person

Another one of my patients displayed symptoms that were more obviously obsessional. A teacher of ailing children, Yves feared that if the bus he was awaiting was preceded by another one that shared the same route, this meant that one of the children placed under his care would have a catatonic fit, another child would run away, and so forth.

These obsessive thoughts centered on buses, but also on various elements of the erotic ceremony. If Yves had trouble getting an erection, if he did not ejaculate, or if his girlfriend chose one sexual position over another, he felt that his young charges would be stricken again with disaster. The logical process behind these rituals can be schematized as follows: homosexual desire for children—a conscious objection to this desire—the onset of magical thinking. The latter favored an indifferent or sexually charged aspect in order to modulate homosexual desire, whose roots were analyzed with respect to the bond between Yves and his father.

Yves spoke slowly and with a very low voice that was almost inaudible, as if he were about to fall asleep or had just woke up—a state between sleep and wakefulness. He seemed to be terrified of something, and he often recalled memories of spankings that were apparently administered by some sadistic female schoolteachers. What is more, he tirelessly yet dreamily (as if sleeping) commented on Freud's article, "A child is beaten." Is the child being beaten or seduced? Who is doing it? Whose child is it? He never ceased to be fascinated with such questions.

Yves rarely spoke to me about his mother, who lived in the provinces and with whom he had a very limited relationship; he wondered if the schoolteachers were perhaps masking a "monster," and he spoke of the uneasiness he had felt as a child when thinking that he had stumbled upon a sexual relationship between his mother and a family friend. Nevertheless, all that remained rather vague, forgotten, brushed aside, and neutralized. Yves displayed a little more interest when his father experienced some professional difficulties. In addition, he began to ruminate about his homosexual desires for his "friends." Indeed, his "girlfriends" always had a designated lover. Hence, Yves was perpetually assuming the role of *a third party* who fantasized about the other man's pleasure and felt "frigid—if there is no man in the scenario."

This continued until the day he sent me a poignant telegram—both the display of emotion and the telegram itself are relevant here—informing me that he would have to miss his session because his mother had just committed suicide.

Yves came back two sessions later (the funeral was in the provinces). I immediately noticed a change in his speech: it had become clearer, more distinct, and more flowing—it was not exactly verbose, but it was richer than ever before. Although Yves made a concerted effort to recall memories that might reveal that his mother had been depressed, he found nothing that was worth reporting. She had been around, busy, taciturn, a dreamer—if he thought about it after the fact, she may have been depressed. Perhaps he unconsciously solicited the sadistic stimulation of "monsters" in order to overcome his indifference to his mother. Or perhaps he did so in order to rediscover a relationship that was passionate yet buried, a relationship that occurred between a depressed mother and her only son (the patient considered himself not as an object but as a substitute for repressed maternal feelings and resentments).

I would like to emphasize that the mother is buried within obsessional discourse. She was already dead, and a part of Yves' personality had assimilated her. As a result of his mortifying speech, his sexual impotence, and the obsessional rituals in which he performed a role-reversal and saw himself as a potential executioner of the children he cared for, Yves bore some resemblance to his mother's tomb. Furthermore, by identifying with his mother's disappointed and depressed desire, Yves was able to accede to masculine desire. The depressed woman withdrew her libido from other people in order to experience it solely within her silent narcissistic sorrow before committing the fatal act.

It so happens that her son was the ultimate offshoot of the desire that she denied. He directed himself toward other people; he moved about and became agitated. Yet he remained tentative, hesitant, and weary from having *assimilated* both his mother's wounded narcissism and her depressive withdrawal from speech or from acts that were directed toward other people. I do mean "assimilated." The fleeting memory of the discomfort Yves felt after stumbling upon his mother when she was romantically involved with a family friend had occurred when this child was in the midst of *eating an ice cream cone*—he was overtaken by fits of vomiting.

I had not really been aware of this devouring, which prefigured a disgust-rejection of a mother who had become the object of desire for someone else. At that point in the treatment, the axis of interpretation focused on the desire-hatred for the other man. I thought about it again, and we reconsidered this scene a few sessions after his mother's death, when Yves dreamt that he was performing fellatio on himself. In the dream itself, he found that this body position was difficult, even impossible, and he noticed that his penis was not his own but that of his mother, "as if we were the same body, and the penis was hers or mine at the same time—I don't know, it was hard to tell."

With respect to young girls and devouring, I have already drawn attention to a similar theme and corporeal topography in the *Original Record* of the Rat Man case. When the son's (oral) demand is immediately satisfied because the depressed mother responds to him by directing her disappointed and worn-out desire back to it, a space is formed in which the other is devoured and preserved—though in the form of a ghost. Sexual difference has no place to inscribe itself. Language is unable to take any distance from a third party in which it could convey affects and from which it could take shelter, for the depressed mother informs her son, who is an object of substituted desire, that in a world of third parties, desire is nothing but a disappointing artifice.

Consequently, in order to make his affects known, the obsessional neurotic has no choice but to resort to violence: raping women-objects—"shadows"—getting raped himself as a passive object—as an animal, cracking the shell of his language and his artificial personality with the help of a break-in that he prefers to be anal, which counterbalances out his archaic oral fulfillment that shields his unspeakable secret.

Yves' mother's suicide nullified his identification with this depressed woman. He freed himself from her, as if he had "vomited" her. He began to speak about her as if she were another person, and he tried to be the subject of his own speech, to speak in his own name.

When a patient is stricken with tragedy, the analyst is inevitably called into question. Had the analyst followed a different course, could it have changed Yves' relationship with his mother and prevented her suicide? Was I not a party to Yves' reticence about his mother? Should I have enabled this woman to escape from the tomb in which she was trapped by both her son's padlocked desire and her own complicity in this necrophiliac, smothering relationship that they found satisfying through their silence and shared blindness? These questions clearly arose out of a counter-transference that had difficulty remaining dispassionate once death got mixed up in it.

In light of the divestment of speech through affect representatives, I have become aware of a technical imperative that concerns the treatment of obsessional neurotics. Although this requirement runs counter to dogma, I shall heed it in the future: not only must analysts occasionally put aside the neutrality and abeyance that are all too similar to obsessional defenses, but more important, they should also propose verbal and affective *constructions* that are relevant to the relation to the archaic object, to the preobject, and to narcissism. As if it were primarily a matter of teaching the obsessional neurotic a *language* that he does not know, even though it affects him as well as those around him—the language of precocious seduction.

If he does not learn this language, the depressed person relinquishes desire (that is, seduction) and embraces the death act after having suffered from asymbolia. If he does not learn this language, the obsessional son creates his own artificial language—a phallic prosthesis of his depressed mother. Treatment is impossible when one is faced with the artificial defense of obsessional discourse, which I see as a variant of the "false self." In such cases, the analytic process must seek links between this dead language and the discourse of a desire that aspires to discover its relationship to the voracious and precocious *demand* that is intensely and immediately satisfied, only to be buried under a dead sign that believes it wields some power.

I have suggested that depressed discourse bases itself upon a disavowal of the signifier—a signifier that is "devitalized" because it is separated from affects. The obsessional neurotic's primary and oral identification with maternal depression leads him *on the one hand* to deny this depression and to replace it (to compensate for it) with an investment of the symbolic (language, thought, homosexual relations). In this way, the obsessional neurotic replaces the depressed woman's executioner; that is, he replaces what he imagines to be the masculine power that his mother lacks and that causes her ill-being. Yet *on the other hand,* the obsessional neurotic preserves the fundamental core of the psychic functioning of this maternal depression: the dissociation between affect representation and verbal representation.

As opposed to the depressed mother, however, the obsessional neurotic does not neutralize—or absorb—affect representations. Instead, he *abreacts* them—he acts them out through other semiotic materials (aural, visual, tactical). Thus, he keeps them to himself and remains loyal to his mother's tomb, whose existence he does not internalize even though he is aware of it.

Traumatized as he is by the depression of his mother, who burdened her child for a while before fulfilling his request in order to survive, the obsessional neurotic continues to be the stubborn and ruthless traitor of such distress—of his own distress, in fact, for he assimilates his mother's helplessness. And he will only reveal it through a reversal—by taking revenge, for example, on the demeaned female-objects of his desires, or by eroticizing the wounded and depressive narcissism of his mother while coming forth as an object of anal aggressions on the part of his peers, an object that is more than just passive and persecuting.

Hence, as long as analysis fails to elucidate this traumatic oral relationship with maternal depression, it cannot work through the defenses that are intrinsic to obsessional discourse and to the anal eroticization that supports and perpetuates them. For analysis is what reorients language toward a hallucinatory psychic activity— acts (-1)—that attempts to correspond to the immediate satisfaction of the demand. The incorporation of obsessional discourse into a paradoxical act can be seen as a conjuration of the trauma inflicted by passion that comes from, and is directed toward, the depressive mother.

4. COUNTERTRANSFERENCE:
A REVIVED HYSTERIA

By identifying with their patients and even adopting their anxiety and excitability in order to identify them more easily, analysts render transference hysterical. We are all hysterics, at least intermittently. We all have our own idea and image (or impression) of the hysteric, and I shall obviously present my own. For what is known as countertransference is perhaps a discreet, if not guilt-ridden, way to concede that analysts' knowledge is maintained through their capacity to take on the lot of their double before playing dead or mourning their fate.

The history of culture and of psychoanalysis is peppered with the impasses and splendors of this close connection between hysterics and their beloved, both of whom could be diagnosed as incarnations of countertransference. I shall give two examples that will place these ideas in their imaginary context.

Jeanne Guyon (1649–1717) was one of the last great French mystics.[1] A quietist and a prophet of "pure love," she practiced and advocated *silence* as the only way to submit to God and to communicate with Him as well as with other people. She described the redemption of desires, wishes, individual interests, "pure love," and "silent communication" as "work without labor," "total deprivation," a "passive night," "a demise," and "a gift." In such an amalgam, the self and its God are deprived of all possible attributes—which amounts to saying that they are deprived of *judgment*. In those days, the Cartesians saw this sort of annihilation of self, thought, and language as a revolt against Port-Royal rationalism. But it was especially the Church, represented by Bossuet, that rose up against Mme Guyon and took aim through her at Fénelon, who had adopted some of his friend's ideas. Jeanne was found guilty of heresy and placed in an institution for six years.

From the time of her birth, the future mystic was seriously ill— she suffered from an abscessed back and legs that resulted in gangrene. Later she also contracted syphilis, and she never failed to find herself in so-called "crisis" states throughout her life. Nevertheless, she managed to forget her pains and to conceal her suffering and sensations. Or rather, she took pleasure in pain, in the sort of jouissance that wastes away without being experienced as suffering. She called it "pure love.":

> The soul "burns to suffer for what it loves." I do not think about it—I know nothing about it. I sense a deep wound in the bottom of my heart, but it is so delightful that I linger in my sorrow and take pleasure in my pain. (A Short Method of Prayer and Spiritual Torrent)

What was the secret of this alchemy? Anguish and pain were attributed to an Ideal Father, the Imaginary Father in prehistory,[2] who loved her, she believed, and whom she called her Beloved. In this regard, Fénelon (too filial) and Bossuet (too logical) would not go as far as did Jeanne.

From the age of nine, however, she seems to have experienced "spiritual torrents," although she declared that she "entertained doubts about Hell." In other words, even though Jeanne's dreams made the throes of the unconscious become apparent, she managed to disregard them. She later continued to infuriate Bossuet by upholding that she did not envision feelings as words (what heresy!), even though feelings come from words and are subordinated to them. Instead, she gave primacy to feelings.

Nevertheless, this follower of an "ineffable silence," of an "angel's language," and of "silent communication" was a prolific writer. An endless correspondence, an autobiography, and poems that foreshadow the automatic writing of the surrealists point to a feverish and uncontrollable sensuality. Fénelon was captivated by this, and he shared Jeanne's fascination for what he would call "the childhood of our being" and "the dark night." Through Guyon's encouragement, even Bossuet, who had once condemned her, began to be interested in the "states of oration" that he had criticized during his early quarrels with this quietist.

What is more, this lover of the ineffable who identified with Baby Jesus was a worldly woman. She created the Brotherhood of Pure Love and founded various social programs. More directly than did some of her predecessors like Saint Francis of Sales, Saint Theresa, or Saint John of the Cross, Jeanne's contradictions and naïve crises made a *strange chiasmus* appear. It was as if the subject had put herself in the very place where drives topple over into a psychic inscription that leads to a symbolic mental organization. Placed at such crossroads, a hysteric would not cease to waver between the unspeakable excitement of drives, on the one hand, and language with its symbolic dimension weighed down by the body, on the other. Fénelon was to engage in a countertransference toward the unnameable, whereas Bossuet was to play the role of the stern father by denouncing a perversion that for Jeanne remained unconscious.

Closer to our day, a young Russian woman named Sabina Spielrein was hospitalized, under Jung's orders, for a serious condition that resembled schizophrenia.[3] A medical student, she became an analyst "between" Jung and Freud. She was the first person to speak of the impulsional bases of phonation (the aggressiveness of the explosives P, B; the fusional eroticism of the liquids L, M), and of the death drive as an immanent counterpart to the life drive. (See her studies: *Destruction as the Cause of Coming into Being*

(1912) and *Reflections on the Various Stages of Linguistic Development: The Origins of the Childish Words Papa and Mama* (1922).)

She was in love with Jung, her first analyst, and she confessed to him that she wanted to have his baby—a blond Aryan Siegfried. Gripped himself by a loving identification with his enigmatic patient, Jung seems to have made his own child out of this union, a child that remained theoretical, as it should be: his concept of the Shadow and the Anima—sorts of female doubles, hysterical or psychotic, that are inherent in each of us.[4]

As for Freud, on the other hand, he borrowed his notion of the death drive from Sabina. Without waiting long to show his appreciation, he started up an epistolary exchange with Jung concerning the merits of their young protégé. Although Miss Spielrein apparently stimulated the erotic life of one man and the theoretical work of them both, Freud remained the more moderate and assertive of the two. In the end, he freed himself from this three-way embrace, and he authoritatively sent this young seductress back to her roots and her maternal obligations. Which was, after all, a way to assume a fatherly role:

> *I am, as you know, cured of the last shred of my predilection for the Aryan cause, and would like to take it that if the child turns out to be a boy he will develop into a stalwart Zionist.*
> *He or she must be dark in any case, no more towheads.*[5]

If forced to choose between these two countertransferences (Jung's and Freud's), I would confess a weakness for Freud's heavy-handed behavior, for he ordered this inspiring woman to take charge of his descendants, whether Jewish or psychoanalytic, and to participate in the founding of psychoanalysis in the Soviet Union. Such a challenge must have seemed infinitely more rash and risky than the one that consisted of languishing in the mirror games or shadows of Jungian esoterism. What followed proved this to be true.

Jeanne Guyon on the outermost bounds of language, Sabina Spielrein within the death drive: the hysteric, in these cases a woman, uses these two means to render imaginary a *spastic* body, a somatic memory that is resistant to representation. Hysterics do this without ignoring the other side of the coin—*symbolic power*—so much so that they enjoy it, make light of it, and suffer from it, if need be. Not only with one, but two fathers, as if to be reassured that He exists.

One could bemoan the fate of hysterics, who are victims of their masters. As for me, I prefer to focus on the revelation that the hysteric (male or female) induces in the master by unseating his cognitive defenses and by rousing him to come up with a new (though still insufficient) understanding of anxiety: that of the hysteric and that of the master. Analysts make progress by identifying with hysterical discourse and its silent exterior. They displace this plasticity into the imaginary, which causes the hysteric to travel from the verbal to the somatic and vice versa; they use their listening to transpose it onto phobias, depressions, and psychoses. Such is the foundation of psychoanalytic treatment, which joins together the shared fates of hysteria and interpretation.

Why do hysterics enjoy such a privileged role, since they also can hinder the evolution of analytic technique if we fail to modify and revive our concept of hysteria or if we remain unaware of the features of other psychic structures that require different techniques and modes of listening? I shall attempt to respond to this question by insisting that two levels, two memories, and two psychic economies coincide in both male and female hysteria.

The Two Memories of the Hysteric

Is the etiology of hysteria a sexual one? That is, does hysteria stem from a trauma inflicted by an external party? Is it a product of an irreconcilable and thus anxiety-ridden phantasmatic structure? Or does the inducement of the trauma and fantasy that cause hysteria require an ego endowed with "a weak level of consciousness," a "hypnotic ego" (as Breuer said) that facilitates the movement of a conscious idea toward a "plastic incarnation" that would be physical suffering (as French psychiatrists like Briquet, Charcot, and

Bernheim believed at the end of the nineteenth century)? If not, was Janet right in saying that since the hysterical ego is too weak to make the statement "I no longer see," hysterics disregard the "I" and the "no longer" and merely retain the "see"—a sensation localized in the subconscious that has become a subconscious *idée fixe?* In that case, hysteria would be "a malady by representation."[6]

Following Freud, analysts were convinced that this subconscious *idée fixe* of an ego endowed with a modest power of synthesis was a sexual fantasy. More precisely, it could be attested that the hysteric's troubles did not stem from the mere representation of an affect, but from a *sexual scenario* that could not be reconciled with a symbolic system that was otherwise left unchanged.

Some recent viewpoints seem to return to the hypothesis offered by nineteenth-century French psychiatrists. These perspectives either dispense with sexual etiology or accept the sexual hypothesis (in the psychoanalytic tradition), though only as a *complementary* determination of hysterical semiology. Thus, they maintain that all emotions (think of the endemic emotionalism of hysteria, even when it puts on deadened masks, including the mask of "pure love") reflect the inhibition of mental or pragmatic plans of action.

According to this hypothesis, anxiety—that companion of the hysteric which replaces jouissance—discharges an irremediable cognitive incongruence. To put it another way, new information makes subjects incapable of mobilizing their mental work and completely subjects them to phantasmatic anxiety. The unconscious fantasy is seen as a psychic response that results from a cognitive incongruence that suppresses the excess of excitement—which is the thrust of desire. The trauma (whether endogenous or exogenous) is nothing more than a cognitive incongruence taken over by a representation that encompasses anxiety. Anxiety appears as a failure of emotional life, incapable of mobilizing the mental work of cognitive, logical, and rhetorical assimilation.[7]

Though stemming from Freudianism, this surreptitious return to psychiatric positions, of which the most subtle variant can be traced back to Janet, may surprise and worry analysts. As for me,

I see it as an opportunity to rattle the current psychoanalytic view of hysteria, so that we might consider the role of analytic treatment in a broader perspective, seeing it as an experimental reactivation of hysteria, at once eased and diverted by an optimal handling of countertransference. Let me explain myself.

Hysterics seek a maximal symbolic and psychic jouissance while simultaneously postulating the impossibility or the futility of this desire. This discrepancy takes on some well-documented forms: endless seduction *and* frigidity, an eroticization of the link with other people and the outside world *and* an untouchable autosensuality, verbal haste *and* the discrediting of speech, a erotomaniac exaltation *and* an inexorable sadness with its underlying depressive tendencies, the incitement of the father and his knowledge *and* a spasmodic, angry, and mute body that can even be morbid toward the rival, the double, the mother. My aim is not to complete this portrait of hysterical symptomotology, but to recall that these elements suggest that the hysteric suffers from two anxieties and two memories.

Phallic identification with the father leads the hysterical subject (male or female) to *compete against maximal symbolic performance.* This results in rapid (thus poorly integrated) language acquisition, an abundant discourse, an intellectual curiosity, and a quest for knowledge. "Tell me what I know. If not, I will not tell it to you"—witness hysterical blackmail.

This is followed by a symbolic or cognitive competence, or even a "supercompetence." This destines hysterics to be the motor, when they are not the leader, of social, communicable, and mobilizing discourses. At the same time, a peerless or fatherless [*hors pair ou hors père*] excitability leads hysterics to crack the phallic framework that supports their cognitive congruence. They counteract it with an *exuberant affect* that can be either distressing or ecstatic, but whose upsurge comes forth through a lack of symbolic synthesis. And then hysterics disintegrate this acquired, cultivated, and fawned-upon coherence in order to oppose it to the woeful delights of their unnameable bodies, if not to the ineffable night of the mystics or the cult of disconnection or death.

Torn between two contracts—the rigorous requirements of the symbolic and the rigorous requirements of excitability—the hysterical subject, who is unable to synthesize these demands, resorts to such compromise solutions as anxiety, somatic symptoms, or irreconcilable fantasies.

I shall call *trauma* the manifested clash between these two demands. This clash may take the form of conversion or of phantasmatic anxiety: two compromise solutions (one being closer to soma and the other to psychic representatives) between symbolic solicitation and the solicitation of desire.

Though it surfaces in childhood, the trauma reverberates in any situation that confronts hysterics with new pieces of information that threaten their psychosexual compromises. In such situations, they leave behind their pragmatic or mental plans of action and fall back onto conversion or phantasmatic anxiety.

Thus, hysterics suffer from two types of reminiscences:[8] the reminiscence of their seductive identification with the paternal authority of symbolic knowledge and cognitive competence, and the reminiscence of a radical excitability that cannot be symbolized, one that is experienced as a gap, as passivity, as female castration, as a narcissistic flaw, or as depressive disregard.

The two-sided influence of psychotropic medicines on anxiety in general and on hysterical anxiety in particular has been noted. Some of these drugs modify the responses of the autonomous nervous system by inhibiting the perception of the activated state that causes anxiety feelings. Others have a sedating effect on the central nervous system—they control its hyperactivity and free up recurrent and sometimes newly adapted plans of action. These influences reveal *the biological substratum of the excitability that underlies anxiety,* and they encourage us to investigate the preconditions of cognitive (symbolic) memory. Biological disturbances upset the hysteric's psychic equilibrium, which leads not to psychotic disorganization, but to a new compromise that is made up of conversion and anxiety.

From this double contract particular to hysterics, I could derive the *fragmentation of their personality,* which often appears in the form of role playing, masks, and multiple personalities. One could interpret these aspects as identity stabilizers of the various attacks on emotional or anxious memory that are initially represented as fantasies and that are then embodied in order to form a series of characters incapable of synthesis.

Indeed, one of the spectacular features of hysteria is that it causes gaps in the realm of knowledge. Such gaps can result not only in personality fragmentation, but also in a *hypersensitive,* almost supernatural intuition—an intuition that can sense the emotions and latent thoughts of other people:

> A patient comes to a session with me and seems upset. She lies down on my couch and tells me she dreamt I had cancer, or that someone close to me was dying of cancer. Sure enough, a letter I had just received informed me that one of my close relatives had been diagnosed with this disease.

Using material from the past, I interpreted the patient's words as a death wish for her mother and for me. Yet it also was true that the patient used an emotional echo (transmissible by bodily signs) to exert a hold on me and to escape from her own conflicts.

Gaps in the realm of knowledge can also give way to *delirious fantasies*—a paralogical hyperassociativeness that sometimes opens the abyss of insanity within the core of a well-adapted hysteria. This reminds me of another patient, who usually exhibited a cold rationality. She came to her session wearing a sweater that she had been given by a friend who had committed suicide—a suicide for which my patient felt responsible. I shall return to the counter-transference that this analysis mobilized by emphasizing its relation to the patient's sensory memory.[9]

When she saw me, she felt a sudden urge to give me her sweater. Her purpose was "to finish off this series of deaths with your own, since I told you I can kill you if you aren't strong enough." She wanted me to die because she could not include me in her love. This does not change the fact that the hysteric's erotic fantasy shatters the surface of rational communication, and that anxiety permeatess the analysand's discourse. Consequently, language exchanges its cognitive coherence for a contagious strength. Signs and objects (words, the sweater) are invested with desire and sensuality. They become "performative": direct agents—erotic and in fact deadly—of a thereby disclosed hysterical intensity. Sustained by the uncontrollable force of drives, unconscious desire permeates speech. Without dissolving speech, unconscious desire endows it with a somnambular logic in which the animism of objects replaces the possibility of a metalinguistic evaluation of its discourse. Can the analyst do anything besides playing dead and adopting a stoic apathy?

This bivalence of the hysterical psyche corroborates the already observed phenomenon that hysterical *sexuality* is disavowed by *sensualization*. The hysteric's presumed aspiration to endless pleasures is not sexual but sensual—an unlimited sensory and emotional excitability. In reality, erotomaniac hysterics are sexual atheists, when they are not frigid. At the same time, they feign a devotion to their oversensitized bodies.

Through the desire by which they encounter the other, the father, and knowledge, hysterics try too hard, make believe, allay suspicion, and fail. The sorrow of unappeased desire, however, draws them into a secret garden, into their sensual, autosensual double. There, they anxiously delight in their want, quivering, abandoned, fascinated by the mirage of another likeness: a passive being, a woman, the castrated mother. With phallic sexuality on the one hand and autosexuality as a mirror-reduction on the other, the hysteric is of neither gender, and is filled with the anxiety of being genderless. When the hysteric is a woman, her frigidity does not prevent her from engaging in a sensory and sadomasochistic perversion. She becomes the victim of true perverts, or she is afflicted with the symptoms of various ailments, paralyses, skin eruptions, or fits of vomiting.

This makes me think of Roberte, a young, successful, and intelligent woman who came to see me because she had been losing her teeth for many years. And when she was not in the dentist's office, she spent her time vomiting up everything she swallowed. I was quickly made aware of her frigidity, which was coupled with oral and gastric troubles. Seen as a whole, these problems formed an "autojouissance" that compensated for her masochistic sexual relations. Roberte claimed to be totally indifferent to these relations, which consisted of rape, physical violence, and wounds that her sexual partners, whom she chose within the outer limits of delinquency, inflicted upon her head and body.

Her younger brother was altogether absent from her discourse, although the analysis revealed that he had played an important part in her trauma. Indeed, phantasmatic anxiety had crystallized around the time of this boy's birth: he cut off the little girl's bond with her mother and steered her toward a sadomasochistic rivalry with her father. The father, who indulged in experiments on his baby girl's body and language, fostered this patient's phallic desire and symbolic performance. Because of such paternal perversity, however, this structure was condemned. It doomed to failure any attempt she might make to have a sexual relationship with a man, and it released an overflowed sensuality that favored the oral and digestive tracts (the preferred link between mothers and babies). Her father fantasy, which condemned Roberte to virginity if she did not allow him to rape her, appeared in the treatment as a compromise solution. It gave support to the patient during her first adolescent fugues as well as in her more recent intellectual escapes.

One might think that the female hysteric would find a rare moment of satisfaction during *pregnancy*. Indeed, she would finally have acquired her father's child and would thus have found herself settled and supported in desire, knowledge, and the symbolic order. But this assumption overlooks the fact that such indubitable satisfaction is coupled with sensory saturation. Dizziness and vomiting or untimely raptures invalidate the gains of desire and the phallic order, thereby drowning them in the pregnant woman's unnameable, self-satisfying, and unapproachable sensuality.

At this point, I would like to say a few words about the hysteric's relation to those two aporia that are the *other woman* (who represents a stolen sensuality) and *language* (the sign of phallic knowledge).

Whether phallic, depressed, loving, or leaving, the *mother of a hysteric* (especially a female hysteric) is not only the other of the father, but also a slave to the phallus or to the incarnation of castration. Horrible for this reason alone, the mother is also a counterpart to that other aspect of the hysterical psyche: its sign-less sensuality, its inaccessible and sublime want-to-be. Thus, repulsion with the mother coincides with submission to her, which results in a desirable, despicable, and abject replica. Consequently, when female homosexuality is not a phallic seizure of sensual anxiety (which crystallizes the other woman and her prototype, the mother), it is not a sexuality, but an indefinite reduplication of the anxiety that punctuates conversion symptoms and bouts of depression.

In the context of phallic performance, language, whose logical coherence is maintained as a mask and as seduction, appears to be removed from anxious excitability. Null, void, and false, language gives in to silence through mute bouts of depression or certain mystic experiences. Otherwise, it is replaced by a feverish accelera-tion of thought, or perhaps by a submersion of an ego disinte-grated by inexpressible emotions. This denial of language is not a psychosis, but a defensive struggle of autoerotic sensuality with desire and its derivative—knowledge.

Hysterical subjects can be differentiated from other psychic structures by their ability to sustain these two levels and to pit them against each other. In so doing, they avoid a profound cogni-tive disorganization, but they pay the price of such compromises as conversion, anxiety, simulation, the inseparable pair of frigidity and sensuality, and communicable thought. Thus, if we bear in mind this hiatus as well as this plasticity between the two memo-ries, can we really say that the hysteric has a soul?

Theologians have asked this question with respect to women, and it is hardly an absurd one. Indeed, if such excitability, which is resistant to language and representation, constitutes the two-sided core of the hysterical structure, we have reason to say that *all* of the hysteric is not to be found in the psyche. What remains is immense, and we can reunite it with the psyche if we take affects and drives to be psychosomatic entities that are constantly excluded from representation, though faithfully geared toward it.

In like manner, if the Freudian *unconscious* is not a language but a storehouse of drives, the hysterical psyche and its unconscious become a privileged space for recording the transit between the psychic and the extra-psychic. Is the unconscious the chosen land of psychoanalysis because it strives to harness conversion and anxiety within interpretation by means of an interposed hysteric? The invention of the unconscious, like the invention of the whole analytic device, appears to introduce a theoretical model that replaces the wrenching effort that hysterics must put forth if they wish to join the two levels of excitability and signification, and it appears to assuage their difficulty or inability to carry out such a junction.

The unconscious is a memory, in the sense of a space of transit or transference between excitability and cognition. Within this space, we discover what is known as unconscious *desire* (since conscious desire is so unstable and hidden that we wonder if it even exists) as well as the *analyst.* As they both (unconscious desire and its analyst) are servants of hysterics, they allow hysterics quite simply to exist. That is, they allow them to exist within the speech that shapes hysterics, but also, one would hope, dissolves them.

Could the unconscious, when combined with the conscious, be an easy way to synthesize the inner life of hysterics, a life that they relentlessly seek because they have trouble mastering it, plagued as they are by both biology and their seducers? Theologians have resolved this synthesis by granting their subjects a single object in which to delight—that is, God (as Saint Augustine said, *res qua fruendem est*). If God no longer exists, the unconscious must reassemble the fragments of hysterical heterogeneity and its masks. Even as we make firm use of the logic Freud has offered us, we must remember that this logic is a *theoretical power play.* The hysteric's symptoms and anguished jouissance also invite us to expose it to that which eludes its definitive nature—the biological body and action (seduction and acting-out).

Analytic Treatment Protects Itself from Hysteria

When Freud crafted the analytic device, he moderated (or neutralized) hysterical seduction on the axis of desire for the father and on corporeal, autosensory excitability: an avoidance of the gaze, the touch, and of motion, and an invitation to translate them into speech. Thus, once the analytic device is put into place, the firm hold of hysteria is depicted as an anxiety fantasy. The body undergoes or must undergo a deformation of conscious representation under the thrust of an inadmissible excitement. Hysteria would thus be a discursive formation, or deformation.

Both of Freud's theories of hysteria bear witness to the development of this maneuver. After focusing on a trauma inflicted by a seductive parent,[10] Freud shifted his attention to an irreconcilable fantasy, a derivative of the hysteric's perverse desires. That was how he discerned the source of the hysteric's anxiety and conversion symptoms.[11] Nevertheless, although the hypothesis that hysteria possesses an exogenous etiology (through biology or an external agent) may be put into question, it is not disproved. The external agent, however, is displaced from hysterical memory and introduced into the treatment itself: *transference* replays the trauma for the analyst and arouses an autosensuality as well as an infantile memory and a phantasmatic anxiety in the treatment's two protagonists.

Because of this insertion of the exogenous (the seductive agent and autosensuality) into the transference-actualized endogenous (the anxiety fantasy), the analyst passes through the unconscious fantasy of the symptom and returns to the reconstruction of an egoistic and cognitive congruence. But we should not forget the resistances that complicated treatment, when it is considered to be a translation of the heterogeneous realms of hysteria, and caused Freud to reformulate his topography as well as the goals of analysis.[12]

Having chosen the sexual fantasy as the mechanism that allows access to conversion and hysterical anxiety, analysis has the advantage of being a pivot between the knowledge level and the emotional level, which is the level that is resistant to representation. Since the role of interpretation is to accede to both levels, the patient's transference and the analyst's countertransference are always required.

It is first a matter of upsetting cognitive congruence—especially that of the practitioner—by discharging the analyst's unconscious, anxiety, and emotionalism in order to return them to the analysand through the intervention of interpretation. Interpretation proceeds to translate them into a repetitive yet varied sequence of fantasies that are given a name and progressively integrated into the subject's capacity for synthesis. If transference begins with a loss of cognitive congruence, countertransference does the same thing. If one wishes to be attentive to the hysterical psyche, countertransference is essential.

I shall return to what differentiates hysterical countertransference from other forms of countertransference. For now, I shall merely note that although the analyst's empathy and understanding are necessarily accompanied by a revival of his own psychological conflicts and unconscious elements, which no training analysis can suppress, this notion of countertransference aims at introducing, seducing, and producing the same sort of psychological work in the patient—with the eventual possibility that the unnameable autosensuality will be converted into a compatible discourse.

When we are faced with a serious case of hysterical anxiety, I believe that we cannot dogmatically exclude the option of treating the patient with the same psychotropic drugs that are used to treat depression and psychosis. Such an intervention also points to countertransference, for it implicates the analyst's unconscious as much as the theory he promotes by assuming that reducing anxiety (without obliterating it) will lead to a more effective interpretation.

In addition to intrapsychic resistances, reversible cerebral possibilities can also be at the base of certain symptoms, including hysterical one. Relieving a symptom while interpreting it is neither an abandonment of analysis nor a relentless pursuit of recovery that ignores psychic effort. Such a process recognizes the dual contract and memory that constitute the hysterical structure, for it acknowledges the diversity of this psychopathological structure, in which one must distinguish between what hysterics desire not to desire (they oppose, sabotage, or prevent their well-being in order to maintain the jouissance of their anxiety) and what they cannot desire (fixated as they are on the domain of nonobjects that border on psychic representation).

Refusing the recourse to medicines discharges another countertransference, that of the romantic or nihilistic debt that the origin of psychoanalysis paid to its ideological context, one that perpetuated suffering and frustration as the sole source of psychic work. This viewpoint is certainly valid. Nevertheless, it can be modified as a result of historical evolution and the continuing growth of those who contribute to it. In the long run, it will depend on the theoretical model that analysts use to approach their patients (in this case, that of hysterics and their dual memory).

Acknowledging an excitability that resists meaning, possibly modifying it through psychotropic medicines, and reinforcing the transferential bond through empathy, seduction, and frustration in order to fortify a psychic space that is hypertrophied or threatened: these are what appear to be the countertransferential modalities of hysteria.

Countertransference: Absolute or Pathological?

Although Freud places little emphasis on countertransference (other than in a 1915 text on transference love),[13] and Ferenczi sees it as a reinforced empathy that is revealed to the patient in an imposed analytical rite of passage, since World War II, the question of countertransference has lent itself to numerous and confusing discussions. One widely accepted definition of countertransference comes from an article by Annie Reich: "Countertransference thus comprises the effects of the analyst's own unconscious needs and conflicts on his understanding or techniques."[14]

Here, countertransference is seen as something unpleasant that may hinder the progress of the treatment. In this perspective, it can be detected in any sign that reveals that analysts have given up their benevolent neutrality, especially through any hostile feelings they may have toward the patient, or toward the repetitiveness, the indolence, the vague discomfort, the irritability, the excessively positive or negative emotions, the difficulty in grasping the meaning of analytic discourse, dreams that implicate patients, the parapraxes, or the various actings-out of unconscious neurotic strivings that may come up in analysis.[15]

On the other hand, Melanie Klein's disciples, most notably Paula Heimann in 1950 and in a later article,[16] not only vindicate the advent of countertransference and the patient's interpretation of it as indispensable to the treatment, but also consider countertransference to be synonymous with intuition and empathy. I myself lean toward such a position. If not through the acting-out of their own unconscious reserve, it is difficult to see how analysts could part with a superegoistic or simply conscious listening in order to aim for the well-known yet enigmatic "benevolent listening." Although this sort of listening clearly requires some distance, it primarily draws on identification, intuition, and empathy.

By referring to Paula Heimann's first article and by completely rejecting the Kleinian point of view, Lacan reinforces the immanence of countertransference within the treatment. He even challenges the notion of countertransference itself, a notion that he finds highly artificial. For Lacan, *transference* has equal implications for the two protagonists. It spares neither the analyst nor his loving or hostile feelings toward his patient.

As if mirroring the hysteric's psychic functioning, of which I said that new information, especially of the affective variety, disturbs the level of cognitive congruence, discharges emotions, anxiety, and fantasies, and thus creates the precondition of transference, Lacan says in so many words that through the analyst's listening, which is already a form of transference, the analyst parts with his cognitive congruence, and uses such a preeminent ignorance to approach the unconscious of the other. As an *object a* of the analysand, the analyst can only accept this gap in his knowledge, within which he can play games—bridge games—with his emotions, loves, and hatreds. Lacan uses the example of a case reported by a Kleinian analyst. Unable to understand his patient's dream, the analyst grew to suffer from the same ailments as his patient. It was only after admitting his mistake and divulging other aspects of the treatment that the analyst could cease to be the projective object, the bad object. The treatment resumed in a very satisfying manner. "It is only when the analyst fails to understand that he is affected and that there is a deviation from normal countertransference."[17] (This is a reference to the Kleinian view that Lacan criticized.)

Yet for Lacan, whether the analyst understands or not is unimportant. Structurally, each analyst is an *object a*—chosen and rejected, loved and hated by his patient. So what must he do? He need not *understand,* but *know* that the two game-players are subject to the desire of the Other. They must play dead by allowing the analyzing subject's own desire to come forth. In order for analysts to understand that they are the object of the patient's desire and vice versa, they need only know what desire means. Since the objects are already in the Other, the two protagonists merely embody *erastes*—passionate love. Thus, transference love (which is the matter at hand) would neither be counterindicative of analysis nor a handicap to it.

> *Transference love is why we are here. This is, if I may say so, its manifest effect. But it also has a latent effect, which is bound to its unknowing, its unknowledge. Unknowledge of what? Of that which is precisely the object of its desire, in a latent, I mean to say objective, or structured, way.*[18]

Transference love (the analyst's and the analysand's) will eventually pinpoint the underlying structural desire of the two protagonists. Thus, a certain ignorance [*nescience*] has a bearing on the two game-players. The specificity of the stoic ignorance and apathy particular to *analysts* stems from the fact that they are sustained by *another desire,* an original desire that they themselves have acquired.

I am possessed by a stronger desire—in my position as an analyst—a mutation in the economy of his desire has occurred for him.

The analyst plays with death, and plays dead: "That means that the analyst must always know what has been dealt" (the bridge game).[19]

If the principle behind these remarks appears to be unassailable, the actual unfolding of the treatment, especially the treatment of hysterics, appears to present pitfalls and make demands that must be taken into account: does ignorance not become complacency? Does the apathy of the one who plays dead not reinforce the hysteric's fear of being rejected from the word of the father, or conversely, the fantasy of unification with his symbolic power? Which abysses of sadomasochism awaken the depiction, if not the acting-out, of transference love? How can one handle countertransference in a way that succumbs neither to the ease of psychotropic self-medication nor to the slave-analysand's submission to his master?

In the treatment of hysterics, countertransference is characterized by two major difficulties. Analysts are challenged to become the positive or negative object of seduction, where desire and knowledge of the other reinforce each other. Moreover, since they are dependent on their sensuality, they could succumb to a fusion with unnameable anxiety, or inversely, they could refuse to lend an ear or a sign to their own wavering. The blind spot and gaps in listening occur when countertransferential traps are so firmly set that they encourage the repetition of fantasies and prevent their mobility. I shall outline this through two examples. The first serves to consider countertransference from the point of view of sensory memory and affect that are resistant to language. The second concerns the phallic ordeal and the particular anxiety that it induces in the hysteric. Of course, these two levels have

a bearing on each other, as do their countertransferential difficulties.

Claire, the patient with the deadly sweater, complained during our
first sessions that her previous analyst had not scheduled her for
regular sessions. Yet during her first two years of treatment, she
did a strange thing: each time I said I was going on vacation, she
would forget the dates. She would miss a session before I left and
would come back before I had returned. This would be followed
by confusion, accusations, and a refusal to pay. On such occasions,
her discourse and behavior, which were normally dispassionate,
would become abruptly disturbed.

Claire was very attached to her mother, for whom she was a
beloved only child. Thinking about this painfully tight bond gave
way to a chronic bronchial asthma, and I interpreted the vacation
symptom as separation anxiety. Claire could make no sense of this
repeated refusal, and she reacted to her confusion by telling me
that all my interpretations "failed" her when they did not "suffo-
cate her." And she reminded me that she required a "set framework" and "strict rules." Nevertheless, the next time we had to
separate, she disregarded these needs as if hallucinating. She even
got me to doubt myself: had I perhaps been mistaken when telling
her about my vacation plans? I came up with other interpretations:
by disregarding the framework of the sessions, Claire was trying
to free herself from her mother's stranglehold, as well as from my
own grasp on her; she was trying to knock me around, to "suffo-
cate" me, disturb me, make me crazy. My interpretations led
nowhere, except to a rational acceptance and her complaint that
she could not accept them on an emotional level:

> I understand what you're saying, but it makes no difference to
> me. Your words have no effect on me. They reach my head, but
> don't go inside.

For Claire, this spastic and painful "inside" was a repudiated
jouissance. She would only open up to me through the acting-

out of the vacations, which resembled an actual staging of her repudiation. A phobic procession followed, as well as a phallic, anal, and oral testing of the analyst. It was not I, but Claire who held the truth of the "framework." It was she who wielded the power to give or not to give her breath, her speech, her money.

I spent a long time (at least I think I did, but was it perhaps a countertransferential impatience that resulted from the frustration I felt when faced with Claire's attempts to eject me from my own mental "framework," my understanding, my clear thinking?) trying to find words that were applicable and acceptable to the patient. I had to find words that could account for her greedy attachment to her mother as well as for the anxiety she experienced from being in such a crushing fusion. Claire protected herself from this fusion by forgetting our agreements, losing her cognitive points of reference, and trying to drag me into her confused state in order to take revenge on her mother, to take her breath away, and to inflict her with asthma.

I stopped interpreting, and thus gave Claire the impression that I had been mistaken. I rediscovered the empathetic role of silence: it allowed her to be in a frenzy, did not respond to her magical conviction that she could kill me, stifled my tendency to interpret in order to "clair-ify" Claire, and kept me quiet even more than usual. Then, it reinvented her condensed, figured, and ambivalent interpretations—loving and hateful ones—that were apparently attractive and primarily sensory and elliptic, almost like baby talk. As in the fatal sweater session:

Me: The fatal sweater—a chain that kills me and warms my breast. Claire: I have never wanted to kiss you, and my mother didn't have any breasts.

It was at the next session that Claire first spoke to me about her father. A new picture of the man surfaced, one in which he appeared to be attached to his daughter as well as protective of her. He also seemed to be a tender antidote for an intrusive and depressed mother. We were working on the axis of desire and knowledge. Claire rediscovered her memory of her points of reference and she never made another mistake about my vacation plans.

A final example will illustrate some countertransferential difficulties with the hysteric that can be associated with preconscious phallic desire. It was reported by Jacob A. Arlow and concerns a supervised treatment.[20] The analyst under supervision brought up the case of a male homosexual. The patient enjoyed submitting his penis to be fellated, but in fantasy, he identified himself with the person fellating in an act of castrating the powerful man. The one who loses his penis was not the one who is fellated but the one who does it. The junction of these active and passive identifications led the patient to a series of crippling inhibitions. The therapist had trouble interpreting these alternating fantasies and seemed inhibited himself when reporting the following dream to his supervisor:

> In the dream the patient is lying on the couch. He turns around to offer him a cigarette.[21]

The analyst admitted to his supervisor that he had been having difficulties with his patient and that he had been "nonplused" by this particular dream. At that very moment, he took out a cigarette for himself, and although he knew very well that his supervisor did not smoke, he offered him a cigarette.

According to Arlow's interpretation, the young candidate had identified with the patient, thus demonstrating countertransference. He had discovered unconscious problems in himself that were similar to those of his analysand (passive homosexuality, offering his penis and his cigarette, identifying with the strong man and desiring to castrate him by allowing himself to be castrated). This seems obvious enough. But Arlow the supervisor neglected to say how he engaged in countertransference himself. Did he not play the role of the strong man who performs fellatio? Did he not put the young therapist in a passive position by inhibiting his mental work when he was under supervision or in a session? Did he not unconsciously submit his candidate to the unconscious voracity of the master that he was, a relationship that the young therapist dramatized by offering him a cigarette? Did I say voracity? In Latin, "desire" is *appetitus*. The appetite of the candidate? Or the appetite of the supervisor who was too fond of the tempting dish that was brought to him?

This is nothing more than a rash hypothesis on my part, one that has the advantage of emphasizing the ubiquity of counter-transference as well as its presence during all stages of the analytic maneuver.

One cannot draw a conclusion about countertransference, which is the driving force behind the analytic profession. I shall merely offer an artificial one, by emphasizing this view of my session, which concluded, you will note, on the phallic appetite of the one who considered himself to be the master.

Although the hysteric has bequeathed transferential ubiquity to analysis in the form of a poisonous gift, let us acknowledge that this implies tasting in order to avoid it more easily, while never developing an actual distaste for it. Nevertheless, how many of us are capable of such supervised hysteria, or rather of such revived hysteria? Without relinquishing its appetite, revived hysteria can lead from an endogenous hunger-dissatisfaction to a pure appetite for words.

What Is a Question?

Analysts acquire knowledge by listening, that is, through interpretive thinking that can be either silent or audible. Such attentive thinking is commonly believed to stem from their desire, if not their erogenous zones. Nevertheless, it must be added that the source in question can only become thought if it is converted into a *question*.

A question is not a negation. It begins, of course, by denying the tenacity of the need and desire that provoke our identification with our patients. Anyone who is unfamiliar with the delightful and dizzying obscurity of such an identification cannot be bothered by this maneuver, which quite frankly is more costly than enriching for psychoanalysis.

As for negation and rejection, *Verneinung* and *Verwerfung*, Freud and Lacan may have said all there is to say. These two analysts have sought to situate speech and the symbolic function that it governs with respect to the impact of castration. By virtue of this operation, meaning can be found, for once, in the very place from which the thinking (thus sexed) being acts. There is one condition that must be fulfilled before I can speak (I-speaker, I-patient, or I-analyst): I must lose my fondness for identificatory need as well as the impoverished latency of desire, and I must articulate a jouissance of the pure Word. By making light of its own difficulties, and by listening to the other and to the depths of passion, such speech can become flesh. To speak in more academic terms, we could compare this transformation to the psychosomatic miracles of verbalization.

If, however, we make too much of the negation and rejection that underlie symbolic castration, we run the daunting risk of rooting it in *mourning* alone, which would guarantee a stoic existence for analysts as well as analysands. Nevertheless, such a position enjoys a certain grandeur, and we are familiar with the therapeutic benefits that the Kleinians have gained by placing the *depressive position* at the heart of our capacity to speak. There is a catch, however, for this grandeur must be neutralized by the amiable suggestion of erotic scenarios. The grief-stricken being is prone to take responsibility for these seductive retributions, for what could be more antithetical (thus pertinent) to mourning than a profusion of tiny trains that continuously go in and out of dark tunnels? To speak more loftily, the recognition of a *lack,* which is intrinsic to the condition of the *speakbeing,* introduces a Carthusian rigor into treatments that are often aphonic and that compensate for actings-out or political scores to settle.

This invites us to ask ourselves if symbolic castration—which is contingent upon negation and rejection, laden with separation and frustration, and responsible for oral, anal, and penile losses—owes its benevolent and brutal impact less to its status as a negation than as a *question.*

What is a question? I want you to tell me. It means that I withdraw myself from the allocution and that I put you at the forefront of this speech transference that I intentionally choose to call an allocution. I implicitly acknowledge that you have *emotions and dynamic characteristics.*[1] No, I shall not grant you the same knowledge that I grant myself as a speaker, although I agree to redistribute our psyches. I assume that there is a part of me in you, and I expect that it will give me an answer to the question that the other part is formulating. You do not necessarily answer me as I think you will; you disappoint me, surprise me (sometimes), out-guess me (rarely), and satisfy me (let's wait and see).

Though analytic interpretation adopts neither the melodic patterns nor the syntactic features of a question, *it adopts the psychological profile of a question*. I think I know something, but I give up and allow you to speak. You are the one who must know, speak, lie, think.

By giving a name to that which cannot be formulated, I put it into question. I make an affect into a question; I elevate sensation to the understanding of a sign; I introduce a secret trauma into an allocution. By formulating a question for the analyst, sensations or affects that are impossible to formulate can make sense to the patient. They can be articulated, displaced, or developed. Analytic name-giving is not a definition, for it is content to repudiate the repudiation[2] (for which it finds a model in *Verneinung*), and—a double negative—it enables the symbolic to expand into an *indefinite questioning*. For even if the patient sees the analyst as a "subject-presumed-to-know," analysts know that they are nothing more than questioning and questioned subjects.

Seen then as a question, symbolic castration is the logical side of the Oedipus complex. It opens the discourse of the *infans* and enables him to employ speech and to approach an infinite horizon. As an indispensable element of the analytic process, symbolic castration confronts patients with what they do not know, and by ousting the analyst's imaginary omnipotence, it makes patients aware of their own ignorance. The end of an analysis is contingent upon the choice of a sexual identity; yet if it were only that, it would simply be a mechanical exercise. The end of analysis also introduces a vast array of questions, about which the only thing I know is that I must respond to them—all alone, so that a new question might surface.

Such a conception of symbolic castration may resurrect more than it relinquishes, for it prompts a certain creativity that can counteract the widespread abandonment that occurs at the end of certain treatments, treatments accompanied by actings-out intended to reconstruct a symbolically beheaded ego.

As a result, the analyst's symbolic castration commands his art of interpretation. Abrupt silence, which serves to pursue rejection and to introduce unsuspected psychoses that have neurotic allures, approaches a fusion with the contagious affect that had allowed me to chart my patient's progress. Because of my affectionate complicity, I respond to my patient with a "pre-language" that is derived from parsimonious agreements or displacements. If I wish to compose a tactful speech, however, I must distance myself from these two contexts (whose temporary effectiveness is, if I may say so, out of the question).

Tact means for-give.[3] Tact is a gift of understanding and judgment that I give to the other. I deprive myself of my own understanding and judgment, and I detach myself from my affect and my silence, whose painful and blissful plenitude poses a problem for me. And I do not cease to ask questions. I do not always tell the other that I am asking myself questions from the very place in which I believe he can be found. My way of knowing that I do not know is my permanent questioning that shows through my tone of voice, my gestures, my body's position and, of course, my discourse. Questioning frees me from the attraction of absolute knowledge, which does not stalk psychoanalysts, but does not spare them either. In the end, questioning has a bearing on the subject, who will perhaps try, armed with the analyst's admiration, to pinpoint his hatred without fixating on a position, a display of knowledge, or an adherence.

Need I emphasize that I see symbolic castration less as asceticism than as an expansion—through asceticism—toward an endless poiesis? This view is my own perversion, my own path to vitality.

Shall I give an example?

Intellectual Acting-Out

Martine is a teacher of French as a foreign language, and she was almost forty when she first came to see me.[4] She wanted to remake her life, to learn more about herself and others, and to "open her mind." A single woman, Martine had lived with a colleague named Edith, who died in a car accident abroad, where Martine had taken her. Martine was reluctant to speak about this painful and guilt-ridden memory, a memory she managed to avoid through crying spells and fits of anger—through various acts that revealed a resistance to remembering. This reluctance coincided with an absence of affect in her language.

From the beginning of her analysis, she referred to two traumatic childhood experiences. The patient spoke about them frequently, employing a *tentative* and *repetitive* discourse that nevertheless revealed a great deal of anger. The patient's father had died during her mother's pregnancy, and that tragedy was followed by her mother's inconsolable mourning. Martine's mother wanted to replace her husband with a boy, and in fact, she never sought a possible name for a daughter. The newborn was thus to be named Martin, after his father (indeed, my patient's mother did often mistakenly call her daughter "Martin"). This sort of violence, which obliterated Martine's own sexual identity to transplant upon her that of a man, was coupled with a sadistic invasion of a sensual and erotic nature. Martine's mother treated her daughter's intestinal disorders with repeated enemas. This ritual dominated and blocked my patient's memory, and it became the one memory that for a long time excluded from the analysis all other recollections of childhood.

Martine was brought up in a strict and religious environment that led to a spiritual crisis and an attempt to take holy orders. A priest discouraged her, however, as he was (understandably) unsure if "her intentions were pure." This was followed by a brief encounter with prostitution that was prompted by a friend who "had some experience in those matters." This led to disgust and to a denial of her sexuality. She did not finish high school, but later returned to school and became certified to teach French as a foreign language.

Martine had begun her studies of French as a foreign language during her relationship with Edith, and she had just completed her certification when she entered into analysis with me. Her studies consumed all of her psychological and sexual life. She assimilated and reconstructed the discourses of other people, and she delved into psychoanalysis as a means of understanding her loneliness and symptoms. For since her childhood and until her analysis, Martine had been subject to rectal-colonic bleeding, as well as to eczema that appeared most often on the edges of her lips, ears, and eyes (which could be interpreted as the limits of her body, or as displacements of inhibited sexual zones).

During the analysis, these symptoms surfaced and then worsened, especially during periods of what I can only call "intellectual actings-out"—rushing to various courses, participating in analytic seminars in order to present a theory that she knew conflicted with that of the seminar director, and developing an infatuation with theoretical writing.

These intellectual actings-out allowed Martine to generate discourse through intellectualization and conscious rationalization—in effect, to prevent free association. Hence, Martine spent her sessions presenting various theories, discussing each of them, and disagreeing with a given philosopher or linguist. My interpretations, which tried to associate these feverish activities with an attempt to seduce or to invade mentally as a compensation for the anal traumas of her early childhood, were accepted with interest, and then neatly filed away into Freudian or Lacanian theoretical categories, only to be replaced by other analytical constructions that Martine would discover.

I was the target of Martine's intellectual actings-out, which resulted from her idealization of me: since I was a theoretician, and I wrote, what better way to become close to me, seduce me, or to attack or rape me than this test of strength between anal penises, a test that consisted for Martine (I imagine), in a comparison of our respective intellectual endeavors! The idealization to which I was subjected reinforced her inhibition of drives and affects, as well as her *translation of traumas into sensory and emotional memory.* This led to an exuberant search for knowledge. All the same, can we really speak of inhibition when faced with so much intellectual curiosity? I will answer "yes" for two reasons.

—Martine assimilated various theories and pitted them against each other in order to display a phallic, anal strength in her seminars and in my presence. She nevertheless saw no relation (and denied the relation that I saw) between her theoretical knowledge and the meager fragments of her past and present that she had confided to me. These intellectual actings-out interested me insofar as she used them as a defense in the transference, a mixture of idealization and rejection of the analyst.

—Furthermore, the texts that she wrote and showed me displayed no cognitive or theoretical inventiveness. They were watered-down versions of the Masters, mere compilations. These texts harbored the incorporation and enraged evacuation of an intrusive mother, which the rectal-colonic bleeding inscribed in the patient's body before she began her analysis, and which her competitiveness (her intellectual actings-out) had replaced in the beginning of the analysis.

Martine's intellectual endeavors enabled her to empower a language of *resistance* to the analysis. Since that was its effect during the treatment, it would be interesting to see how such an effect of resistance produced by the economy of her discourse could respond to the premature aggressions of an archaic period before language existed, a period in which affect and the body were the only thing that could defend the baby and the child. Yet this archaic affective defense against castration as well as narcissistic disintegration had already revealed itself as too threatening to the patient's identity (as shown by the example of her violent relations with her mother and with Edith). She abandoned it only to replace it with the screen of cognitive discourse and with psychosomatic accidents that clearly threaten the body, but also preserve affects and sexual identity. I would say that Martine's motto was "Better mind and body than sexual feeling."

"I"-Cogito and "Ego"-Sensation

I would describe Martine's speaking style as governed by the *subject of the cogito,* separated from the *ego* and from the advent of the unconscious.

In this case, I identified inhibition through a separation between the discourse of the cogito and its subject, on the one hand,
and the *iconic, gestural, or paralinguistic expression of ego affects
and of the advent of the unconscious,* on the other. If I refer to a
"separation" between the discourse of the "I"-cogito (constructions
and theoretical activities) and the paralinguistic expression of the
ego and of unconscious processes, it is because "separation" is a
more common term than "splitting" or "isolation" (terms that
usually refer to psychosis). The neutrality of the term renders it
suitable for describing the hesitations, arrested states, and stupe-
faction that characterize hysterical discourse, a discourse that remains in the shadows of the affects and traumas that it represents.
In this way, Martine acted out the wishes that were implicit in her
speech, yet *not directly expressed.*

She clearly acted out these wishes through her intellectual endeavors, but only by disguising them as "analized," "fecalized"
concepts. She inhibited her production of free associations during
her sessions by making sure that her speech remained primarily
cognitive in nature. Martine had very few dreams, no fantasies.

There was a price to pay for these two inhibitions: her symptoms of eczema and of rectal-colonic bleeding.

Nevertheless, transference encouraged the strengthening of
both the ego and the unconscious. This first became apparent
when Martine attempted to use psychodrama to take charge of
the sessions. Paralinguistic and nonlinguistic signals attracted her
attention. She underwent a series of osteopathic manipulations
that led to orgasms that were "beyond description." I shall highlight a few steps along her path toward a sort of "sensory autism."
During the analysis, we witnessed an affective production that was
to explain this sensory autism and place it within the context
of transference.

Martine was very aware of the signals that embellished her
environment: the security code of her apartment building, the
intercom, doorbells, the computerized entrance to her own apartment, as well as the slightest changes in any of these signals. Her
attention was drawn to borders, entry ways, and orifices.

After presenting one of her theories, she was abruptly overcome by an anxiety that her language-cogito was unable to express: she burst into tears or threw fits of rage directed toward herself, a given professor, or (inevitably) me.

Martine married one of her students, who did not speak French at all. She tried to defy me by insisting on how much she enjoyed communicating uniquely with her body, since her husband was not much of a student and was in no hurry to learn the language of his new country.

Furthermore, to stimulate her organs so that she might have a baby despite her age, Martine underwent a series of uterine massages administered by a woman. "Incredible pleasures, no comparison with what my husband gives me." Me: "This woman touched you." Martine: "I don't even know her name, I never look at her face. Nothing but her hands, and my stomach that enjoys such exquisite sensations, everything is directed toward me."

Martine made me think of the difficulty that Freud and Lacan had with the question "What does a woman want?" Perhaps the answer is nothing more than the autistic withdrawal of affect, or the swallowing-up of the other. That is, a woman does not *want*. She invaginates herself in self-stimulation without eroticism, the hidden side of her refusal of castration (that is, her refusal of men) and her intellectual inhibition or acting-out. What we call frigidity may resemble this sort of a sensory autism, an autism that repudiates our image of our own bodies and thus makes the word "autoeroticism" seem inadequate. Indeed, Martine's image of her body was negative and fecal. Her only pleasure came from autistic affect that preceded the representation of her body. The secret code of this affect is that of the sensations. Through sensation, analysis can discover this hidden affect, in order to leave autism behind and to aspire to autoeroticism and eroticism.

It seems to me, then, that hysterical inhibition is a *separation* between:

—a discourse of the *cogito* (in this case, a discourse strengthened by the patient's anal traumas, which counterbalanced an exter-

nalized anal eroticism, since thought hinders anal eroticism),
and

—a pre-linguistic or paralinguistic indexing of ego effects and of
the advent of the unconscious, in which we note the refusal of
castration up to and including symbolic castration within the
masochistic abundance of soma.

On the Brink of Psychodrama: Splitting and the Desire to Die

This structure of separation takes advantage of the inhibition
caused by analysis. Clearly, it also takes advantage of the analyst's
reluctance to force the patient to escape from such an organization,
which could entail the risk of repeating the mother's enemas. I
thus let Martine cogitate. As for me, I interpreted—in vain.

The turning point of this analysis came about when we were
faced on two occasions with the boundaries of psychodrama that
Martine tried to impose onto the treatment.

1. The *separation* between thoughts and feelings developed into
a *splitting of the ego*. Martine's diminished perception of the other
(her "autism") grew into an actual suspension of perception. Martine never knew what so-and-so actually said to her (which implies
that she did not know what I said to her). She remembered "the
general idea," but not "the words." She never remembered how
so-and-so was dressed, if he or she had brown or blond hair, and
so forth. This obliteration of perception and sensation came to
worry her during the analysis, though they continued until the
advent of two actings-out in which my patient completely denied
her perception of other people.

Martine is waiting for a friend outside a restaurant, and her
friend is running late. Martine leaves the restaurant, sees a taxi,
and decides to get in and take off. Someone gets out of the taxi
and pays. Martine becomes so impatient that she almost shoves
aside the object of her anger, before finally realizing (after sev-

eral moments of "blank" blindness) that this person is in fact her friend (more specifically, her friend cries out and shakes her to arouse her from her stupor).

Note her negative hallucination and her suspension of perception-sensation that comes from holding back the impassioned ambivalence she felt toward this friend.

Martine told me she was in the midst of writing two very personal texts that were causing her difficulty because she was unable to find the necessary theoretical references. She was working on a study of Nerval and on a paper on Céline's abjection that she was to present at one of the seminars she attended. She described the ideas she wanted to develop in these texts, and I could easily recognize my own articles. I told her: "By way of your ideas, you wish to get closer to me. Will the desire to be like me and to be in my shoes spare you from realizing that you want to touch me, to touch my body?" She got angry, screamed, made faces: "You're always criticizing my homosexual inclination. I really don't know what you mean."

We see here how taking refuge in theory can be a refusal to acknowledge affects. Martine rattled off "homosexuality," but only as a theoretical label. Her words obliterated the violence and elimination that her writings inflicted upon me. Two sessions later, she told me that while writing her articles and discussing them with me, she had not realized that she had plagiarized my work.

Destruction of the loved-and-hated object. Suspension of perception and sensation. Construction of a subject-cogito by psychotic phagocytose of the other during the act ("I'm taking a taxi," "I'm writing") or of knowledge itself.

I began to focus on the senses of touch, taste, sight, and hearing. I made note of various sensory indicators in Martine's theoretical remarks, and I drew attention to her intellectual and defensive discourse by reiterating the presence of an inhibited *sensory capacity* as well as an inhibited discourse (she said nothing about it; she felt nothing, grew restless, and suffered).

2. The analysis began to resemble a psychodrama that included

the participation of the philosophers and professors whom Martine saw regularly. Through one of my patient's more important intellectual actings-out, we analyzed her *desire to die*.

Martine asked her institute of French as a foreign language if she could practice psychopedagogical therapy under the supervision of Mme X (the director). After a few months, Martine became nervous and anxious. She confided to me that the first name of Mme X was Christine, and that she thought this had a connection with me, as well as with Edith, whose middle name, I learned, was Christine.

I first linked this sudden recollection with what we had already analyzed as her desire to see her sister die, with her desire to do away with me through her writings, and finally with my emphasis on the prevalence of touch, taste, sight, and hearing in the theoretical remarks that Martine kept making. I had indeed decided to point out the sensory signs in Martine's cognitive productions, and to permeate her defensive discourse by locating the whereabouts of inhibited sensory production and discourse. Martine claimed she was upset about identifying Mme X with a *dead person*. "You do understand, Edith is dead and no longer exists! She never meant anything to me! I have no picture of her in my head, I don't remember anything about her. Yet she somehow makes me feel guilty and torments me continually," she said with pathos, gesticulations, and contortions on the couch.

Giving a name to sensations and to the desire to die opened up the *time* of a memory. It was a memory filled by Edith, Mme X, myself, and, in the background, a memory that referred to Martine's relationship with her mother—a memory that was sensory-based and guilt-free from that point on. It was related to the enemas, the hatred, the love, and the sadistic rages that Martine directed against her mother. I caused her to notice that the Dead One was not Edith, but Mme Christine X or perhaps myself after all, since Mme Christine X simply replaced me by allowing Martine to be a therapist.

Once again, there was an expression of rage and more tears. Martine came to the next session and said she had just read a text on transference that completely confirmed what I had been saying. She needed to calm down and to reflect with a book in hand, yet everything seemed much more dangerous when she was in my office with me sitting behind her.

To conclude my summary of this one segment of an analysis, I shall simply emphasize that inhibition (the discourse of the cogito *separated* from an ego ridden with affects) caused the analysis to overflow its setting (acting-out). This required a consideration not only of the events that happen outside such a setting, but also of the linguistic and even sensory aspects of communication.

The patient "acts out instead of remembering," said Freud.[5] Martine believed she was thinking, but her discourse was more likely an *inhibition of the sense of time.* The time excluded from my patient's mental experience was the time of childhood memories: a sensory and trans-cognitive experience.

Analytical Technique: A Genealogy of Cognitive Signs

Faced with such problems, analytical technique has two possible solutions:

1. To mobilize affects, without hesitating to encourage the psychodramatic aspect of the treatment that tends to attract hysterics, since this mode enables them to express affect. The mobilization of affects is an anti-inhibitor of the signifying process. New affects realized in the transference disrupt the intellectualization and the inhibiting function that are characteristic of intellectual acting-out. Analysts mobilize affect by openly presenting themselves during interpretation as a magnet of libido. This emphasis on the analyst's ego is an "imaginary-ization" of the treatment, one that is able to combat the hysteric's sensory autism.

2. A verbalization of perception and sensation can then free up the signifying process that defensively withdrew itself through intellectualization, that is, in order to restore an image of the eroticized body, to restore sensation and perception by giving

them a name. Subjects can only be revived if they endow perceptions and sensations with *signifiance*. Without signifiance, we are faced with the separation between the I-cogito and an ego linked with incommunicable affects. What is the figure of inhibition? The I-cogito interrupted by the affect-ridden ego, the affect-ridden ego blocking the I-cogito. Could the subject be the advent of one in the other, of the I-cogito in the affect-ridden ego, and vice versa?

The type of memory brought about by free association is a search for the past. This memory enables subjects to confront their traumatic experience with speech, yet we cannot solicit this traumatic memory without opening up the *genealogy of cognitive signs*. That is, to topple the *cogito* over into *sensation*. The taste of Proust's madeleine depends on the possibility of remembering it. Inversely, what is memory if not the (verbalized) taste of the madeleine and the pleasure that accompanies it? Time regained is nothing if not the subject, but only insofar as he is able, through cognitive language, to unmask the perception itself.

Yet acting-out lacks sensation.

The discourse of sensations directed toward the Other, and the discourse of the self as other, is by nature an uninhibited discourse. I would rephrase Freud's formula "The patient acts out instead of remembering" as "The patient repeats due to an inhibition of the sense of time." The sense of time is that of symbolic castration, without which there is neither time nor subject.

Resistant to oral, vaginal, and anal castration, Martine reinforced her unconscious anal penis fantasies by destroying the other as well as herself. She accomplished this through the deadly violence of her symptom, that is, through her rectal-colonic bleeding. The analytic setting gave her an opportunity, moreover, to add symbolic consolidation to her refusal of castration. Her refusal of symbolic castration resulted in her idealization of the analyst, shadowed as it was by a liquefying hatred. Although such a refusal of symbolic castration is naturally less deadly than a somatic symptom, it nonetheless handicaps the associative process and bars the advent of unconscious truth.

One cannot approach the ascent to symbolic castration without first addressing what I call the *genotext* of the symbolic[6]—the affects and their primary signs (sensations) in which real and imaginary traumas are resistant to symbolization. Our analytical work had to face two modes at the same time: first, the affect and the sensation that entombed the refusal of oral deprivation, vaginal and anal castration, and Martine's deadly defenses against these, and second, language, which questioned the traumatic need and the unthinkable jouissance by designating them. What is more, language prompted the patient to pose the question of the analyst as a *sensing-and-thinking* being.

While giving this sort of attention to the patient, analysts are forced to confront their own affects. Through its appearance within countertransference, my affect links me to the first phase of the refusal of castration that I share with my patient through my own questioning of this refusal. The same approach implies that analysts compromise themselves. Their symbolic neutrality is challenged and they join the patient in the very place of their passion, a passion that is unamenable to castration. From then on, a path can be cleared, one that will lead to examining (not "cognitively," but from the reality of oral, anal, and vaginal castration) the very refusal of symbolic castration that had once been the source of intellectual inhibition.

By bringing the Oedipus complex to a close, symbolic castration calls forth enigmas. It arouses a certain curiosity about oneself and the world, which entering into analysis and the analytical process itself may seek to obliterate. We must revive the question of active and sensory knowledge while preventing the treatment from degenerating, for the sake of our own mental reassurance, into a refusal of symbolic castration.

And as for the analyst? Does symbolic castration not *also* appear in the form of this intellectual phagocytose, which the analyst's patients, colleagues, friends, and enemies often criticize? More specifically, these phenomena, to which we are all exposed, are like minor narcissistic wounds that a little sense of humor will help to "bandage." Nevertheless, the real difficulty of our work is to confront symbolic castration. Analysts' ability to work with symbolic castration resides in their willingness to redo the course of affect-language-demand-negation-question. And I mean in both directions, forward and backward, from inexpressible traumas to their conscious manifestation and vice versa. In a banal and harsh manner, the art of prompting questions requires the art of constantly questioning ourselves. Not mentally, but from affects-sensations to the I-cogito.

Thus, could symbolic castration be the indefinite anamorphosis of affects into questions and questions into affects? That is one way to define the trials and rewards of interpretive speech. And one way to define the impossibility of assuming such a role in the world, unless you are a stoic or a comedian. Yet after all, these are only two of the many possible bents of the analytical profession.

6. THE INEXPRESSIBLE CHILD

The Imaginary Between Biology and Language

Certain delays in language acquisition as well as similar difficulties in learning logical and grammatical categories appear to have physiological causes that are difficult to identify, and that are even more difficult to treat at the somatic level. Nevertheless, if these lesions in the star-structure of the brain are not too serious, they may allow access to the *symbolic*. The child, however, must first be given the opportunity to make rich and extensive use of his *imaginary*.

By *symbolic,* I am referring to the discursive practice that adheres to the logical and grammatical rules of speaking. And by *imaginary,* I mean the representation of identification strategies (introjection and projection) that mobilize the image of the body as well as the ego and the other, and that make use of primary processes (condensation and displacement).

Of course, the imaginary is contingent upon the mirror stage. The imaginary offers the developing subject an image of himself by using the myriad representations of the child's world to mobilize a whole array of identifications—narcissistic identification accompanied by a grasping of the mother's image, or by fusion with her, primary identification with the benevolent father in "personal prehistory,"[1] secondary identification within the Oedipus complex as well as its important variant—hysterical identification with a phallic role, and so forth.

The imaginary is a kaleidoscope of ego images that build the foundation for the subject of enunciation. Yet we must remember that the imaginary extends its effects through psychic modalities that precede specular identification, that is, through the psychic representatives of affect that are subjected to the fluctuating rules of assimilation and rejection as well as condensation and displacement.

It could be hypothesized that this imaginary level of semiotic *meaning* (as opposed to linguistic *signification*) is closer to the drive representatives particular to the lower layers of the brain. Thus, it can act as a relay between these layers and the cortex that controls linguistic production, thereby constituting supplementary brain circuits able to remedy any psychobiological deficiencies. Consequently, when we are faced with a child who fails to make active use of symbolic communication, and who is unlikely to retain much of what he takes in from the outside world, the imaginary is a way of gaining access to more archaic affective representations, if not to linguistic signification itself. It can also be a way of accessing the drama that underlies these representations, a drama that never ceases to overwhelm, torment, or amuse the child.

I therefore distinguish between the *semiotic,* which consists of drive-related and affective *meaning* organized according to primary processes whose sensory aspects are often nonverbal (sound and melody, rhythm, color, odors, and so forth), on the one hand, and *linguistic signification* that is manifested in linguistic signs and their logico-syntactic organization, on the other. As opposed to the semiotic level, this linguistic level requires that supplementary biological and psychological conditions be met.[2]

Of course, when the imaginary implies creative work and fiction, it involves linguistic signification and is thus indissociable from grammar and logic. Through linguistic performance, however, *psychological preconditions* keep us in the imaginary. In some children, these preconditions do not appear to be innate, or perhaps they have been damaged *in vitro* or at birth. Therapists can attempt to reconstruct these preconditions by working with the imaginary whenever possible.

I shall go one step further. Such difficulties in accessing the symbolic, which cause certain children not to have a spontaneous and natural access to *signification,* though they can access *meaning,* may result in a depression whose perceptibility and seriousness vary from one case to another. Let us recall that from a linguistic point of view, depression is characterized by a disavowal of the symbolic.[3] "Language means nothing to me; I am indifferent to what you say; I am different from the rest of you; I want to withdraw; I won't even fight with you like an emotionally disturbed child would; I won't break down meaning as an autistic child might; I want to enclose you in my inexpressible meaning"— this is what children with "language problems" seem to be saying. Such children are often depressed, though this may go unnoticed.

Unable to use his symbolic, the young *infans* who prolongs his baby stage buries himself in a crypt of unexpressed affect while exasperating those around him, becoming frustrated himself, or becoming accustomed to his hiding-place. He does this, however, without arousing the attention of adults, who remain unaware of the secret signs of a distressed and regressed internal language. In sharp contrast to autistic or emotionally disturbed children, these children give the impression that they are paralyzed with a phobic inhibition that hampers their access to discourse—as if language scared them. Perhaps what really scares them, however, is a depression caused by their inability to use language: they are afraid of being inadequate when faced with a world of speakers—afraid of being "bad speakers."

The therapist's task is twofold. First, the therapist must be an analyst who fosters desire (including of course the desire to speak) despite inhibition and depression. Second, the therapist must be a *speech therapist* who maps out an individual program for each child (since "theoretical givens" do not apply to everyone) and then helps these children understand the linguistic categories that will allow them to add symbolic productions to their subjectivity.

We need not force such cognitive (I would call them "symbolic") processes to occur too quickly. The excessiveness of that sort of approach neglects the fact that the imaginary of this *infans* (who experiences *meaning* but not *signification*) must patiently work out the semiotic preconditions for accessing discourse. After all, the imaginary economy is what makes the *subject of enunciation* come forth—which is the psychological precondition for language acquisition.

I would like to shed some light on these ideas by making a few clinical remarks.

An Opera

I have been aware of Paul's neurological difficulties since his birth. At the age of three, he was still unable to say anything other than some repetitive vowel sounds jumbled with some unidentifiable pseudo-consonants. He did not like it when his parents spoke to each other and obviously rejected any exchange of words between his therapist and his mother. This resulted in dramatic scenes of screaming, crying, and frustration, more than of actual anger.

I interpreted his reactions as an oedipal refusal of the bond between his parents, and thus of any seemingly erotic verbal exchange between two adults, since these kinds of exchanges made Paul feel left out. Not only did my interpretation have no effect on him, but I soon realized that it had been made prematurely. I thought that Paul was refusing a signifying sequence that he was unable to produce, and his *awareness*—perhaps I should say his precocious *consciousness*—that he was so incapable made him feel worthless, depressed, and afraid.

I decided to communicate with Paul and his mother by using something that was accessible to him—*song*. The *operas* we would improvise, which must have seemed rather absurd to any onlooker, were composed of signification that I (or we) wanted to share. Yet, they were initially composed of the meaning of the affect and drive representatives encoded in the melodies, the rhythms, and the accents that were more easily (if not the only thing) available to Paul. "Come over here" (do-re-mi); "How are you" (do-si-la).

Thanks to this game, which was not only vocal, but also multifaceted (semiotic and symbolic), this child gradually overcame his fears and began to vary his sounds with increasing success. In like manner, he began to listen to different records and to reproduce their tunes, as well as, eventually, their lyrics. I felt as if I were tuning up a musical instrument, getting to know this child, and encouraging increasingly unexpected and complicated possibilities to spring from his resonant body.

Hence, opera enabled him to develop the specific articulation of phonemes through singing. We did not focus on technical pronunciation work itself, but on the possibility and pleasure of hearing oneself and articulating sounds through the help of melody. Once he felt confident that he could pronounce words by singing them (that is, with his breath, his sphincters, his gestures, and his body), Paul agreed to use his new-found opera phonemes in everyday speech, which he did with a capacity for precise articulation that few children possess. The singer became a speaker.

Although I shall refrain from describing the specifically analytic work that we accomplished, I should like to emphasize that it remains inextricably linked to the advent of language that it fostered.

"I'm Coming, Dad"

Some difficulties cropped up during later stages of Paul's development, but the imaginary enabled us once again to overcome them. Let me give an example: Paul was unable to distinguish between 1st and 2d person pronouns (*I/you, me/you*). Such a confusion revealed that Paul was dependent on his mother. The participation of this young woman, who eventually detached herself from her narcissistic child-prosthesis that had made her depressed about her son's deficiencies, became the key to the treatment.

The suspension of the *I/you* distinction coincided with Paul's

identification with Pinocchio (of fairy-tale fame). More specifically, Paul identified with the episode in which the little boy saves
his father Gepetto from the jaws of Monstro the Whale. "Help,
Pinocchio," cried the old man. "*I* am coming, *Dad,* wait for *me,*
don't be afraid, *I* am here for *you,*" answered Paul. This tale
allowed Paul to escape from the might of the devouring whale, to
be its victim no more. Furthermore, Paul could seek revenge
against his father. He could now say "I," as long as he did not feel
threatened about being gobbled up or castrated.

The "you," that is, the sign we used when referring to Paul—
the unhappy child, the pain-sufferer—was another character in the
fairy tale. He was the dreaded other ("you") that merged with the
bad part of himself; he was thus able to love this unfortunate
victim. For he appeared in the tale as Gepetto, the kind and
blessed father. A good "you" replaced the bad "you." Through
this idealization, the other ("you") could separate from itself ("I")
and be called something else. At the same time, Paul attained the
status of a hero, and in this capacity, he could refer to himself as
"I" and not as the "you" that his mother used when speaking to
him. This "you" also found a different place from that of the bad
"you." It was the place of the other (Gepetto) who could face
challenges without being a helpless child. Through the acknowledged misfortune of this victimized position, the "you" designated
the role of an important person who was clearly in danger, but
who was noble and lovable (*you* was another hero, the other of the
hero), with whom Pinocchio the hero could swap places—as two
equals, that is, as two different beings.

I shall draw some conclusions from my preliminary comments
on these few aspects of my work with Paul.

Though not all analysts are speech therapists, I believe that
when speech therapists push children toward language, they are
incorporating the analytic function. And I would like to pay tribute to the tenacious and often unappreciated art—analytic art—
that speech therapists practice, I imagine, at the heart of what one
often considers to be a simple method of mechanical learning.

Discourse is a complex psychological event that cannot be reduced to what I call the *symbolic* dimension of grammatical categories and their organization. Discourse also includes the semiotic modality, which is independent from language. In this modality, psychic representatives are displaced from affects as well as from the drama of desires, fears, and depressive fits that have a meaning for children, even though they are unable to join the world of everyday language's coded signification.

In order to be sensitive to the semiotic meaning of this internal language, the analyst-speech therapist must make optimal use of maternal listening. I trusted Paul's mother, or rather, she convinced me that Paul experienced meaning, since she thought that she could understand and respond to him even though he never spoke to her. I adopted her listening and her ability to decipher Paul's meaning.

Although contemporary science is ready to consider most women to be genitors, we must try to reassess the *maternal function,* which somehow manages to mark out the child's path toward signification, despite the child's assigned role of being a narcissistic prosthesis, a counterphobic object, or a temporary antidepressant. When a mother endows her child with language, which is a process that society has deemed maternal, she is often all alone. She has to rely on the therapist, especially when neurological difficulties complicate the passage from meaning to signification, a passage that is already difficult enough for any speaking being. Ideally, mothers give us meaning. We analysts are the ones who must discover signification. This means that our role is *more-than-maternal:* through our identification with the mother-child relationship, we recognize and often anticipate the meaning of that which remains unsaid. Our potential to understand the logic of walled-up affects and blocked identifications enables us to allow suffering to rise up from its tomb. This is the only way in which the signifier that we use—the signifier of everyday communication—can cease to be a lifeless and foreign membrane for the child. Moreover, it may find a home in a subject whom we have accompanied on his path to a second birth.

Since their own past or present boxed-in suffering latches on to their child's, there are very few mothers who can single-handedly endow their handicapped child's inexpressible meaning with signification. When this problem becomes apparent, the mother must solicit the help of the third party who noticed it (whether it be the therapist, the father, or another person)—someone who has helped the mother to recognize, to admit, and to free herself from her unnameable depression before helping her child follow the same route. For even if the causes of the child's depression are primarily biological and the causes of the mother's are psychological, from a linguistic point of view, the result is the same: both the mother and the child are unable to translate psychic representatives of affect into verbal signs.

The Fairy Tale as a Dramatization of Grammatical Categories

In reality, the imaginary dramatizes the psychological conditions that underlie grammatical categories. The imaginary prevents language, which is sometimes acquired by imitation or by the dint of repetition, from becoming a device used by the "false self." Despite his delays, Paul never displayed the symptoms of the "as-if" personality. This child impressed us with his ability to handle all his performances in a creative manner, performances that were quite modest in the beginning and "not what you would expect from a child of his age."

After all, the *time* of the imaginary is not that of speech. It is the time of history, of the footnote to history, of Aristotle's "mythos"—a time in which a conflict is formed and a solution is revealed, a solution that consists of a path that the subject of speech can follow. It is a tortuous time, a time that incorporates the atemporal unconscious, the toilsome repetition of the eternal return, and sudden outbreaks of suffering that can take shape as anger. And finally, it includes the bright spot of understanding that allows us to appreciate the preceding twists and turns of the confusing inexpressible and enables us to see them as something they had not appeared to be at first—as latent potential, as an implicit step toward a distant goal. But how many dark nights, waiting periods, and frustrations are there in the internal maze of this imaginary time? We must wait for the arrival of the time of speech (of the symbolic), that is, the linear time of syntax (subject/predicate) in which the speaker imagines an act that is an act of judgment.

Nevertheless, although we may be relieved to hear a child speak during this enlightened time of judgment, let us remember that when he gets confused or when he steals from us the syntactic and judging signification that we thought he would have forever, we must return to the labyrinth of imaginary time, for stumbling around in it again will enable us to knock down the logical dead-end that blocked the child's growth.

Paul employed verb tenses (present, past, future) correctly when he had to conjugate a verb or do a grammar exercise. But when he told a story, he always used the *present tense*. The adverb indicated if he considered himself to be *before, during,* or *after* the action, but his personal utterances of verbal phrases failed to obey this distinction: "Before I am a baby, now I am big, later I am an astronaut." In an abstract sense, Paul understood the categories of verbal tenses because he could recite their conjugations, but he could not incorporate these categories spontaneously into his speech. Through the help of fairy tales that spoke of metamorphoses, we were able to integrate the function of temporal shifters into Paul's discourse.

Love Establishes the Sense of Time

Let us consider one of those fairy tales, *Sleeping Beauty*. The princess is sixteen years old when the Wicked Witch puts her to sleep. One hundred years later, the love of a prince awakens her from her sleep so that she might recapture the freshness of her sixteen-year-old youth, though at a different moment in time.

This theme of resurrection, in which someone thought to be dead reappears in his original living form and which transports his past beyond the lapse of sleep into a new unknown and unexpected

context, enables us to chart the passage of time. The child identified with Sleeping Beauty's childhood ("she was"). He then identified with the zero yet essential time of her sleep, which also
represents the stagnation of the present time, in which he floun-
ders in his difficulties, understands nothing, and "sleeps" ("she
sleeps"). Finally he identified with the time of revival, which
means a project, a future life that is nonetheless already realized
("she is reborn through love, she shall live"). He was thereby freed
from the threat of separation, and reassured that his future would
be a reunion, a rebirth.

More specifically, it seemed to me that Paul's experience of
meaning was triggered by the distinction that the fairy tale makes
between a burst-present and a confusing present (sleep), and an
initiating-present of act and realization (waking-up)—the first
present creeping toward the past, and the second opening up a
new life. The fairy tale gave Paul a grasp on the past and the
future, and it enabled him to travel through the world of temporal
categories.

It should be noted that tales like this one, which structure the
subject and consequently create the necessary preconditions for
linguistic categories, are tales of love. Let us reflect on that for a
few moments and remember it the next time we are faced with an
inexpressible child.

Two. HISTORY

Two Approaches to the Sacred

The idea of reading the Bible as we might read Marx's *Das Kapital* or Lautréamont's *Chants de Maldoror,* unraveling its contents as if it were one text among many, is without doubt an approach born out of structuralism and semiology. Although such an approach may seem reductive or even outrageous, we must not forget that any interpretation of a religious text or occurrence assumes that it can be made into an object of analysis, even if it means admitting that it conceals something that cannot be analyzed. Of course, we may question this interpretive obsession that tries so desperately to make the Holy Text say what it does not know it is saying, and I shall return to what I believe to be the motivation behind this eternal return to divinity, a return that may be glorious or profane.

When the "human sciences"—which rely upon a rationality that seeks to reveal the universal logic embedded in a myth, a hieratic text, or a poem—turn to the Bible, they are forced to limit them-selves to the logic or rhetoric of the text. At first they disregard its sacred powers, although they hope that their positive and neutral analysis will guide them toward the mechanism—if not the enigma—of what is seen as "holy" and of what appears to function as such. Perhaps the Bible lends itself to semiological analysis more easily than do other forms of writing. Indeed, by paving the way for interpretations, the Talmudic and cabalistic traditions are always inviting us to make yet another one. . . .

What is more, the Book dominates the Judaic religious experience. It overshadows and ultimately governs the ritual, which enables it to bypass the ritual in favor of the letter, or of its interpretive values and a Single yet Infinite Meaning that supports human desire in the face of God. Are reading and interpreting the Bible perhaps the dominant ritual, the very eruption of the Judaic ritual and sacrament into language and logic?

This paradigm of biblical interpretation has resulted in studies inspired by various schools of thought, but that are unified by their common goal of specifying the profound logic that has generated the sacred value of the biblical text. Let us take the example of Mary Douglas' functionalism. While working independently from specialists in religious studies like Jacob Neusner,[1] Douglas has shown that the Levitical food taboos obey the universal law of exclusion, which states that the impure is that which falls outside a symbolic order. The Bible's obsession with purity seems then to be a cornerstone of the sacred. Nevertheless, it is merely a semantic variant of the need for separation, which constitutes an identity or a group as such, contrasts nature with culture, and is glorified in all the purification rituals that have forged the immense catharsis of society and culture.[2]

J. Soler has proposed a reading of the Levitical abominations that is more "semiological" in approach. He has unearthed the way in which a taxonomy that bases itself on the separation and exclusion of food combinations has been transformed into a narrative and a ritual.[3] This taxonomy, which is initially dominated by the dichotomy between life and death, also corresponds to the God/Man dyad and provides a schematic version of the commandment "Thou shall not kill." In the end, the code of Levitical abominations becomes a veritable code of differences that seeks to eliminate ambiguity. In this sense, one might think of the food taboos that pertain to fish, birds, and insects, which are respectively associated to one of the three elements (water, sky, earth): any food product that mixes and blends these elements is considered impure. According to this interpretation, the Levitical taboos would suggest that the fundamental confusion is incest—an inference that can be drawn from the well-known precept, "You shall not boil a kid in its mother's milk" (Exod. 23:19; Deut. 14:21).

Using a different approach, Evan Zuesse has delved into the hypostatized value of this exclusionary figure. He has noted that the Bible comprises a metonymic logic of taboos (which rely on displacement) that could be contrasted with the metaphorical nature of the sacrifice (which relies on deletion and substitution). This has led him to suggest that the Bible marks out the end of sacrificial religion and replaces it with a system of rules, prohibitions, and moral codes.[4]

That is all I shall say about these recent studies, which have helped clarify the inner workings of biblical thought in a way that can be distinguished from the historical or philological approach to religions, especially Judaism. I believe that the conclusions they have drawn are essential to any understanding of the Bible. These studies can be characterized, however, by an important omission: no attention is paid to the linguistic subject of the biblical utterance, nor by way of consequence, to its addressee. *Who is speaking in the Bible? For whom?*

This question is especially relevant for our purposes because it seems to suggest a subject who is not at all neutral and indifferent like the subject described by modern theories of interpretation, but who maintains a specific relationship of *crisis, trial,* or *process* with his God. If it is true that all texts considered "sacred" refer to borderline states of subjectivity, we have reason to reflect upon these states, especially since the biblical narrator is familiar with them. Such a reading would tend to focus on the intra- or infrasubjective dynamics of the sacred text. Yet even if these dynamics are manifested in the figure of the text itself, interpreting them would require that we recognize a *new space,* that of the speaking subject, who henceforth ceases to be an impenetrable point that guarantees the universality of logical operations, and who opens himself instead to analyzable spaces. If I am alluding to Freudian theory here, it is because Freud's theory is capable of using the results of the biblical analyses I have mentioned and of transporting them into subjective space. Were an interpretation to internalize these discoveries as devices proper to certain states of the subject of enunciation, it could go beyond a simply descriptive framework and account for the impact that the Bible has on its addressees.

To return to the characteristic figures of biblical food taboos, I have come to realize that the object excluded by these rules, whatever form it may take in biblical narrative, is ultimately the mother. I cannot review the logical process that has led me to this position, but I shall take the liberty of referring you to my *Powers of Horror*.[5] Let me simply state that it is not enough to study the logical processes of exclusion that underlie the institution of these taboos, for attention must also be paid to the semantic and pragmatic value of the excluded object. We notice, among other things, that separating oneself from the mother, rejecting her, and "abjecting" her; as well as using this negation to resume contact with her, to define oneself according to her, and to "rebuild" her, constitutes an essential movement in the biblical text's struggles against the maternal cults of previous and current forms of paganism.

Now, the analyst is another person who sees such abjection as necessary for the advent of the subject as a speaking being. Studies on early childhood and on language acquisition have shown that the rejection of the mother causes her to be the originary object of need, desire, or speech. Yet she is also an ambiguous object who is, in fact, an *ab-ject*—a magnet of fascination and repulsion—before (in both the logical and chronological sense) she can be established as an object. This suggests an immersion in that which is not "one's own," as well as a dramatic distortion of the narcissistic dyad.

What is more, phobic and psychotic symptoms, which act out uncertainties about the limits of the subject (myself versus other people, inside versus outside), internalize this sort of aggressive fascination with the mother. In the discourse of adults, the mother becomes a locus of horror and adoration. She is ready for the entire procession of part-objects of *disgust* and *anality* that mobilize themselves to support the fragile whole of an ego in crisis.

Therefore, it could be said that a biblical text (the Book of Leviticus), which delineates the precise limits of abjection (from skin to food, sex, and moral codes), has developed a true archeology of the advent of the subject. Indeed, this Book recounts the subject's delicate and painful detachment—moment by moment, layer by layer, step by step—as well as his journey from narcissistic fusion to an autonomy that is never really "his own," never "clean," never complete, and never securely guaranteed in the Other.

I am suggesting, then, an interpretation that compares the Book of Leviticus to the preoedipal dynamic of the subject's separation. My interpretation is rooted in the fragile status of subjectivity, and it thus serves to explain, at least to some extent, the cathartic value of the biblical text. The Book of Leviticus speaks to me by locating me at the point where I lose my "clean self." It takes back what I dislike and acknowledges my bodily discomfort, the ups and downs of my sexuality, and the compromises or harsh demands of my public life. It shapes the very borders of my defeats, *for it has probed into the ambivalent desire for the other,* for the mother as the first other, *which is at the base, that is, on the other side of that which makes me into a speaking being* (a separating, dividing, joining being). The Bible is a text that thrusts its words into my losses. By enabling me to speak about my disappointments, though, it lets me stand in full awareness of them.

This awareness is unconscious—so be it. Nevertheless, it causes me, as a reader of the Bible, to resemble someone who lives on the fringe, on the lines of demarcation within which my security and fragility are separated and merged. Perhaps that is where we might discover what is known as the sacred value of the text: a place that gives meaning to these crises of subjectivity, during which meaning, disturbed as it is by the object-abject of desire, eludes me and "I" run the risk of falling into the indifference of a narcissistic, lethal fusion.

Across the ages, sacred literature may never have done anything but use various forms of sacrifice to enunciate *murder* as a condition of Meaning. At the same time, this literature has emphasized the breathtaking threat that *fusion libido* inflicts upon meaning, which it can carry, destroy, or kill. The message of the biblical abominations, however, is particular and unique: you must be separated from your mother so that you do not kill anyone. Meaning is what guarantees desire and thus preserves the desire for death. You will displace your hatred into thought; you will devise a logic that defends you from murder and madness, a logic whose arbitrary nature shall be your coronation. The Bible offers the best description of this transformation of sacrifice into language, this displacement of murder into a system of meanings. In this way, this *system,* which counterbalances *murder,* becomes the place where all our crises can be exploded and assimilated. In my view, the fulcrum of this biblical process can be located in its particular conception of the *maternal:* the maternal is a promised land if you are willing to leave it, an object of desire if you are willing to renounce and forbid it; the maternal is delight as well as murder, an inescapable "abject" whose awareness haunts you, or which may very well be the constitutive double of your own awareness. "For your hands are defiled with blood/ and your fingers with iniquity" (Isa. 59:3).

Love that Cannot Be Represented

The Bible draws attention to the love that the Jewish people have for their God, and it demands or denounces this love when it is found to be insufficient. On the other hand, ancient texts have much less to say about God's love for Israel. Only two references to this love can be found:

> And David comforted his wife, Bathsheba, and went in unto her, and lay with her; and she bore a son, and he called his name Solomon; and the LORD loved him.
> And he sent by the hand of Nathan the prophet; and he called his name Jedidiah, because of the LORD (2 Sam. 12:24–25).

The queen of Sheba affirms that the Lord loves Israel:

Blessed be the LORD *thy God, which delighted in thee. (1 Kings 10:9).*

Christian agape was to turn the situation around and posit that Love falls from the heavens even before we know it as such. The love that the biblical God has for His people is expressed in another way. As direct as it may be, it demands neither worthiness nor justification, for it is interspersed with preferences and choices that immediately establish the loved one as a Subject. Ancient biblical texts do not make a great deal of this love, and when they do intimate it exists, they imply that it cannot be represented. For instance, note that Nathan is the one who says, though without any words, that Solomon is beloved. What is more, the name of Jedidiah the child ("Jedidah" meaning loved by God) does not reappear in the narrative. As for the second passage, a foreign woman is the one who refers to God's love, and she speaks in riddles.

This brings us to the central problem of the biblical God: He cannot be seen, named, or represented. That these traits are particularly applicable to His *love,* as is shown by the passages I have cited, may give the analyst some insight into the infinitely complex question of the Bible's *prohibition of representation.*

When analysts listen to evocations of narcissistic wounds, or better yet, when they listen to subjects who are constituted by a narcissistic wound, they become aware of a ghostly yet secure presence of the father before they become aware of any oedipal hold on the father's love or on love for him. This archaic mirage of the paternal function, which is placed against the background of primary narcissism as the ultimate guarantee of identity, could very well be considered to be an imaginary Father. Although his actual existence may be hallucinatory, he appears to edify the keystone of the capacity to sublimate, especially through art. Freud characterized this particular Father, who is necessary for the Ego-Ideal, as a support for "primary identification." He referred to him as the "Father in personal prehistory" (*Vater der personlïchen Vorzeit*). Freud postulated that apprehension of this father is "direct and immediate" (*direkte und unmittelbare*), and emphasized that he internalizes both parents and both genders. The immediacy of this absolute, which the young child of a Mother-Father in personal prehistory brings back to a mysterious and direct grasp, guarantees his ability to idealize.

This sheds some scandalous light on the theological or antitheological orientation of philosophy. We know, indeed, that philosophers from Hegel to Heidegger have tried to ascertain the meaning of Being by interpreting the absolute presence of Parousia. We are obliged to note that this two-sided and double-gendered figure of kinship, which is what creates the symbolic, limits the extent to which analysis may search for that which is not simply narcissistic in origin. This, however, does not guarantee symbolic autonomy (or the separation between subject and object that it presumes).

As the zero-degree of symbol formation, this imaginary Father, who is most likely the father desired by the mother (her own father?), is thus the focal point of the processes that lead not to the appearance of the object (along this path, we have found the *abject* and a separative obsession), but to the *position of subjectivity,* that is, a being for and by the Other. The early onset of this moment, as well as its mediation by the mother's desire, causes the subject to believe that this moment is resistant to representation, despite the array of signifiers brought about by the oedipal complex. Those who believe in the God of the Bible do not doubt His love. God—who is impossible to represent, fleeting, and always there though invisible—eludes me and invites me to let go of my narcissism, to venture forth, to inflict suffering and persecution upon myself in order to earn His love. Does He not force these roots into that ineradicable, archaic, and deeply felt conviction that occupies and protects those who accept Him? That is, the conviction that a preoedipal father exists, a *Vater der personlichen Vorzeit,* an imaginary father?

Is Psychoanalysis a "Jewish Science?"

Interpreting the meaning of the sacred text as an elaboration of psychic conflicts that border on psychosis assumes, as I have made clear, that the psychoanalyst is attentive and even vulnerable to the biblical text. Why is it that ever since Freud, analytic attention has invariably focused on the sacred, and more specifically on the biblical sacred?

One might answer that such an orientation stems from the interpretive posture itself. I am made to use silence or speech to listen to and to interpret a discourse that no longer has any meaning for its subject, and that is consequently experienced as painful. I am struck, however, by the fact that analysands are privy to a meaning that is "already there," even if this meaning takes the form of the most dramatic explosions of subjective identity or of linguistic coherence. Does this stem from the conviction that there is an imaginary father? Whose father is it?

In like manner, the interpretive construction made by the analyst, who assimilates this speech through transference or countertransference, also presents itself as a barrier to possible meaning (when I communicate an interpretation) or to a meaning that is arbitrary, if not eccentric (when I resort to silence). This interpretive construction, which can be as portentous as my own desire will allow, is nevertheless my only way—*the* only way?—to guide the analysand's speech from being completely eclipsed toward a state of relative autonomy. Interpretive constructions do not deny that crises occur, but they save us from getting trapped in them or reveling in them. I am proposing, then, an imaginary construction that can serve as an indefinite and infinite truth. As opposed to a positivist interpretation, which would delimit reality by giving itself the last word—the strongest word—analytic interpretation, as an imaginary discourse that serves as truth, makes no attempt to hide its status as fiction, as a *text*.

As a sacred text? This hypothesis, which we should not be too quick to reject, will attract the attention of rationalists on all sides, for a psychoanalyst would be unthinkable, it would seem, at the Collège de France. Nevertheless, we can easily understand that the text of analytic interpretation defuses all beliefs: a psychoanalyst appears suspicious; he is banished from churches and temples. Why?

By normalizing and understanding desire, psychoanalysis does not repudiate it, as commonly believed. It is true that analysis shapes and molds desire, but only as the wings of the Paragon of Faith, as the *subjection of desire to a fascinating object,* perhaps an unnameable one. The analyst remains fully aware that this object drapes itself in the attire of the mother Goddess, who extols our fantasies of origins and our desire for interpretation. Consequently, analyists are obliged to distance themselves from Faith in the Goddess of Reason as well as from religious Faith.

Hence, analysts find that the Bible offers a particular narration that suggests a treatment for the very symptoms that they are called on to interpret. Yet, this close relationship with biblical narration opens up the possibility of choice. Faced with the hypostatized Meaning of the Other, analysts maintain their interpretation by negating the intriguing power wielded by this Other, Father, or Law.

The analyst is not unaware that interpretive desire, which is abrasive and frustrating for the fantasy of the other, is tied to the fantasy of returning to the mother. It is true that under the demands of monotheism, such an attitude reveals the obsession with the pagan mother who has shaped it. Nevertheless, psychoanalysts can only avoid the trap of an archetypal Jungianism by admitting that their own sadomasochistic jubilation—which stems from approaching the source of that which is said—masks a certain hold on the unnameable Object (by way of the Law of the father as well as the fascination with the mother). What is more, analysts, as providers of meaning, should eventually saw off the branch, as well as the limb they are sitting on, for the driving force behind faith is the fantasy of returning to the mother, from whom biblical faith specifically distances us. The ensuing ambiguity causes Judaism, when it is completely internalized, to be the least religious of religions.

By laying bare the splendors of the Virgin Mary, Christianity, after having relied on a neo-testamentary discretion toward this subject, has unintentionally revealed what lies behind faith. In contrast to Freud, it could be maintained that the presence of the

Virgin throughout Christianity is less a return to paganism than an acknowledgment of the hidden side of the sacred mechanism (of any sacred mechanism), which draws us into its soothing and grinding motion in order to leave us with a single path to salvation: having faith in the Father.

Psychoanalysis does not fall short of this, but goes even further: it is "post-Catholic" by X-raying *meaning* as a *fantasy,* and then going on to take various phantasmatic functions to be an original fantasy in the form of an adoration of the object-*abject of maternal love* and a cause of eternal return. Finally, it is "post-Catholic" in that it includes *its own process* within this same course of eternal return. Through this three-way loop, the experience of psychoanalysis results in a sort of combustion.

Let us say, then, that everything ends up as fire—the fire of Heraclitus, the fire of the burning bush, the fire that burned Isaiah's tongue, or the fire that bedazzled heads with Pentecostal tongues. The truth of the matter is that I envisage the fate of meaning during an analytic session in a similar fashion—as a meaning that is multifaceted, indefinable, set ablaze, yet One Meaning that exerts its influence everywhere. We can admit that this meaning requires the analyst to cling to the Bible's rigor, logic, and love, so that this fire might *be* and not die down right away. All the same, it must not blind us into thinking that this fire is the only thing that exists, for it need only state the truth at one point or another.

Neither biblical, rationalistic, religious, nor positivist, the place of the analyst is always elsewhere and deceptive, notable for the attention it gives to emptiness. This ambiguous position generates an ethics of construction if not of healing, and it bases itself not on hope but on the fire of tongues. This is enough to irritate believers, which amounts to almost everyone, in spite of what we might think. As Freud said, analysis "exasperates" human beings; it forces them to contradict themselves.

Nevertheless, the central focus (as well as the stumbling block) of this avoidance-through-profusion that constitutes the serene delicacy of the never-attained end of analysis is analogous to the logic of the Bible. Denying the extent of its impact, which means cleansing the Father in order to decipher the Mother or to decipher a walled-up desire, can easily leads to an anti-Semitism in good faith. In a clinical sense, this anti-Semitism may portray a patient caught in the maternal bosom of fantasy, hope, and dependence. The un-being of a chosen yet excluded being is extremely difficult to assimilate.

On the other hand, one could delight in a strict, "mathematical" reading of the biblical text, a reading that avoids all ambiguities, especially the pagan aspect coiled up beside the maternal body, which borders, as I have said, on the logical desire that serves as a foundation for monotheism. This sort of "scientific" reading would encourage us to make analytic practice into a preferred space for hysteria (in men as well as women), a space targeted by what Lacan would call a paranoid "lovehate" for the Other. Have we not seen a great deal of this recently in the various schools of thought and their schisms?

What might be done about this?

We should read the Bible one more time. To interpret it, of course, but also to let it carve out a space for our own fantasies and interpretive delirium.

8. FROM SIGNS TO THE SUBJECT

In the Gospel According to St. John (written around A.D. 90), chapter 6 could be read as a semiological debate in which Jesus contrasts his own conception of signs with the one held by the "people." He incorporates these signs into what might be called a theory of the subject.

These "people," "them," the "Jews," are clearly opponents of John's community. Historians debate whether they were members of the Synagogue, dissenters from it, disciples of Jesus' brother, supporters of John the Baptist, or members of a Judeo-Christian sect.[1] It is not this sociohistorical aspect that interests me here. Let me simply state that in order to found his "high Christology," John engaged in a semiological debate. His narrative begins by likening the miracles that Jesus performed to the magical signs that founded the faith of the believers, which preceded the true Christianity that was advocated by John. He went beyond this magic, however, in order to incorporate it into another understanding of faith. Let us take a closer look at these transformations.

At first, Jesus is a magician: "And a multitude followed him, because they saw the signs which he did on those on those who were diseased" (John 6:2). At the height of his powers, he takes five barley loaves and two fish from a lad, distributes them to five thousand people, and satisfies their hunger. Naturally, everyone believes he is "the prophet who is to come into the world" (6:14). Finally, he "walks on the sea" (6:19) toward Capernaum.

From that point on, however, the Evangelist purports to assign a new meaning to his miracles. Do they have the same value as the ones familiar to the "people" and described by the Bible? Are they merely a recollection of the episode of the "manna in the wilderness" that Moses gave to his people?

What sign do you do, that we may see, and believe you? What work do you perform? Our fathers ate the manna in the wilderness; as it is written, "He gave them bread from heaven to eat."
(6:30–31)

In sum, are Jesus' signs a renewal of biblical signs? If so, how might we recognize them? It is at this point that John has Jesus create a new semiology.

First, according to the Evangelist, a sign does not formally indicate something for the person who receives it. A sign only has a value for its addressee if it responds to the sensory needs of the receiver. Therefore, we must acknowledge our corporeal needs (hunger, thirst), since responding to them allows "signs" to attain the power that grants them their status as signs. Through the words of Jesus, John thus *adds a sensory layer to signs,* and he interprets them as a satisfaction of the primordial need to survive: "Jesus answered them, 'Truly, truly, I say to you, you seek me, *not because you saw signs, but because you ate your fill of the loaves*'" (6:26).

Hence, John's interpretation of signs starts off as a sensualism, if not as a replenishment of affects (what the Evangelist essentially says is "you are hungry and thirsty."). This replenishment will continue through the symbolic heart of the Eucharistic rite.

John insists that the *sense of sight* alone does not represent the intensity of your experience with these "signs." You should cease to be fascinated with your sight of this sign-gift that you have received from Moses-the-Giver. Instead of being subjugated by it in this way, transfer yourself—into your own space, for you are not simply addressees of this sign-gift: you *are*. As John's narrative progresses, he will tell you what you *truly* are. For the moment, acknowledge that you are hungry, thirsty, needy. . . . If you do so, a second shift will become possible, one that John is quick to initiate. It is a matter of going from these signs-foods of your needs to *"I,"* to place your trust in *"I."* "I am the bread of life" (6:35). Who is this "I"?

> *Labor not for the meat which perisheth, but for the meat which endureth unto everlasting life, which the Son of man shall give unto you; for Him hath God the Father sealed, (6:27)*

The absolute subject is a "son of man" who is sustained by a close relationship with God our Father. The idea of *paternity* implies a carnal genealogy. This evocation of a generational link located in a restatement of signs-miracles automatically reintroduces the body and the sensations. Once again, it incorporates the community of constituents (in the form of bodies) into John's new semiology.

What is more, the verb "to seal"[2] evokes the indissociable proximity of the one who represents (the Son) to the represented (the Father). On the one hand, they are "squeezed" against each other like a seal and its imprint, a break-in and the clue left behind, the gift and its acceptance, the offering and its reception, which only becomes satisfying through suffering from a wound. On the other hand, the verb "to seal" implies a relationship of meaning between the two entities: the Son "means" the Father, and this signification is to be deployed by *you,* as addressees of the evangelical narrative. Since the Son put his faith in the Father, you should trust Him yourself. *Signification* means *trusting* the other, whose own confidence binds him to his father.

This multifaceted movement is what accommodates subjective interpretation. A preexistence of meaning is proposed in and through the figure of the Father. Nevertheless, the Son, who is "sealed" to him, rises immediately to this level. The journey of his passion—his subjectivity—reveals the differences among the constituents as well as the beliefs shared by them all. Finally, this journey reveals the preexistence of Jesus himself: "I say to you, before Abraham was, *I am*" (8:58).

In other words, it will be necessary to "come" to I/me,[3] and not be content with just "seeing" or seeing again a given sign. From that point on, the sign is the subject's trajectory, which replaces the sign-gift. In this perspective, I am reminded of the following polemical passage: "Truly, truly, I say to you, it was not Moses who gave you the bread from heaven; my father gives you the true bread from heaven" (6:32).

To participate in signification, it is not enough to pinpoint a sign that reveals the presence of the Giver. It is important to open up this space, which must be qualified as subjective, and which primarily uses representation (the "sense of sight") to displace the trust between the self and the Father into *a new interiority*. "I will not cast [him] out" (6:37). "But I said to you that you have seen me and yet do not believe. All that the Father gives me will come to me; and him who comes to me I will not cast out. For I have come down from heaven, not to do my own will, but the will of Him who sent me" (6:36–38).

By opening up this interior, invisible space, the sensory foundation of John's semiology is transformed into an intensely symbolic dimension. It is not a matter of "seeing" the Father or of "knowing" that the son is "bread which came down from heaven"—in the same way that one "knows" one's own mother and father (6:41–46). Only he who "comes" from God has "seen" the father: "Not that any one has seen the Father except Him who is from God; he has seen the Father" (6:46). Visual *representation* is replaced again by a *provenance* that is at once physical (traveling, filiation) and symbolic (giving meaning), for it is because the Son *believes* He is signified and generated by the Third Party (the Father) that He ensures His trust and incites the trust of other people. When meaning is subjective, it is derived from this trust. Having been one of Jesus' beloved disciples, John was able to subject his trust or love to the very roots of his conception of signification.

In John's community, where might we find the mechanism of access to this sort of subjective semiology? In the Eucharistic rite, through which the communicant is invited to "eat the flesh of the Son of man" and to "drink his blood" (6:54).

We can see that within the believer's oral and symbolic assimilation of the Son of God, there lies the participant's intense identification with the absolute Subject-Christ, who was defined earlier as "sealed" by trust in the Father and trust of the Father. It appears to function as a phantasmatic identification that mobilizes images as well as sensations and affects, and that is displaced all the way to the abstract signification that consummates this process. Furthermore, a veritable "transubstantiation" is invoked by the dynamism of this Eucharistic identification, which exposes the believer to the diverse realms of subjective experience—from affects to sublimated love, from an all-consuming violence to an assimilating trust and vice versa. "He who eats my flesh and drinks my blood abides in me, and I in him" (6:56).

We find ourselves displaced again. The identification of "I" with "him" leads the communicant to share the passion of Christ, the absolute subject and a model for the believer, and not to benefit merely from his gifts. From a semiological perspective, this paroxysmal osmosis between "him" and "me," an osmosis that occurs in the Eucharist, causes those who were formerly sign interpreters to become subjects. These subjects, who are not satisfied with merely accepting the Giver's indications, are able to decode *his* meaning, which in the heart of this identification, proves to be *their own.*

According to John 6:6, there are two advantages to this sort of subjectivation. First, phantasmatic participation in God's infinite meaning opens the subject to the infinite time of interpretation, a time that might be considered eternal. Second, symbolic identification with the Son of God, which is centered on speech, has a direct effect on the body. Here, we rediscover that signs have a sensory and affective foundation, which has been suggested from the beginning. And now there is a reversal, for by realizing that speech unites him with the absolute Subject, the believer discovers that his own body has been revitalized. This experience of sensory and corporeal regeneration through the effect of transport—of transference—onto the love of the other is imagined to be a guarantee of immortality and resurrection. "As the living Father sent me, and I live because of the Father, so he who eats me will live because of me" (6:57).

This rejuvenating effect of speech, however, is only a retroactive effect of the acceptance of meaning. John's narrative closes with a challenge to sensory indications, to the benefit of the "spirit" and of "words." "It is the spirit that gives life, the flesh is of no avail; the words that I have spoken to you are spirit and life" (6:63). Indeed, John's Christology is *very high*. It does not deny the carnal presence of the subject. Although John bases the regenerative effects of the mass upon an identification with this presence, he secures faith in an identification between the ego and the Meaning of the sealed (offered) Son, surrounded by the passion of the Father. "This is why I told you that no one can come to me unless it is granted him by the Father" (6:65).

The problems of this requirement are understandable, as it transcends both rational awareness and the fetishism of erotic sects. Not surprisingly, this is followed by abandonment and betrayal: "After this many of his disciples drew back and no longer went about with him." (6:66)

It is nevertheless a fact that John's reflection offers psychoanalysts an exemplary course of action. By beginning with the sign-gift that subjects "the people" to the power of an Other, John's thought develops a two-tiered theory of love-identification (between Jesus and God, between the believer and Jesus) that serves as a foundation for a complex subjectivity. When placed within this sort of subjectivity, the sign ceases to be a gift. Indeed, the sign-gift that satisfies needs and causes them to subside inevitably inscribes itself within the finality of a power for death ("not the dead ones that were eaten by the fathers"). From that point on, the sign acts as a more-than-metaphor: a transport of the father, a hold on the violence of affects, a revival of infinite interpretive activity, and a return to corporeal identity.

First Model of the Sign (the "People")

He who requests—*object*—He who gives

gift

sign of the giver

presence of the giver

satisfaction

Second Model of the Sign (John's sign)

sign

Subject——affect—Son sealed to the Father

metaphor

"trust," "love," "signify"

In summary, two models of the sign can be derived from a reading of this text: the first one is defeated and the second one proposed. Through John, a new dynamics of *signification* becomes possible, one that is circular (from the Same to the Other), heterogeneous (meaning and affect), and infinite (the play of interpretation). In these dynamics, the "gift" that the Son gave to the Father—that is, the death of Jesus—is inscribed in trust (transport, love). They revitalize the infinite nature of meaning and life, without getting caught in death-satisfaction or in deadly regal power, which is precisely what Jesus rejects.

This movement could be seen as a sort of passage. Jesus' "miracle" of crossing the sea is without doubt a most impressive one. Nevertheless, this crossing cannot be narrated. The "boat touches the ground" abruptly, and imagination alone is invited to follow Jesus' walking on water. As imaginary as this crossing may be, it could also be a spiritual one.

We can be sure, in any event, that John transforms Jesus the conjurer into Christian interiority. This transformation was the beginning of a story that would be developed by Plotinus, the Church Fathers, Descartes, Hegel, and many others. It is a story for which Freud may have offered an incisive perspective that allows us to understood from the *inside,* so that the ritual of Eucharistic assimilation might be transformed into an "epiphany" of the subject.

Writing for Adolescence

The adolescent, like the child, is a mythical figure of the imaginary that enables us to distance ourselves from some of our failings, splittings of the ego, disavowals, or mere desires, which it reifies into the figure of someone who has not yet grown up. Moreover, the adolescent allows us to see, hear, and read these subjective fluctuations.

Certain eras were crazy about childhood. Through the figure of Emile, the age of Rousseau longed for the progressive stability of a new social contract. The time of Freud and his followers sought the reserved yet cogent knowledge of perverse polymorphous children. Other eras have identified with the ambiguity of young pages, picadors, troublemakers, or terrorists—from Casanova to Milos Forman and Mad Max, and it would seem that contemporary life partakes in such identifications. Whatever the actual problems of today's adolescents may be, when I speak here about the "adolescent" and more specifically about "adolescent writing," I am suggesting that we inquire into the role of the imaginary in countertransference as well as its practical effectiveness for the patient and the analyst.

When I say "adolescent," I mean less a developmental stage than an open psychic structure. Just as biologists speak of the "open structure" of living organisms that renew their identity by interacting with another identity, it could be said that the adolescent structure opens itself to that which has been repressed. At the same time, a tremendous freeing-up of the superego permits it to initiate a psychic reorganization of the individual, a reorganization that is followed by the onset of pregenitality and an attempt to integrate it into genitality.

After the oedipal stabilization of subjective identity, adolescents begin to question their identifications, as well as their capacities to speak and to symbolize. The search for a new love object reactivates both the depressive position and the manic attempts to resolve it—which range from perversion to drug addiction and membership in ideological and religious groups with universalist strivings. Insofar as the keystone, the Other medium of writing, is much closer to the ideal ego than to the ego-ideal, such psychic structures and their corollary—writing, that is—take on narcissistic and perverse characteristics.

Just as there are *"as-if"* personalities, there are *"open-structure"* personalities. The latter incorporate the "as-if" personality as well as other characteristics that can appear in perverse structures, even if they do not necessarily harbor any actual perversions. Because of such factors as changes in the contemporary family, the blurring of sex roles and parental roles, and the lifting of religious and moral taboos, subjects are no longer structured according to rigorous prohibitions or laws. The boundaries between differences of sex and identity, of reality and fantasy, of act and discourse, and so forth, are easily crossed without entering the domain of perversion or borderline states, if only because these "open structures" easily mirror the free flow (the flimsiness?) of our mass-media society. Such structures resort to sublimation in order to conceal one's complaint. The adolescent represents this structure *naturally,* and it could only be termed a "crisis" structure within the context of an ideal and consistent law.

Let us attempt to sharpen our definition of this *open structure* and to emphasize the value that it might have for the practice of writing. This relationship could be approached from at least three angles:

1. Semiological activity as a generator of written signs. Although supported by its linguistic substratum, writing also provides a motor dimension, muscular and anal control, an aggressive appropriation of the body of the other as well as of one's own body, and finally, a masturbatory and narcissistic gratification.

2. The production of a novelistic fiction. As an imaginary activity, novelistic fiction makes use of the codes of representation and the available ideologies that screen individual fantasies. The "screening" may amount to a suppression of unconscious materials and lead to a stereotypical, cliché-ridden form of writing. It may also lead to an actual inscription of unconscious material within language, thereby giving adolescents the impression that they are employing—after a long wait and for the first time in their lives—a living discourse that is not empty, not an "as-if." More real than a fantasy, fiction generates a new living identity. If an atheist like Mayakovsky was able to believe in resurrection, it would seem that his faith had been inspired by the experience of writing.

3. Evading the judgment of the other. The solitary economy of writing protects subjects from phobic affects. Though it enables them to reconstruct their psychic space, it shelters them from reality testing. The psychological advantages of such sheltering are obvious; but this does not eliminate the question of the subject's relation to reality in his own experience, as well as in psychoanalytic treatment, when therapy makes use of patients' writings.

I shall make a few remarks about an eighteen-year-old female patient whom I treated once a week in a psychotherapeutic setting. This patient, who was not capable of any real phantasmatic development and was prone to states of delirium and acting-out, wanted to become a police officer. Moreover, she constantly tried to seduce policemen, security agents, and the like.

In the beginning of her treatment, Anne was bound to a single discourse: that of her desire-delirium and acting-out, which she perceived with no objectivity. By way of her transference and her insistence that she, like myself, could write about love, she began to create comic strips that depicted the life and sexual escapades of police officers. Onomatopoeic effects were gradually replaced by balloons that surrounded words and dialogues of increasing complexity. "These cop stories are like dreams or novels," she said.

During the next stage of the analysis, Anne saw herself as a writer of love songs—in English. It is notable that drawings, as well as a foreign language, were used to strive for an increasingly precise representation of unconscious materials. Following this period, Anne wrote a series of letters addressed to her analyst that gave freer expression to her troubles and psychological suffering. I noticed some changes in Anne's discourse within the scope of the sessions where she brought along her letters and other writings. Her speech became richer and less aggressively demanding, which meant it became more depressive, thus more polished. Writing had replaced "law and order." Her writing, a "peace warden," was clearly provisional, though I believed it gave Anne a chance to make amends with her memories of the past.

In this specific case, as well as in other cases of adolescents who do not display Anne's borderline symptoms, I would tend to see writing as a semiotic practice that facilitates a renewed organization of psychic space—a process that precedes an idealized maturity. The adolescent imaginary is an amorous one, and the love object, prone to being lost, revitalizes the depressive position. Basing itself upon this position of the object, adolescent writing (written signs added to a fantasy that is screened by available codes of the imaginary) makes another attempt to manifest the symbol. Hannah Segal attributes this materialization to the depressive position, and she sees it as a result of the "symbolic equivalent" of the paranoid position.[1] During adolescence, moreover, this depressive revival of the symbol is accompanied by a rather free phantasmatic development in which fantasies facilitate an alteration of the underlying *drives* and *signs* of written and spoken language.

In this sense, imaginary activity and especially imaginary writing (through the narcissistic gratification and the protection from phobias that it offers) give the subject a chance to elaborate a discourse that is not "vacuous" and that is experienced as genuine. To the view put forth by Hannah Segal, I would add the following nuance: although adolescent writing finds solace in reactivating the depressive position, it sustains itself through a manic position. As a denial of loss and a triumph of the ego through the fetish of the text, writing becomes a necessary phallic complement, if not the phallus par excellence. For this very reason, writing is contingent upon an ideal paternity.

It is important to note that our society does not forbid adolescents to make this sort of phallic affirmation; in fact, it clearly allows adolescents to have an imaginary. Modern societies have come to offer an invitation to engage in imaginary activities that replace—or merely water down—the rites of passage that other societies require of their adolescents. Nevertheless, an adult could be entitled to this imaginary only as a reader or spectator of novels, films, or paintings—or as an artist. For that matter, what, if not an "open structure," could motivate someone to write?

Novelistic Writing

Understood as the elaboration of a style, writing resembles the subject's fight against schizophrenia or depression. The very genre of the novel, with its characters and the logic of its plots, is quite dependent on the "adolescent" economy of writing, although these are two separate matters. This view would imply that a novel is the work of a perpetual subject-adolescent. As a permanent witness to our adolescence, the novel would enable us to rediscover the state of incompleteness (which is as depressive as it is joyful) that leads in some respects to what we call aesthetic pleasure.

My attention is drawn less to a given writer's splitting of the ego than to the distance between the ego and the ego-ideal, the superego being suspended. Yet this suspension is what allows *free motion* to occur between the representations of an ego identified with the adolescent economy (depression, projection, pregenitality, narcissism) and that of an ego-ideal. It enables the ego-ideal to bear witness to ego conflicts by way of condensation and displacement.

This free movement represents another open structure. Nevertheless, it differs from the open structure of adolescence because the ideal ego that governs adolescent writing is replaced by an ego-ideal that is much more stable. In men, the ego-ideal bases itself upon the mother's object of desire, who is often the mother's father (the male writer's work grows out from the space inhabited by his maternal grandfather, who observes the adolescent that he himself is). In female writers, this ego-ideal is maintained by the incestuous father or his equivalent. Securing women's writing in an incestuous father leads to a dramatic burst of ambivalence (love-hate) toward the mother, an ambivalence that is laden with more psychotic dangers for women than for men.

Whether the novelist plays the role of an adolescent represented by an ego-ideal, identifies with the adolescent, or is himself an adolescent, the theme of the adolescent is one of the most salient characteristics of Western novels.

The Betrayed Page Betrays: Ambivalence as a Novelistic Quality

In the *Marriage of Figaro,* Mozart immortalized the figure of the page who, like a happy Narcissus, yearns day and night without ever knowing if he is in love. I believe we have not sufficiently emphasized that the themes of the earliest modern novels—those written just after the Middle Ages—are developed through the loves of pages. These loves constitute the very framework of novelistic psychology.

It is commonly believed that the first French prose novel (that is, neither an epic nor a courtly lyric) was a text written by Antoine de la Sale (1385 or 1386–1460) entitled *Le Petit Jehan de Saintré* (1456).[2] We are right in the heart of the fifteenth century. The author lived around the time of the Hundred Years

War (1337–1453), the Battle of Orleans (1428), and Joan of Arc's death (1431). A feverish ecclesiastical activity attests to the symbolic upheaval of that era; one need only think of the Council of Basel (1431–39) and the Council at Constance (1414–18). Although these historical events do not imbue the text itself, the novel attests to the transition between the Middle Ages and the Renaissance through its use of medieval discourse (especially its erudition) as well as its introduction of new forms of discourse.

At the age of fourteen, and following his early studies in Provence, Antoine de la Sale began his career as a page in the Court of Louis II, king of Sicily. Around 1442, he became both a writer who compiled historical, geographical, legal, and ethical texts and a tutor who wrote manuals for his students. Then, as if merging his own experience as a page with the lives of the students who were the object of his didactic writings, Antoine created the character of Jehan de Saintré.

I would first like to emphasize the unpolished and "transitory" characteristics of this first French novelist, who was so clumsy that he lay bare the narrative threads he interwove: classical erudition, citations from courtly literature, and the use of dramatic dialogue remain unchanged in the text of this novel. Such borrowings point to an author who was still unsure of his competence, and who was still seeking an authoritative discourse. To this adolescent quality can be added the rather ambiguous relation that the novel sets up between text, theater, and reality. In this sense, each utterance is preceded by an indication such as "Author" or "Actor" or "Lady." These clues reveal that the author wished to distance himself from his fiction, as if he wanted us to know that his choice to use these artifices was a deliberate one. In addition, they present the reification of text into spectacle, into an act, as though the author wanted us to see these creatures of speech in the hallucinatory or real form of actual bodies. The writings of this first French novelist do not yield to the efficacy of drama (of psychodrama), though they call out to it, over and above the peaceful activity of reading. Nevertheless, the element that centers this specimen text on the adolescent structure is the particular relationship between the young page, on the one hand, and the Lady and her lover, the Abbot, on the other.

Young Jehan is in love with the Lady. The Lady, however, employs a perfidious discourse. She says one thing to Jehan and another to the Court, thereby betraying her young suitor by way of the Abbot. The novel makes our young hero confront his oedipal scenario through "deferred action" so that Young Jehan might learn of the duplicity of adolescence. His incestuous love for the Lady will be transformed into an imaginary identification with her. As time goes on, Jehan will build up his own double language; he will at once love and despise the Lady, whom he will eventually punish. The story ends there, but the novel, which becomes a summary of the hero's adventures, continues until the time of his death.

The interest of this novel resides in its portrayal of the adolescent who conquers his incestuous object, the Lady, by way of an imaginary assimilation of her discourse. A whole revolution in mentalities plays a role in this little adventure. Before the birth of the novel, the hero and the villain were single-minded. In the *Song of Roland* and in all of the *Tales of the Round Table,* the hero and the villain pursue each other with a relentless hostility and without any possibility of a compromise. Roland and Ganelon have nothing in common, and they negate each other in the courtly tradition, in which betrayal disgraces the characters and arrests the text. This is hardly the situation, however, of our adolescent and his world: Saintré is at once child and warrior, page and hero; he is deceived by the Lady but a conqueror in battle. He is cared for and then betrayed; he is the lover of the Lady and loved by the King and by his brother-in-arms, Boucicault. Saintré is never completely masculine; he is the Lady's child-lover and the playmate-friend of his tutors and of his brother, whose bed he shares. In sum, this protagonist is the perfect androgen, the innocent and vindicated pervert.

This ambivalence is, in fact, at the very origin of psychology. For that matter, there is no psychology without dissimulation and betrayal. Ambivalence and psychology are much more characteristic of the novel than of the epic or the courtly romance. In the fifteenth century, if a French writer wanted to write about loss or betrayal, he first needed to imagine a mediator, a figure of incompleteness but also one of every possibility, of the "anything is possible." Jehan de Saintré the Page triumphs over the Lady as well the Abbot, and a new genre is born: the adolescent novel. The writer as an adolescent is someone who could betray his parents—by turning them against each other—in order to be free. If that does not make him grow up, it certainly frees up his superego! And it serves to reward the reader, a speechless child who simply wants to be an adolescent!

The Eighteenth Century: Which Sex? Or, How to Build a Psychic Life

Psychoanalysts tend to see psychic space as an interiority whose revolving motion circumscribes the subject's experiences. The basic principle of analysis, which is rooted in speech and introspection, encourages this sort of conception. Analysis presents itself as an ideal model of functioning that leads (or may lead) to adaptation and ongoing development.

For a literary historian, however, psychic space—which was foreseen by Plotinus and developed through prayer and theology—is without doubt an imaginary creation that was brilliantly realized in the nineteenth-century psychological novel.

Conversely, seventeenth-century man had no interior. In any event, that century offers us portraits of men who lack interiority. The clearest image of this individual without interiority, this "man without a name" (as Tirso de Molina says about Don Juan) who adheres to a surprising and versatile inconstancy, can be found in the baroque spectacle. By using images of the "enchanted isle," the sparkling water and sumptuous sets (which were often burned after the show) informed the audience that nothing was true except God. Everything was "staged," everything was "make-believe."

Two centuries later, the nineteenth-century realists no longer accepted this kaleidoscopic and artificial psychic space. They feverishly attempted to restrict it by suggesting that this sort of activity, which was implausible and irresponsible, was of a "secondary nature!"[3]

The transition from the baroque man, who had neither interior nor exterior, to the psychological man of the romantics, of Stendhal and George Sand, occurred during the eighteenth century. More specifically, this transition is intrinisic to the very genre of the novel, which adopts the peripeteia, theatrical effects, implausible disguises, and other forms of "acting-out" characteristic of picaresque and libertine novels and subjects them to another order: that of the "social contract," of the "natural" individual, of novelistic practice. We should note, moreover, that the adolescent character acts as a model for this shift from the baroque man ("neither inside nor outside") toward the psychological man of the nineteenth century.

Among the many questions that center on the eighteenth-century adolescent, it is the issue of sexual identity that will be the object of my attention here. If we peruse the novels of this era, we see that the eighteenth century explicitly formulates the notion of sexual difference as an unresolved, if not impenetrable, concept.[4] Let us recall that Rousseau's *Emile* posits that there is no difference between the sexes at the origin of society or at the moment of its perversion-perdition. The teacher's primary goal would be to distinguish between the sexes and their roles, such that Emile becomes a tutor and Sophie a nanny. Yet the child remains undifferentiated: "Up to the nubile age, children of the two sexes have nothing apparent to distinguish them: the same visage, the same figure, the same complexion, the same voice. Everything is equal: girls are children, boys are children; the same name suffices for beings so much alike."[5] Furthermore, there may still be a lack of differentiation once children have assumed sexual identities: "Emile is a man and Sophie is a woman; therein consists all their glory. In the confounding of the sexes that reigns among us, someone is almost a prodigy for belonging to his own sex."[6]

Before being endowed with a stable sexual identity, the Rousseauian child is subjected to a true educational journey. These rites of passage are different from the incredible exploits of the adventure novel, for they require children to confront the feminine realm [*le féminin*] in order to guard themselves from it more easily and thus discover their own "other." Now, although this is what the teacher aims for, accomplishing it is far from easy.

Rousseau wrote a lesser tale called "La Reine Fantasque" (1752), which was followed by the "Lettre à d'Alembert" (1758), a text that warns us of the danger of a generalized feminization ("not wishing to suffer from separation and unable to become men, women make each of us into a woman"). Rousseau's short story seems to enjoy exploring the possibilities of sexual confusion— confusion, that is, and not infantile asexuality. This philosophical tale covers sexual hybridization, the double, and twins. Rousseau wagers on writing a tale that is "tolerable and even gay, but which lacks plot, love, and perversity." All the same, we are brought to the height of perversity: Rousseau fails because his tale recounts a bizarre story. From their birth, a pair of twins—a brother and a sister—possess the attributes of the opposite sex. The ensuing theatrical imbroglio affects the natural chain of events, for when these children become adolescents, they are unable to carry out their assigned social roles without some help from the outside world.

This tale, which is much more erotic than its author may have intended, delves deeply into sexual ambiguity: Prince Caprice is as feminine as can be, and Princess Reason is a born leader. They both become involved in a plot that is absurd and twisted, that speaks of hybridization and insanity. The ambivalence is such that no logical or pedagogical means seems capable of ending it: only providence or chance can bring things back to normal. What is more, Rousseau repeatedly tells his characters that this order appears to be quite arbitrary. For all practical purposes, he tells them to make themselves crazy: "The best way for you to cure your wife is to join her in her madness," says the Discreet Fairy to the King. And then, "whether because of these oddities or in spite of them," everything will return to normal." Rousseau hesitated a long time before publishing this tribute to gender confusion that depends in the end on the mother's fantasies and that needs to be resolved providentially by the end of adolescence. The story comprises a couple of twins, a couple of hybrids, a couple that runs the risk of incest through the mother's desire: "In any event, I am sure they will love each other as much as they can."

Man and woman, brother and sister, adult and child, the figure of the adolescent becomes, in the works of Rousseau, a figure who apparently lacks "perversion." We are familiar with the romance of the rural and incestuous societies of the Valais, which are filled with ambiguous adolescents ("His voice falters, or, rather, he loses it; he is neither child nor man and can take the tone of neither") who become "husband and wife without ever ceasing to be brother and sister."[7] Rousseau tones down the extravagant perversion of the twins in "La Reine Fantasque" through the mirage of a Golden Age.

Diderot, who was more of a libertarian, shaped the protagonists of *Rameau's Nephew* (1773) and *Jacques le Fataliste* (1777) as adolescent prototypes who question paternity, normality, and religion; whereas for Restif de la Bretonne, generalized incest—which is omnipresent in rural society and novelistic logic—deprives the adolescent of his sallies and makes him into one incest victim among many.

One final process by which the adolescent figure integrates and disintegrates both personality and sexual identity can be found in a lesser-known text of the eighteenth century: Jean-Baptiste Louvet's *Les Amours du chevalier de Faublas* (1787–1790).

Faublas excels at the art of disguise, which enables him not only to switch genders at will, but also to accumulate all sorts of false names in a way that would seem worthy only of Stendhal. This young man, who was born to the Baron of Faublas but who lost his mother at an early age, lacks an identity. He accumulates masks with so much gusto that he seems to get less pleasure from his gender reversals than from his betrayals, which leave him completely guilt-free. His art is one of disguise, but his essence is elsewhere: he moves about like a ballet dancer, gliding between masters and mistresses, brothers and sisters. Like a sexual amphibian or a series of disguises, he goes by Faublas, Blasfau, Mlle du Portail, or the Chevalier de Florville (borrowing the pseudonym that Mme de B., one of his mistresses, uses when she dresses as a man at whim). He is the Baron's son and Adelaide's brother, then the Baron's daughter, Adelaide's sister, and Porter's daughter and then son, only to become his own brother. Was he looking for some sort of "dead mother"?

His breathtaking disguises serve as a strong defense against madness. In fact, once two of his mistresses are dead (like his mother), he can no longer *play* between them. And when the game is over, the masks fall to the ground. They do not unveil nudity, but emptiness, no one, madness. Indeed, when Faublas is set free by the disappearance of his mistresses, he is in no hurry to choose a wife, for without the enactments that enable him to accost fake mothers, he has no reason to search for one. It is revealing that Faublas' madness is what arrests the narration, and that letters (fragments, in the end) are what point to his insanity. The father will have to bring things back to normal and to impose himself onto his son in order to cure him and to make us hear the final cry of "he is ours." The disguised lunatic becomes a real adolescent.

Sexual ambiguity, cross-dressing, multiple identities—Faublas is an eighteenth-century punk. Once you stop playing your game, madness is on its way. This means that you become aware that the baroque game (Don Juan, Casanova) could and should end. From that point on, an interiority opens up, one that emerges, at first, as madness, chaos, or emptiness. It will become necessary to organize it by setting up both paternal figures and their cohort, the doctor, but also by relying on *novelistic discourse*. For following the letters that report the disintegration of madness (mutism, cries), the narration goes on to incorporate psychic occurrences. These disguises are followed by dream narrations, comparisons, analogies. Writing becomes associative and interpretive. It is also worth noting that incestuous acting-out, in the works of Restif de la Bretonne, for instance, is always described through the devices of a sophisticated text: dreams that relate to each other, signs, allusions, discourses that summon their complements, notably in his writings that fall between *Le Paysan perverti* (1775) and *La Paysanne pervertie* (1784).

Whether because of the eccentricity of perversion, or because of the fact that perversion comes so naturally, the eighteenth-century adolescent comes forth as a fundamental figure. As a symbol of a subjectivity in crisis, he is also the figure that allows the novelist to extend psychic disintegration to psychosis and to include it in the unity of the novel. Novelistic interpretation, polyvalent as it is, creates a totality that envelops all disguises and games. Whatever their themes may be, subsequent novels will stem from this adolescent universe. They are ambivalent, hybrid, disguised, and "baroque." The novel prolongs the adolescent and replaces his acts with a narration as well as with polymorphous and indecisive interpretations.

Fathers and Sons: On the Body and the Paternal Name

Dostoevsky's *The Adolescent* (1874–75), which is often considered to be one of the great writer's lesser texts, was written in between such masterpieces as *The Possessed* and *The Brothers Karamazov.* What attracts me in this rich text is Dostoevsky's often-stated interest in adolescence, and more specifically his treatment of Arkadi's lineage.

In 1874, Dostoevsky wrote in his *Notebook* that he was planning "a novel about children, only about children, and which has a child for a hero." Later, in 1876, in *Diary of a Writer,* he made a definitive choice: "as a test of his ideas," he wished to work with "a boy whose childhood is past: a young man who is quietly eager to go out in the world." Note that to "test his ideas" about writing, Dostoevsky was led to rely on an adolescent hero. And then, if we look at his remarks on the evolution of his novel, we can trace the writer's identification with the adolescent through his eventual decision to write in the first person: "A young man in pain, with a strong desire to avenge his hurt and an insatiable love for himself. Let's start with the word 'I'. . . . An extremely succinct confession."

First, Dostoevsky sees the adolescent as "a true predator . . . the lowest form of coarseness combined with the greatest degree of generosity. As well as seductive and repelling." These characteristics are eventually attributed to Arkadi's father. The novel recounts the adventures of Count Versilov, a womanizer and an atheist who represents high society (as decadent as it is fascinating) and who is the Adolescent's biological father. At his side, we find a holy paternity that is entirely symbolic: Makar Dolgorouki, the muzhik, the father in the eyes of the law. He bestows his own name onto his wife's illegitimate son, and he then devotes himself to a mystic nomadism in order to spread Christ's word throughout the Holy Land of Russia. In this historical and familial context, the adolescent has an "idea": power—financial power, to begin with, for he wishes to be rich like Rothschild, and then the monetary power to triumph over women and his inferiors. In the end, he seeks "something that can be acquired through power and only though power: that is self-sufficiency and a calm awareness of my strength."[8] A strength that is entirely symbolic, by the way, for the adolescent has absolutely no interest in using it: "If only I could acquire power . . . I wouldn't even have to use it. I'm sure that I'd always be content to remain modestly inconspicuous." And then he turns to his reveries: he would be like a Rothschild who "just ate a ham sandwich" but whose "knowledge of what I could have had if I chose to would satisfy my palate." This symbolic affirmation of triumph likens the adolescent's position to the writer's power: "It must be my way *all the way* according to my perverse will just in order to prove *to myself* that I have the strength to renounce it all."[9]

This sort of longing, which is megalomaniac even in its humility, is forced to confront a two-sided paternal figure: the saint and the seducer. The adolescent exhibits an attitude of love-hate toward them both: he is fascinated by Versilov's erotic life and religious skepticism, though he has a devout admiration for the mystic renunciation of Dolgorouki, the peasant. In turn, he will become Versilov's wife and Dolgorouki's alter ego, all the while experiencing a whole range of homosexual feelings for an elusive father, since Arkadi is never really sure that either of these two fathers is his own. It is as if this novel contained two "novels of origins" that struggled to cast permanent doubts on the father's existence.

At the same time, the writer-adolescent's implicit rejection of the father is accompanied by a love for him, a love that seems to reproduce, in a secular fashion, Christ's corporeal and spiritual adherence to His Father. The Son separated from His Father desires to join Him in the Trinity where the Spirit proceeds only from the Father (*per filium*). This fruitful theme of Russian Orthodox theology differs from "egalitarian" consubstantiation, which posits, according to the Catholic tradition, that the Spirit proceeds from the Father *and* the Son (*filoque*). For the Orthodox Dostoevsky, it is as if the adolescent had not directly absorbed this libidinal and symbolic identification with paternity, but had to construct it through his desire. A subtle elaboration of homosexuality ensues, one that takes into account all the ambivalence of the father-son relationship.

In his study of Dostoevsky, Freud is too quick to associate the writer with "parricide."[10] In fact, it is possible to extract, even from the symptoms of epilepsy, the preverbal expression of a sustained contradiction (love and hate). This insoluble contradiction afflicts the subject with a motor discharge (just as it can lead other subjects to actings-out). The adolescent's novelistic elaboration of his problems with his father's body and name could be interpreted as an attempt to analyze Dostoevsky's early, nebulous relationship with his own tyrannical father. The father, who is said to have been killed by some incensed muzhiks, seems to have unleashed the first convulsive symptoms, which were rekindled, as we know, by the even more tyrannical treatment of the penal colony. *The Brothers Karamazov* was to return to these themes of the father and of guilt, of the brothers and of homosexuality, and the father figure was to remain the pivot of desire. Nevertheless, *The Adoles-*

cent is the work that seems most pertinent to this question, which it addresses in a direct, familial manner.

The Seduction of the Formless and Immature

When modern novels question either themselves or their inevitably patriarchal values (which stem from an inevitably adult society), their writers often claim to be directly seduced by the adolescent or by adolescence, as in Nabokov's *Lolita* (1955) or Gombrowicz's *Trans-Atlantyk* (1950) and *Pornografia* (1958). In this way, of course, writers can rediscover a means to display their exhibitionism or their essentially latent homosexuality. In all these texts, the narrator's identification with his seductress or seducer is an important element, especially since adolescents supersede the categories of codified perversion. They impose themselves onto novelists like metaphors of that which is not yet formed—a mirage of pre-language or an indecisive body.

In this sense, Witold Gombrowicz, who has devoted his work to the pursuit of narrative forms appropriate for the fluidity of experience, including its annihilation in aphasia or in absurdity (see his *Cosmos,* 1964), nevertheless writes that "form is not in harmony with the essence of life."[11] He glorifies "that which is formless and inferior, immature—the essential characteristics of youth, that is, of everything that lives."[12] To the adult world, including its most baroque characters (like Gonzalo the pervert in *Trans-Atlantyk*), Gombrowicz opposes the fascinating adolescent world: Ignace, Karol, and Henia. "My first goal, of course, is to bring the minor term of the boy, the adolescent, into prominence, into the world of official altars, by adding still another one that is a tribute to the young God of the Worst, of the less good, of the inferior, the 'unimportant' that nevertheless finds strength in its inferior power."[13] To achieve this goal, the pornography that the writer creates relies on adolescent erotic games. There is no obscenity, nothing scandalous, and not even any explicit behavior. Instead, there are suggestions, approximations, allusions to reconciliations or evasions: nothing but *signs.* Could the pornography of

the uninitiated, as well as that of writers—adolescent pornography—constitute a desire to name, to bring to light a wavering
meaning that lies upon the boundaries of words and drives?

Betrayal by and of the page, bisexuality and cross-dressing, filiation, fledgling seducers: these certainly do not exhaust the adolescent images and conflicts that articulate the great moments of
novel-writing. To these characteristics could be added the sort of
Bildungsroman that recounts the close connection between adolescence and the novel (Tristram Shandy, Julien Sorel, Bel Ami).
Nevertheless, these themes provide a general indication of the
degree to which the polyphony of the novel, its ambivalence, and
its postoedipal (albeit perverse) flexibility are indebted to the open
adolescent structure.

For the reader, is the written representation of an essentially
open, incomplete structure much more than a drug? In any event,
the novel, which is closer to catharsis, offers a certain working-
out that is not unrelated to the one inspired by transference and
interpretation. I would call it *semiotic:*[14] a party to the primary
processes that recur in adolescence and reproduce the drama of
adolescent fantasies by assimilating stereotypes, but that are also
capable of viable inscriptions of unconscious materials that rise to
the surface in the adolescent preconscious. This semiotic working-
out provides the frame (the form), or simply the mirror of the
adolescent passage. Thus, we might reasonably ask the following
question: must we choose between sending an adolescent to an
analyst or encouraging him to write novels? Or should we perhaps
write them together? It is a frivolous question, an adolescent question, yet it brings up another question: is the analyst a grandmother or an adolescent? If analysts wish to sustain their listening
to an open structure, they may need to fulfill both these roles.

This inquiry into the adolescent and writing has brought us to
the problem of perversion and its relationship to writing. The
history of novel-writing can teach us how to approach perversion
with empathy and without complacency. Analysts, aware that
their "well-meaning listening" includes a degree of perversion, can

sustain this inquiry by subjecting their own technique to it, which may mean the closure of the frame or its expansion, the decision of whether or not to employ signs that are different from speech, the recognition that real events occur outside the realm of transference, and so forth. These are a few of the technical ramifications that the recognition of such "open structures," that is, of adolescents, can bring to the analyst's awareness.

10. THE WHEEL OF SMILES

> *I make men aware of the*
> *first, or perhaps second,*
> *origin of the second*
> *origin of their being*
>
> —LEONARDO DA VINCI

You creep into the orange light that splashes the eyelids of Saint Anne. Its brightness causes you to skim past the Virgin Mary's shoulder as well as the enigmatic smile of this dancing Mona Lisa. You make your way down her sensual and firm arm that takes Jesus from between her knees and places him on the ground, though she may also be drawing him nearer to her. You immerse yourself in a green the color of Venetian water, a green that flows along with the veil on these graceful thighs and legs. You pause for a moment on the chubby and already impish face of the child-God and of his extension, the lamb—his passion and his resurrection.

Now you make an about-turn, and while lingering in the dazzling movement of the reflected light, you are lured into the face of the mother-daughter double, of Anne and Mary. And you begin again, in an endless progression through these revolving reflections.

It seems that the petals of a mysterious rose of joy are unfolding, and you are soothed by a kaleidoscope of faces. By means of a circular reflection of gazes exchanged between a mother and her son, a very human story is about to be born beneath your eyes. *She*

Leonardo da Vinci: The Virgin Mary, St. Anne, and Infant Jesus
(*Louvre, Paris*)

has a twofold grace, in memory of a past maternal caress. *He* is
already engaged in an instinctive and erotic flight toward glory.

Modern man lacks the words and images needed to celebrate
this imaginary prehistory of the individual. However this may be,
the next time you go beyond the tenderness of a dream in which
you are both he and she, the skin barely detached and the image
barely unfolded, or the next time femininity acknowledges its

155

Leonardo da Vinci: The Virgin and Child with St. Anne and John the
Baptist, cartoon (*National Gallery, London*)

maternal side, from one end to the other, from body to body, fold
upon fold of an exquisite separation, all of which are silent when
faced with the delicious torments of amatory or narcissistic uncertainty, go to the Louvre to see this Leonardo painting.

From a theological perspective, Leonardo condensed the Immaculate Conception and the Incarnation into the already accepted

model of a "triple Saint Anne" (it is more clearly expressed in Italian and German: *santa Anna Metterza, heilige Anna Selbdritt*). Between the thirteenth and fifteenth centuries, this theme emerged as a double of and counterweight to the classical Trinity, which is composed of the Father, the Son, and the Holy Spirit. This required that a perspective for the Virgin Mary be created, and that Anne accept Mary's immaculate conception (in the form of *praeredemptio,* as Duns Scotus says), and, in the same vein, that both the ternary logic of Christianity and the treatment that it inflicts upon the consecration of a Goddess-mother be enhanced.

Leonardo, who was haunted by Dante's *Paradiso,* envisioned a female Trinity that was also a humanistic celebration of Jesus' body growing out of the iridescent flesh of an Anne lovingly coiled up beside her daughter, Mary. The Creator, like the creator of paintings, would be a man who possessed a glowing femininity that shone in the lamb's brow and guaranteed the Apocalypse as well as a universal smile. For a Renaissance man, then, Jesus had a sexuality. Was his sexuality sublime because he had a mother? We are right at the heart of the Western imaginary.

By grafting an autobiographical novel onto this canvas, Freud made it into a new object of meditation. In reality, no vulture and no kite seems to trace this mystic flight,[1] which nevertheless remains a cult of ideal maternity that the artist has absorbed. If there is a phallus, it may be elsewhere. Indeed, what are Jesus and the lamb actually doing? The animal leg extending the child's as if suggesting a continuity between baby and beast, those fists firmly encircling long, erect ears that resemble horns, this interlocking of the lamb between Christ's legs—is the autoeroticism of the child and the creator the guarantor of maternal exaltation?

Even if this were the case, I would wager that Leonardo's problem was most of all a *plastic* one: how might the *circle* be reconciled with the *triangle?* Mary's head is at a right angle to Anne's shoulder. Mary's legs could be Anne's and vice versa; they form two triangles that lean against each other like two pivots. The angle of Mary's knee points to the oval shape created by her arms. In the group of three feet, the one on the far left creates a mirror image of Mary's right foot. Finally, in the heart of the construction, the curves of Mary's body draw the angles toward an ellipse that points to Jesus, who completes the curve by turning his head. He is aided by the lamb, who reinforces this backward gaze.

Leonardo da Vinci quotes Dante: "If a triangle can be made in the semicircle so that it has no right angle" (*Paradiso,* 13.101). And he elaborates on this: "Any body placed within the luminous air emanates in a circular manner and fills the surrounding space with numberless enactments of the self. The whole appears within the whole, and within each part" (*Notebooks*).

The painter wrote in order to be deciphered in a mirror, perhaps in response to Plotinus. As opposed to the sketch from the National Gallery, in which Anne's index finger points to the heavenly origin of the group, the Louvre canvas depicts the source of the history of Christianity as mutual mirror-effects. "In the beginning" was the reflection of loving gazes. One child and two mothers: without beginning or end, a wheel of smiles.

II. GLORY, GRIEF, AND WRITING

> *(A Letter to a*
> *"Romantic" Concerning*
> *Madame de Staël)*

I would like to thank you, my dear friend, for having asked a "nonspecialist," a "nonromantic" like myself to give her impressions of Mme de Staël. As an individual, Germaine de Staël fascinates me, but I find her writing style a bit too wordy. I believe we have not yet unveiled the secret and the influence of the wide-ranging speculations that this woman made during a tumultuous era. Nevertheless, I can only offer my hunches and conjectures about this matter, and I certainly do not wish to interfere with the scholarly research that has been done on the subject. I have reread Mme de Staël's work, of course, which I did with pleasure, intensity, and empathy. The latter characteristics could also be applied to the Priestess of Coppet herself, and they reflect my unconscious identification with this famous Baroness. Of course, I shall brush aside this identification as quickly as I allude to it.

At first glance, an intellectual woman—and Mme de Staël (1766–1817) was the first member of this awkward species—is not an agreeable person. De Staël felt that everything was worthy of her attention, from the French Revolution to suicide, from literature to love, from happiness to betrayal, and I will leave it at that. This reasoner loved to confound her statements (think of her many convoluted sentences, highbrow allusions, and erudite or self-centered digressions), but she eventually fell upon a stroke of inspiration that went to the heart of the matter and could stand the test of time. With much élan, she grafted insipid imbroglios onto sentimental plots that had already been imbued with the local color of her novels (think of the many moral schemes of *Delphine* or the homosexual and incestuous innocence that taints the Italian setting of *Corinne!*). What is more, Mme de Staël wanted to be the best of lovers, that is, the most distraught of lovers. And to conclude, or perhaps to begin, she brazenly staked out her place in glory, although she acknowledged that glory was not without its perils!

What was her motivation for all this? She wanted to have more control over her addressee, who first was her lover, then the general public, and finally the World at Large, for Mme de Staël was a cosmopolitan woman. But as she herself admits, she mainly sought to fill the "emptiness" of a life that was viewed by others, in fact, as being already too full.

As opposed to the misogynists, I resist the assumption that Mme de Staël diffused her thought in order to compensate for her lack of objective charm, or simply to compensate for her worries that she might not be charming enough. Personally, I find that Germaine Necker (the wife of de Staël) was not without physical attractiveness, which I find in her round eyes, wide with curiosity, and in her slightly plump and voracious arms that bare her forceful character. Her attractiveness also stems from her eagerness to accumulate worldly culture, especially the German variety, and from her desire to impress not only her father (whom she saw as "the man who, of all the characters of the present time, has reaped the greatest portion of glory, and to whom the impartial justices will confirm the possession in its greatest extent"),[1] but also all the distinguished or simply attractive men of Europe. Of course, not being a man, I am unfamiliar with the drawbacks of this sort of exuberance, and I am unaware of the dangers of this passionate and verbal Niagara. Yet had I been in Goethe's shoes (should I dare contemplate such a substitution), I believe that I would have been less interested in avoiding a visit from this French traveler than in making her laugh about her own naïveté and flights of fancy, which were not at all classical but cruelly romantic.

To begin with, Germaine de Staël was an intellectual because she was not a woman of wit, learning, and taste as were the illustrious letter writers and novelists from the seventeenth century to the French Revolution, and she was not really a specialist or a scholar in the spirit of the brainy women who lived at the end of the nineteenth century. She lacked the rhetorical grace of a Mme de Sévigné, and although she had a knack for mathematics, she did not have the single-minded infatuation with science of an Émilie de Châtelet or the sheer brilliance of a Sophie Kovalevskaya or a Marie Curie. Even if we limit ourselves to the humanistic disciplines, we must admit that she did not have the passion for empirical truth that a Melanie Klein would have. Instead, Mme de Staël was driven by the spirit of commitment that was able to transform philosophical drudgery into a Simone de Beauvoir placed at the side of a Sartre.

Necker's daughter might have been less zealous had she met a man who was her intellectual equal, instead of the rather dull M. de Staël, the good-looking Narbonne, the adaptable Rocca, or even the famous but excessively restrained and inconstant Benjamin Constant. But I am only making allusions and assumptions here, if only because of the rather casual natural of the "letter" genre.

Placed between two forms of feminine intelligence, and historically situated between *l'ancien régime* and *le nouveau régime,* Mme de Staël was a figure of encyclopedic curiosity. Everything interested her, and she relied on her intuition to supplement her vast array of knowledge. What is more important, in a world of growing complexity, she was able to publicize her arduous contemplations, which normally have been the province of clerics. This engaged thinker was one of the first "women of the media," and I shall say more about this later. For now, I would like to convince you that she *resembled* an *encyclopédiste*. Note, however, that there were no women among these illustrious *philosophes*. These enlightened men had freethinking woman friends and confidantes who were cultured and even highly educated, but who never strove for universality to the extent that they did. I would say that Germaine de Staël was a belated *encyclopédiste*. She appeared in the aftermath of Montesquieu and Voltaire, whose influence can be detected in her writings on political and literary institutions. Nevertheless, this woman, who lived through the Reign of Terror, guided the intellectual triumphalism she saw as inherently human (in men as well as women) toward the private realm of the passions, of grief, or merely of doubts about other people. Yet she never abandoned her conquering spirit, even when peering into her own disappointments and defeats. Was she a fearless hysteric who ruled over her terminal depression in the same way she tried, with fairly good results, to rule over men?

Whatever the response may be, only a woman could have led this transition from social or natural man to distraught and pretentious man. But she also had to remain strong in order to avoid falling into the trap of melancholic woe that is so tempting and threatening for the second sex. She managed to do so by suppressing her sorrows with the power of reason, which was not diminished but aided by what would become known as "romantic" angst. Theory contemplates depression and protects us from it. The intellectual women who followed Mme de Staël were privy to this experience that she herself initiated.

Although this observation may enable me to extract the genealogy of an extremely complicated lineage of female intellectuals, of women who subsist on thought and writing (Mme de Staël impressively built her own character without relying on her social status and wealth, which helped her without hindering her), I must note that no one reads Mme de Staël anymore, with the obvious exception of you and your colleagues. Of all the pages that this gifted writer bequeathed to us, only one great whimsical remark has survived: "Glory is the radiant grief of happiness."

It is a real pity that the rest of her work remains so little known. Be that as it may, this maxim, which one could easily challenge (personally, I do not agree with it; I would have expressed it differently, but that is another story), is *very powerful*. Although I do not mean that the subject is exhausted, I shall simplify the matter by suggesting that the essence of Mme de Staël can be found in that one sentence, for between the two poles of *glory* and *grief,* which provide a glimpse of her life and her era, this woman's *happiness* wove through a maze of various passions and disappointments—so that she might *write* about them. This is why our romantic was a true modern thinker, for her emotional romanticism was the laboratory of an exaltation of *writing for its own sake,* beyond its ardently fostered affective content. The notion of glory, whose subtleties were painted by Mme de Staël, mirrors this kinship with the authority of writing—a by-product of the passion that is solicited by passion itself. Through Germaine de Staël, the *Goddess of Reason* was replaced by the *glory of writing,* via a celebration of adversity.

Indeed, for Mme de Staël, nothing was more important than glory. She brought it down from its theological heights, and by appropriating its phallic attributes (*Gloria Patri et Filio et Spiritui Sancto*), she rooted it in the opinion that other people have of our worth, in the flattering positive image that the general public bestows upon us. This lover, who aimed to please, was a psychologist and a sociologist, for Germaine de Staël saw glory, which emanates from narcissism and from the ego-ideal (if you will pardon my using the terminology of a later era), as eminently "primitive" and inevitably "social":

> *Of all the passions to which the human heart is susceptible, there is none which possesses so striking a character as the Love of Glory. The traces of its operations may be discovered in the primitive nature of man, but it is only in the midst of society that this sentiment acquires its true force. In order to deserve the name of passion, it must absorb all the other affections of the soul, and its pleasures as well as its pains result only from the entire development of its power.*[2]

She goes on to say that "the love of glory is the most exalted principle which can activate the soul."[3] Of course, glory is only a "relative celebrity," and "we [must] always summon the universe

and posterity to confirm the title of so august a crown." Nevertheless, it is "a most fascinating enjoyment [*jouissance*], to make the
universe resound with our name, to exist so far beyond ourselves
that we can reconcile our minds to any illusion, both as to the
nature of space and the duration of life, and believe that we constitute some of the metaphysical attributes of the Eternal."[4]

Were a man to make such a confession, it would seem unconvincing, even megalomaniac. In the ecstasy of this lay Saint Theresa, however, we witness a weighty justification and a plea for a
female narcissism that de Staël quite unoriginally focused on the
mirror, although her thoughts on the subject also posit a sort of
universal narcissism. The writer of these lines felt confronted by
the "acclamation of the multitude [that] agitates the soul," though
modesty made her focus entirely on other people: the fact "that
grand events ripen and unfold themselves in your breast, and in
the name of the people who rely upon your knowledge, demands
the most lively attention to your own thoughts."[5]

Although Mme de Staël was aware that there are a *wide range*
of glories, of *writings,* and of *actions,* especially military ones, she
was predisposed to be interested in the different forms of glory.
Although it resembles "solitary pleasures," this celebrity of writing
is "rarely contemporary," however. Our incisive psychologist's
love for this sort of glory was so insatiable that it left her hungry,
distressed, and envious: "Since there is never anything that suffices
in the pleasures of this glory, the soul can only be filled by the
expectation that they will come, those pleasures that it attains only
serving to link it with those that it desires."[6]

I shall not belabor my point that Mme de Staël's diverse writings bear witness to a rare understanding of glory and its contents.
I shall merely emphasize what I find to be their most impressive
feature: that psychological analysis goes hand in hand with historical observation. The "reign of terror," she tells us in the introduction, led her to compare the advantages of monarchies and republics with the nature of glory. Attracted by republics yet interested
in both personal worth and the social characteristics of nobility,
Mme de Staël was one of the first people to be concerned with the

ruthlessness of public opinion: "Nothing is more difficult than to know to what degree we ought to cultivate the desire of popularity by which we enjoy unpopular distinctions. It is almost impossible always to know with certainty the degree of deference we ought to show for public opinion."[7]

It must be remembered that our democrat was unfamiliar with totalitarianism and the influx of the mass media. We are a long way from Hannah Arendt, yet the historical distance between these two philosophers does not rule out certain similarities in their thinking. During the Reign of Terror, Mme de Staël observed what we might call the "new types of media" that characterized that era, for the invention of the printing press made her very aware of the "freedom of the press" and the "multiplicity of newspapers." As a source of freedom as well as useful and important information, these phenomena, which "make public each day the ideas that circulated the previous day" make it "almost impossible [that] there can exist, in such a country, what is called glory."[8] The author continues:

> There may be esteem; for esteem does not destroy equality, and he who extends it to another acts upon judgment instead of resigning its exercise. But an enthusiastic attachment to men is banished—in the present state of the world, he who endeavors to distinguish himself is at variance with the self-love of others. . . . In a word, every discovery which knowledge has produced diminishes the empire of the individual by enriching the mass.[9]

As useful and as beneficial as this process may have been, our writer was unable to hide her distress. She sketched out one of the first *indictments* of *equalizing democracies,* although the rest of her text is careful enough to challenge the desire for glory, in the name of a value that is judged to be supreme: happiness. "Man's bliss is more important to him than his life, for he would kill himself in order to escape from pain—the passion of glory, like all sentiments, should be judged according to its influence on happiness."[10]

This cult of happiness is maintained, however, for the sole purpose of revealing its futility:

Happiness, such as the mind of man endeavors to conceive, is an object beyond the reach of human efforts; and happiness that is attainable, can only be accomplished by a patient study of the surest means that can shield us from the greater ills of life. To the investigation of these means the present treatise is devoted.

Thus, there is no more glory, nothing but the avoidance of pain in the place of a supposedly wished-for happiness. Did you say "guillotine?" Indeed, the horrific blade prompted what Mme de Staël called her "sacred cult of adversity" (*Réflexions sur le procès de la Reine*). We cannot reduce her taste for melancholy to a single historical determination, even an extreme one. Yet when Mme de Staël implores grace for Marie Antoinette, I am convinced that her plea harbors the wounded ego of a humanist who despised massacres, the wrath of an aristocrat who was subject to the brutality of popular opinion, and the rebellion of a "feminist" far ahead of her time who fought against the oppression of women. For the most part, these experiences were enough to sustain, if not to induce, a certain taste for being unhappy. Germaine de Staël pleaded that the Queen was innocent, feminine, foreign, and maternal. She maintained that the higher you are, the harder you fall. In fact, she felt that all women were ridiculed by this sacrifice because of the weakness of their social position and their maternal fragility. In her own words:

Arbiters of the queen's life, I wish to speak to you in accordance with your wishes: I seek to implore you to be just and tolerant towards Marie Antoinette, and, moreover, to be envious of her glory. By immolating her, you make her last forever.[11]
I appeal to you women, who are immolated in a loving mother, who are immolated by a would-be attack on weakness, by an annihilation of pity; such will be your influence if tyranny reigns supreme, and such will be your fate if your tears flow in vain. I beg you to defend the queen with all the strength you can muster.[12]

Even when faced with great hardship, Mme de Staël never stopped thinking about glory. Yet she saw feminine weakness and sorrow, swept away by the tyrannical French Revolution, as even more powerful than glory.

Thus, while the Reign of Terror and public "opinion" tried to abolish glory and prevent happiness, *adversity* fell to the bottom of the alchemical vase that was the romantic psychology developed by Mme de Staël—a woman who investigated a heartbreaking story. Adversity is the only thing able to join glory, and adversity is what Mme de Staël would elaborate in her novels and essays.

By inducing guilt, the highest moral standards and a ruthless superego brought about this dependence on adversity. Mme de Staël wrote that "Richardson was asked why he painted Clarissa to be so unhappy. 'Because,' he responded, 'I have never been able to forgive her for leaving her father's house.' "[13] (I shall note in passing that these words are not without interest if we apply them to Germaine Necker.) Our novelist continues: "Hence, I can sincerely say that in my *Delphine,* I was unable to forgive the heroine for having succumbed to her feelings for a married man, even though her feelings remained innocent." The social constraints exercised against women played their own role in this predisposition to suffering. Thus, "I also wanted to show that the society's unbending judgment of her may be worthy of condemnation itself."

All this coalesced and helped show our author that the essence of human life stems from feelings more than reason: "Finally, I believe that there is a class of people whose pains and joys result only from affections of the heart, whose completely interior nature remains unknown to the common run of men."[14] Even more daringly, and in an unabashedly melancholic manner, she saw traces of "the emptiness of life" in the will to succeed and in the religious passions. Finally, through the words of one of her heroines, Corinne, and in the novel that shares the same name, Mme de Staël seems to have advocated the depressive character of her genius: "The poor woman! My brilliance, if it still remains, can only be felt through the strength of my pain; it can only be seen in relation to the traits of a powerful enemy."[15]

Nevertheless, we must refrain from projecting our own notions onto these words, for this is not a matter of pathology. Conceived as such, adversity is a sign of worth; it points to a noble soul. All of Mme de Staël's thinking—a product of our first *militant liberal*—was geared toward preserving differences. As a staunch opponent of egalitarian democracies, she only sought equality (an idea that did, in fact, interest her) if it could be reconciled with her desire *to categorize* people not according to feudal distinctions but according to "levels of education" and other evidence of "personal worth."

> *Purity of language, dignity of expression, that bespeak and picture out the nobility of the soul, are eminently necessary in a state that is founded according to democratic principles. Elsewhere, certain factitious barriers prevent the total confusion of different educations, but when power is only to be supported and upheld by the supposition of personal merit, what care should be taken to surround that merit with all the splendor of its external characteristics!* [16]

In light of these ideas, if melancholia is neither completely nor exclusively a form of "glory," it is without doubt something positive because it paves the way for glory. Why is that? Because Mme de Staël saw melancholia as a product of liberty that contributes, moreover, to excellence in the arts. She uses the example of England to support this notion:

> *It may be asked why the English, who are so happy in their government, and in their customs and manners, should have been so much more melancholy in their disposition than the French. The reason is that liberty and virtue, the greatest consequences of human reason, require meditation, and that meditation naturally leads the mind toward serious objects.* [17]

In another (though similar) vein, Mme de Staël predicted that Germany would become prosperous if it made better use of the

French Enlightenment by focusing on its sentimental and "efficient" (as we would say today) values.

Yet of all the ways to be worthy, the nobility of the arts shines through, for the arts can tie adversity together with glory. What is more, as time goes on, the only possible glory will be that of the arts, which are capable of unleashing the passions—especially adversity—with the intent of mastering them. This impelled Mme de Staël to promote style to the rank of "one of the principal powers of the free state":

for style, not consisting of the grammatical turning of a period, cannot be looked at as a single form, but as closely connected with the ideas and nature of the mind. . . . The purity and grandeur of the language add greatly to the consideration of those who govern, particularly in a country where a political equality is established. Real dignity of language is the best method of pronouncing all moral distinctions: it also inspires a respect that improves those who experience it. In short, it is possible that the art of writing may one day become one of the principal powers of the free state.[18]

Did this reflection not serve to guide France's most powerful statesmen? It should remain a convincing measure of what we call "human qualities" in a democracy that must relativize values or even abolish them.

Nevertheless, although a woman of letters contributes to the dignity of the arts in the same way that men do, she is more susceptible to the adversity of glory than a man would be. She experiences glory itself as misfortune. In this regard, Mme de Staël yields to the spirited and unfortunately timeless admission of suffering that lies behind the invulnerable façade of an intellectual woman. Who would suspect that this wounded warrior was in pain, since she was the first to hide her susceptibility behind the mask of the one in charge, even if it meant raising suffering to the rank of a supreme virtue?

In reality, the woman of letters "drags on her isolated existence like the *Pariahs of India,* amongst all those distinct classes, none of which will ever admit her, and who consider her as fit only to live by herself, as an object of curiosity, perhaps of envy, although, in fact, deserving of [pity]."[19] Along with Montesquieu, Voltaire, Condorcet, and André Chénier, Mme de Staël is thought to be one of the first people to believe that political institutions contribute to the great literature of each nation. It seems to me, however, that she considered political institutions to be various *styles* comparable to the art of writing.

How delightful are the first steps taken in the hopes of acquiring reputation; what satisfaction to hear our name recited, to obtain a rank in opinion, to be distinguished among the multitude! But alas! when we have arrived at this envied height, what terror takes possession of the mind, what a frightful solitude surrounds us! We then wish, but in vain, to reenter our wonted associations, but the time has passed. Nothing is so easy as to lose the small portion of fame we may have acquired, but it is not so easy a matter to obtain that benevolent reception which is accorded with pleasure to an obscure individual.[20]

And yet, the solitary activity of writing about pain is what allowed Mme de Staël to continue her tireless pursuit of the horizon—forever unsatisfied but nonetheless radiant—that envelops the glory we owe to literature. Her many loves (Narbonne, Ribbing, Constant, O'Donnell, Prosper de Barante, François de Pange, and John Rocca, among others), her break-ups, disappointments, sorrows inflicted by rivals and unfaithful lovers are worthy of a romantic novel. Germaine de Staël's life was a novel of sorts—and her biography offers us proof of this.

At the same time, if we consider the strength with which she revealed and overcame her amorous disappointments, it would seem that these setbacks are indispensable conditions for writing. All these woes and demands, which would eventually irritate even the most easygoing of lovers, do not really constitute a melancholic masochism that embraces pain as the sole object of love, though in some ways, they appear to be a neurotic self-punishment on the part of an extremely moralistic daughter who aspired to experience no authority other than the paternal one she harbored in her own self. Despite her whole string of lovers, Germaine de Staël was not a libertine—her erotic pleasures did not capture her attention when she wrote, and as for their "reality," which is debatable in any event, witnesses are always cruel. What she sought, rather, was the mastery of psychic space—which ranges from suffering to pathos—through words, phrases, judgments, or logical and novelistic constructs. To attain that sort of restricted yet eternal glory, our author endlessly intensified the pretenses of passionate pain.

Could romantic sensibility be a stepping-stone to the cult of writing? Could it be the advancement of a new sacred object? Terror, death, the absurdity of conventional wisdom, the emptiness of life: these are all facts of life. You still have to survive—by writing. But from that point on, the written word is no longer a secondary entity that Divine Creation can master by making it subtle, modest, or more insolently, ironic. The written word is turned into the immanence of transcendence. It is an altar that harbors a rattled religiosity that is uncertain yet tenacious, flattered as well as frightened by popular opinion, and predisposed to delight in the gaze of the other. Mme de Staël called this sort of enthusiasm a form of glory, which was the driving force behind her writing that constituted her life.

I know that we no longer believe in this "glory." We do not even believe in "it" [*ça*]. Yet when someone wishes to write, "it" reappears, surreptitiously and intermittently, and Mme de Staël seems closer to us then we had thought.

With warm regards,

12. JOYCE "THE GRACEHOPER" OR ORPHEUS' RETURN

Perversion or Sublimation

We all know that any attempt to speak about Joyce proves to be difficult, disappointing, absurd, and ridiculous. Literary criticism, or what is left of it, remains fascinated by the liveliness of the imaginary movement that amasses representations and then makes associations, displaces, disappears, and dissolves with a speed that undermines the identity of the verbal sign in *Finnegans Wake,* while it already seduces and frustrates us in *Ulysses.* Critics have been reluctant to associate this maelstrom of images with the *symptom* or with its *traversal,* or even with its cost, which may be likened to a sacred ceremony that defies the worship of meaning.

I see Joyce as the anti-Mallarmé par excellence, for he writes within a dimension that is contrary to that of poetry. In some ways, Joyce was not too far from Mallarmé, who said, "I have been afflicted by some highly disturbing symptoms caused by the mere act of writing." Yet, unlike the master from the rue de Rome, Joyce was satisfied neither with encumbering the symptom nor with exploring formal possibilities by interweaving music and literature or by making infinite meaning into the absence of meaning. He analyzed the *symptom* of writing within its intrapsychic dimension, which is contingent upon the speaking being's capacity to *identify* with an aspect or feature of another subject or object. Identification has a bearing on the imaginary as well as the uncanny adventure of human meaning, which literature portrays through its characters, verisimilitude, cathartic effects, and many other *topoi* that have been categorized by traditional and less-traditional literary theorists. Nevertheless, Joyce is the author who possesses the daunting advantage of having mirrored, experienced, and revealed the inner workings of identification, which governs the evolution of the imaginary, that is, fiction.

These remarks inevitably raise a few questions: How do analysts conceive of "identification," and how does this universal psychic process govern the imaginary? What made Joyce particularly able to confront this specific aspect of imaginary functioning? And finally, which of his themes and narrative techniques appear to support the view I have proposed?

Identification with a *relation* or an *object* (the mother, the father, or any one of their traits) is a transference between my body and my ever-evolving psychic apparatus—which is incomplete, flexible, and fluid—and an *other* whose immutability provides me with a guide and a representation. I see myself as one of them, I become them (note the metaphorical side of this *transport,* which is known as *metaphorien* in Greek). I become One, a subject capable of preverbal and verbal representations. This sort of identification calls to mind oral assimilation and amorous fusion. Indeed, the love I give and receive makes such identification possible, an identification that coexists with this love. Let us think of love, then, in the sense of Greek eros—which is violent and destructive, though it enjoys a Platonic side that ascends to the Ideal—and Christian agape, which I receive from another person without my having to earn it.

Joyce's Catholicism,[1] which consisted of his profound experience with Trinitarian religion as well as his mockery of it, impelled him to contemplate its central ritual—the *Eucharist*—which is the ritual par excellence of identification with God's body and a springboard for all other identifications, including that of artistic profusion. This ritual is also prescribed by the Catholic faith. It is likely that the cultural context of Catholicism—which Joyce had completely assimilated—was challenged by a biographical event that endangered his identity and enabled him to focus his writing on the identificatory substratum of psychic functioning, which he so masterfully laid out against the backdrop of the grandest religion.

The obsession that Joyce "the Gracehoper" had with the Eucharist theme is exemplified by his many references to transubstantiation or to Arius' heresy, to the consubstantiality between father and son in Shakespeare's *Hamlet* and between Shakespeare, his father, his son Hamnet, as well as to Shakespeare's complete works in the sense of a veritable source of inspiration. Let us recall, moreover, the condensation of "trinity" and "transubstantiation" in Joyce's umbrella word "contransmagnificandjewbangtantiality."

In a more indirect fashion, many phenomena lay bare the displacement and realization of identification within narrative themes and within the very dynamics of fiction, such as the orality of Bloom, who loves to eat livers, gizzards, and other animal innards, Mulligan's and Stephen's dizzying absorption of knowledge, the meal during which Stephen and Bloom meet, and even the narrator's assimilation of Molly in the final monologue. Nevertheless, I see the two variations on amatory experience—Stephen Dedalus' agape and Leopold Bloom's eros[2]—as the most important manifestations and the most analytically correct vision of the identificatory movement that characterizes artistic practice.

The unveiling of intrapsychic identification in a literary text could be interpreted as a "return of the repressed"—we repress the processes that have ruled over our psychic space, and it is only through a breach of repression or a modification of its obstacles that this repressed process can come to light. In this sense, the clear presence of themes or narrative techniques ought to be seen as a symptom. Hence, a proliferating, unstable, and problematic identification becomes the symptom par excellence of Mallarmé's "act of writing." Yet Joyce is aware of this, perhaps unconsciously, but in a way that is clearly informed by theological ignorance [*nescience*]. As a result, he turns the symptom upside down, voids it, and proclaims that its most profound logic is necessary for our day-to-day living.

We all require manifold plastic, polymorphous, and polyphonic identifications, and even if the Eucharist has lost the bewitching power that enabled us to partake in such identifications, we will have two choices: we can read literature or we can try to reinvent love. The experience of love and the experience of art, which serve to solidify the identificatory process, are the only ways in which we can maintain our psychic space as a "living system" that is open to the other and capable of adaptation and change.

This sort of integration of polymorphism or perversion is coupled with a type of linguistic production that is not limited to the calculation of "pure signifiers," as impressive as this calculation may be. Such a language practice integrates pre- or transverbal representations that span the whole array of semiotic phenomena—from gestures to colors and sounds—and it makes language into a theatrical ritual or a carnavalized liturgy instead of a formal exercise.

Would this proximity to psychosis (which stems from treating words as if they were things), exaggerated as it is by an identificatory polymorphism of an exceptional diversity, be caused by an ultimate identification with an archaic mother or with the supreme authority that harbors the plastic identity of a narrator who unabashedly defies the "law of the father" that guarantees all normalized identity? Carl Jung seems to think so when he states that Joyce "knows the female soul as if he were the devil's grandmother." Joyce is a rather strange grandmother, however, one who assumes the role of a sensual Jew (Bloom), and whose phallic jouissance and veritable transfusions into female bodies (Bloom's masturbation in front of Gerty) are inspired in the end by the power of the text, and especially by the sacred imposition of the proper name.

If not, would Joyce be a *"saint homme"* who completely inverted the perverse symptom of identification with the woman, and who caused the sally of style to replace castration, as Lacan has suggested?[3]

I would put it another way: Joyce succeeds where Orpheus fails. His adventure represents the modern, post-Christian version of Greek myth. The artist-hero is forbidden to see anything: to look for Eurydice in Hell, to turn toward the mystery of women. If he does so, Orpheus loses his beloved, and this impossible love is paid for by a sacrifice (he is torn to pieces by the Bacchantes) and by immortality (he survives dissipated in his song). As opposed to this, Dedalus-Bloom does not divert his gaze from the infernal night that engulfs Eurydice, although he himself does not vanish. At least, he does not vanish any more than does Joyce, who overcame the difficulties of his existence and sacrificed his social being to the myth of the accursed artist, though ironically, he navigated his passage by means of women who were patrons and lovers of literature.

Tragically, the madness suffered by Joyce's daughter, Lucia, may bear witness to the playful metamorphoses toward a father who could not keep still. Still, the Joycean odyssey toward the fatherland of his works is not spared from returning to the invisible secret of femininity, which Freud said was unknowable in men as well as women. The narrator gazes at her, his Eurydice-Molly, insolent, aggressive, and obscene, and we are reminded of Joyce's scatological letters to Nora.[4] He rescues her from the inferno of passion by allotting her this final chant-monologue, whose origin can be traced to the figure of Nora herself.

Some people claim that this end of *Ulysses* contains a recognition—or a silencing—of female sexuality. I believe, rather, that it depicts a male artist who is sated with a final appropriation-identification and who returns to us a Bacchante swallowed by Orpheus.[5] Only in this way can Dedalus-Bloom achieve the plenitude of his text-body, and thus release his text to us as though it were his body, his transubstantiation. The narrator seems to say, "This is my body," and we know that he sometimes identifies with HCE [Humphrey Chimpden Earwicker] in *Finnegans Wake*. As for the reader (like the Bacchantes), he assimilates the true presence of a complex male sexuality through textual signs and without any repression. This is a prerequisite for enigmatic sublimation: the text, which restrains but does not repress libido, thereby exercises its cathartic function upon the reader. It is clear, however, that this removal of repression also serves to explain the reader's irritation, discomfort, captivation and, ultimately, surrender. Everything is to be seen and all the places are available; nothing is lacking and nothing is hidden that could not indeed be present. In this way, the inferno of passion and the diabolical woman are absorbed into themes as well as language before developing into comedy or farce. The secret of the individual can be kept, but not the storehouse of sentiments that nurture psychological life, for it is absorbed into the ubiquitous nature of an identificatory writing that is both greedy and relentless.

Of Identification: Eros and Agape

The psychoanalytic term "identification" refers to various aspects in the process of becoming a subject, such as narcissistic identification, hysterical identification, and projective identification. If I concede that I am never ideally One under the Law of the Other, my entire psychic experience consists of failed identifications as well as my impossible attempts to be an autonomous being, attempts that circumscribe narcissism, perversion, and alienation. Despite its divergent uses, the term "identification" is maintained throughout analytic theory and practice for at least two reasons. First, whatever the different varieties of identification may be, the general term of "identification" presupposes the speaking being's tendency to internalize a foreign entity, in a symbolic sense and in reality. We should be aware that this structure requires two processes of representation: a verbal one and a trans- or preverbal one. In addition, identification functions within transference as an axis of knowledge and interpretation of the other.

Second, with regard to the economy of writing in general, and more particularly in the case of Joyce, the problem of identification shifts the emphasis from the Oedipus complex (which many authors feel has little importance for someone like Joyce, who was more interested in wanderers like Telemachus or Ulysses than in such deadly Greeks as Oedipus or Orestes) to another intrapsychic experience, which precedes and surpasses the Oedipus complex, and which avoids the generic labels of psychiatric "structures."

Hence, I am suggesting that we think of identification as the movement that causes the advent of the subject, insofar as he unites himself with the other and makes himself identical to the other. I am not saying that subjects model themselves *after* the other, for this sort of imitation would point to the realm of the plastic incertitude of comparison. On the contrary, the "I" transferred to the Other becomes One with the Other through the entire range of the symbolic, the imaginary, and the real. Freud has described the intensity of *Einfühlung,* the *empathy* that is characteristic of certain amatory, hysterical, or mystic states. He has also brought to our attention that the subject's *primary identification* stems from a primitive form that he refers to as a "father in personal prehistory" (*Vater der Persönlichen Vorzeit*) who possesses the sexual features of both parents.

In current analytic practice, the growing number of narcissistic, borderline, or psychosomatic patients has called upon the analyst's *Einfühlung* more than ever before. As a result, a transverbal identification rooted in primary identification becomes a fundamental part of treatment. The problematic repression of these new patients (as well as of artists?) sets into motion everything from verbal representations to psychic drive representatives. Indeed, transference incites the analyst's words as well as his affect. To guide my speech to the psychic place in which my patient acts out her convulsive crises, for instance, I must participate in her *affective* suffering before rushing into the *language* of signs and giving a name to our shared affect that we had not been able to name.

This entails a *metaphorical* experience similar to Baudelaire's "mystic metamorphosis," as opposed to a mere comparison. This is precisely the *sine qua non* condition for the advent of the subject:

a metaphor that would be a *transport* of drive representatives and verbal representations instead of an other that makes me One with him, the metaphor of body and soul. Narcissistic reiteration (when I say "mama," it is not yet a stable identificatory metaphor but a simple repetition) or projective identification (since I do not wish to know that I hate her, she hates me) are elements in a series that will be completed—for the time being, never permanently— through a metaphorical movement of identification with the imaginary Father, a movement that Freud calls "primary identification." As is the case with Christian agape, this identification comes from above, from a third party (whom the analyst sees as the work of the mother's love for the third party), but that the child need not elaborate. Delightful and soothing, a ghostly debt and the ultimate aim of existence—such is Joyce's filial agape, if we are to have faith in the Hamlet, Shakespeare, Bloom, Rudy, and Dedalus figures that he created.

Although the domination of drive representatives over verbal representations is especially pronounced in narcissistic identification and projective identification, this predominance characterizes all forms of identification, since the logic of identification is always *unstable* and *in motion* ("a vague entity"), whereas its *economy* is *ambiguous,* at once symbolic *and* real. Identification is a "transcorporation." At the most fruitful moment in treatment, my body is my patient's body—a source of my weariness, my youthfulness, my rebirth. By way of the interpretation or the verbalization that our relationship enriches for my patient, I replace the symptom that brought him to me. Otherwise, we become lodged in the same identificatory inscription with respect to transference and countertransference.

Within the scope of this analytic and artistic agape, we find ourselves led from identification to transubstantiation. Is the father consubstantial with the son, or is the son merely conceived in the father's image? Is the Eucharist the actual body of Christ that I identify with by absorbing it, or is it merely a representation? Or, as the highly logical and Jansenist *Logique de Port-Royal* (1662) puts it, was the Eucharist *previously* bread and wine and *now* the body of Christ? I shall not pursue the nuances of these debates, which racked Christianity until the Council of Trent (1545–63), and which are also at the heart of our inquiry into the psychic side of identification. Instead, I shall examine this debate through two secular perspectives: Joyce's, of course, but first Galileo's.

You will not be surprised to learn that this debate about transubstantiation was resurrected, and indeed, made defunct, by modern science, especially by Galileo.[6] Galileo's Copernican heliocentrism, which was eventually accepted by the Church, does not seem to have been the primary focus of the accusations brought against him, which were provoked rather by his conception of matter. In fact, his *Saggiatore* (1623) revealed to all that he was an atomist. If matter is thoroughly atomic, there clearly can be no transubstantiation—even though it was definitively recognized by the Council of Trent in 1551. Of course, no physical science could display the *symbolic-and-real* side of identification. At best, science could relegate it to subjectivity: you "imagine" that you are identical to X. It would be necessary to wait for a Freud—the Galileo of the unconscious—who would propose a new way to look at the *real* value of symbolic identification, including its somatic modifications.

Though a seasoned explorer of similar psychic landscapes, the artist nevertheless discharges the identificatory symptom into an original discourse—into style. Neither subjugated like the believer nor converted into somatic symptoms like the hysteric—though sometimes one or the other—the artist is constantly generating identifications. At the same time, he gives them a voice, because, I would venture to guess, he clings more than anyone to the "father in personal prehistory." Despite the widespread myth that the artist submits to his mother's desire, or rather to the necessity to defend himself against this desire, the artist sees himself not as the mother's phallus, but as that ghostly third party to which the mother aspires, as a loving version of the Third Party, a preoedipal father "who first loved you" (according to the Gospels), a conglomeration of both genders (as Freud suggests). "God is agape."

The Transubstantiation of the "Childman"

In *Ulysses,* Joyce makes some significant allusions to transubstantiation. He was intrigued by Arius' heresy, which was condemned
at the Nicene Council (325) for having cast doubts on the consubstantiality of the Father and the Son and which prefigured the
great schisms within the Church (Orthodox currents, Protestant-
ism). Hence, "Arius, warring his life long upon the consubstantiality of the Son with the Father."[7] And later, "is that then the
divine substance wherein Father and Son are consubstantial?
Where is poor dear Arius to try conclusions. . . . Ill-starred here-
siarch?"[8]

Stephen's reflection on *Hamlet* and his bond with the father-
ghost is clearly a most striking passage, for it condenses Joyce's
obsession with the mystery of Christ with his increasing conviction
that writing serves as a resurrection. Far from being a "lofty
impersonal power," the author naturally relies on his biography to
give life to his works (which explains the importance that he
attaches to the relationship between the death of Shakespeare's
father and son and his writing of *Hamlet*). What is more important,
however, is that he physically survives through his works, which
are his true "begetting." In this way, Joyce becomes sensitive to
the idea of an osmosis that is not only symbolic but also real, and
that functions between the creator and the created, the father and
the son, the lover and the beloved.

That this osmosis contains a certain absorption of homosexuality is of less importance than the more startling consequence of
this process: *style.* If style is a symptom within language, its hol-
lowing-out into a derisive sainthood, a light neutrality, and a costly
expense ("erigenating from next to nothing," *Finnegans Wake*)
from the body to meaning could be derived from this transfusion
between two entities (father and son). This transfusion, which is
clearly phantasmatic, guarantees the real and infinite flexibility of
the writing subject as well as his incredible theatricality, his perversion incited by the father's worshiped suffering, and his almost
unlimited capacity to create imaginary resurrections. It always

replaces the father who is put to death (like Christ, but also like
the King of Denmark): a domesticated and gentle character in his
traits of a man without qualities (like Dedalus the engineer) and
especially in his carnal weaknesses (like Bloom, who, as we know,
proposes his ambiguous and frustrated paternity to Stephen). Stephen says it admirably in connection with *Hamlet:*

> *A father, Stephen said, battling against hopelessness, is a neces-*
> *sary evil. He wrote the play in the months that followed his father's*
> *death. . . . The corpse of John Shakespeare does not walk the*
> *night. From hour to hour it rots and rots. He rests, disarmed of his*
> *fatherhood, having devised that mystical estate upon the son. . . .*
> *Fatherhood, in the sense of conscious begetting, is unknown to*
> *man, it is a mystical state, an apostolic succession, from only*
> *begetter to only begotten. On that mystery and not on the madonna*
> *which the cunning Italian intellect flung to the mob of Europe the*
> *church is founded and founded irremovable because founded, like*
> *the world, macro- and microcosm, upon the void. Upon certitude,*
> *upon unlikelihood. Amor matris, subjective and objective genitive,*
> *may be the only true thing in life. Paternity may be a legal fiction.*
> *Who is the father of any son that any son should love him or he*
> *any son?*[9]

Joyce patiently traces the equivalence between the dead father,
Shakespeare the author, and his artistic transmutation that leads
from being a "spectre" to being his own son—the text.

> *It is the ghost, the king and no king, and the player is Shakespeare*
> *who has studied* Hamlet *all the years of his life which were not*
> *vanity in order to play the part of the spectre. He speaks the words*
> *of Burbage, the young player who stands before him beyond the*
> *rack of cerecloth, calling him by a name:*
> *"Hamlet, I am thy father's spirit"*
> *bidding him list. To a son he speaks, the son of his soul, the prince,*
> *young Hamlet and to the son of his body, Hamnet Shakespeare,*
> *who has died in Stratford that his namesake may live forever.*

—Is it possible that that player Shakespeare, a ghost by absence, and in the vesture of buried Denmark, a ghost by death, speaking his own words to his own son's name (had Hamnet Shakespeare lived he would have been prince Hamlet's twin) is it possible, I want to know, or probable that he did not draw or foresee the logical conclusion of those two premises: you are the dispossessed son: I am the murdered father: your mother is the guilty queen. Ann Shakespeare, born Hathaway? [10]

The father dies so that the son might live; the son dies so that the father might be embodied in his work and transformed into his own son. In this "Dedalean" maze, we must search for the woman. The Christian agape of transubstantiation was in opposition with Greek eros. Before Plato sublimated love into a mystic quest of the Good and the Beautiful under the guise of Diotima in the *Symposium* or in the second part of the *Phaedrus,* he described it as a violent psychodrama: a sadomasochistic and lethal force between the lover and the beloved, whom Plato did not hesitate to compare to the wolf and the lamb. Is this tale lost forever?

The loving consumption of the father that concludes the act of identification with the Eucharist must not obscure the violence of its underlying aggression, which is aimed toward Him, and specifically His body, insofar as it is The Body. The father's body carries the memory of the mother's body, which was a body-envelope of the time of the archaic symbiosis between the ego and its narcissistic attributes. Imagining the degeneration or simply the sexuality—weakness, jouissance, sin—of the father's body frees me from my dependence on my mother's body. What is more, this sort of imagination-transposition makes my own reproductive deficiency into the fate of another. It is not I, but he who is the crazy one, the passionate one, the sacrificed one. He, that is, the father.

Yet in the fantasy, and through the movement of idealizing identification with the father, the mother is the one who bears the brunt of rejection. To sum up, identification, understood as a heterogeneous transference (body *and* meaning, metaphor and mystic metamorphosis) onto the realm of the father, begins by placing me in improbability and uncertainty—that is, in meaning. Nevertheless, it is by separating myself from *amor matris* (a subjective and objective genitive) that I may enter the official fiction that constitutes my subjective identity. At the same time, however, this endless erotic separation from my mother's body is the matrix of my eroticism—an eternal accompaniment for my agapeistic identifications.

Stephen's eroticism is cunningly shaped around his mother, and he is ready to assume responsibility for her death (what causes a mother to die: her son or cancer?). She is the recipient of Stephen's violent passions: "Raw head and bloody bones!"

Stephen's mother is shown in her death rattle, but her discourse is no less passionate because of it, and it also serves to incite her son's negative passions:

> [*The mother pleads*] *Have mercy on Stephen, Lord, for my sake! Inexpressible was my anguish when expiring with love, grief, and agony on Mount Calvary.*
> STEPHEN: Nothung!
> (He lifts his ashplant high with both hands and smashes the chandelier. Time's livid final flame leaps and, in the following darkness, ruin of all space, shattered glass and toppling masonry.)[11]

By blurring the relations between Stephen-agape and Bloom-eros such that no character ever becomes the symbol of a single passion, Joyce entrusts Bloom with the search for filial love: the son of his flesh, who died when he was eleven days old, would be replaced by an entirely symbolic, though extremely tangible, filiation—by Stephen. We know, however, that Bloom is the one who incarnates eroticism, and even if his tolerance of Molly's adultery, among other matters, reveals some homosexual sentiment, the female body is what arouses his autoeroticism and the variegated forms of his heterosexual libido. Furthermore, it is through Bloom, not Stephen, that Joyce chooses to relate his own amorous experience of 1904. Bloom constructs his well-known apology of love with regard to a *love song.*

> Words? Music? No: it's what's behind.
> Bloom looped, unlooped, noded, disnoded.
>   Bloom. Flood of warm jimjam lickitup flowed to flow in music out, in desire,
> dark to lick flow, invading. Tipping her tepping her tapping her topping her. Tup.
> Pores to dilate dilating. Tup. The joy the fell the warm the Tup. To pour o'er sluices
> pouring gushes. Flood, gush, flow, joygush, tupthrop. Now! Language of
> love.[12]

And in a more derisive manner, Bloom speaks of love with regard to uncertainty and to the avoidance of the love object: "Love loves to love love. . . . You love a certain person. And this person loves that other person because everybody loves somebody but God loves everybody."[13] Furthermore, the Christian variant of love is ironically described and attributed to "the reverend Mr. Love. He's a minister in the country somewhere."[14]

Artistic practice unites two forms of love, which are two variants of identification—the paternal, symbolic variety and the maternal, drive-related one. In a "consubstantial" manner, the experience of art prompts the artist to identify his psyche with his characters and their experiences. That *Ulysses* concludes with Molly's monologue is the best example of such a transfusion, which is at once passionate (through the identification and replication of the beloved woman) and symbolic (through the assimilation of her speech). This transfusion characterizes the evolution of all literary characters, and it calls to mind Flaubert's *"Madame Bovary, c'est moi."* This ending allows us to have a better understanding of the episode of the baby's birth (or of the work of art?) in "The Oxen of the Sun" chapter of *Ulysses.*

It cannot be denied that the creator's fantasy includes a narcissistic, mirror-image replication of a bountiful maternal power. This repetition is only possible, however, if its passionate nature is turned into words through a paternal, agapeistic identification. This sort of transformation occurs in a secular and ironic form during the scene in which Bloom and Stephen look at each other in a mirror and see Shakespeare's beardless face "rigid in facial paralysis." As an image of both the derisiveness of the father's ghost and his sublime yet impotent ambivalence, this scene reveals how much the artist needs to idealize a paternal figure, as long as such a figure remains unstable (in order to be constantly engaged in identity formation) and rigid (in order to add to it the life of the maternal body, by means of a mimetic rapport). The ongoing exchange between eros and agape must never end, for it guarantees not only a certain androgyny but also the belief in the *life* of *signs* as well as the reduction of *life* into a *text*.

Hence, this "childman" or "manchild" is a greedy consumer of both his parents. If Joyce was reluctant to recognize himself in the Oedipus complex (he had read Freud and Jung before 1915), it is because his interest is not in the traditional Oedipus complex, but in the sort of supple identifications that later attracted the attention of psychoanalysts who studied narcissism and psychosis. This entails an unmistakable element of parricide and matricide ("woman killer," says Nora Barnacle as well as Richard's wife in *Exiles*), though not in the sense of a purely erotic aggressiveness directed toward the father or, in a more projective manner, toward the mother. It is perhaps more accurate to speak of a *narcissistic-and-loving* assimilation that seeks to apprehend the external poles of narcissism within the fluid identity of an everchanging subject who lacks interiority, other than his potential to assimilate (people, texts, recollections . . .). Such assimilation has neither an exterior nor an interior, for it is simply the permanent transference that occurs between the two.

In 1916, Joyce wrote down one of Nora's dreams. "A new Shakespearean play is being performed. Shakespeare is there; there are two ghosts in the play; Nora is afraid that Lucia might be frightened." Joyce observes that Lucia is "herself in little," whereas Nora's fear is perhaps due to "that either subsequent honors or the future development of my mind or art or its extravagant excursions into forbidden territory may bring unrest into her life." [15] Would glory, or the development of Joyce's spirit and art through their foray into forbidden territory, be capable of disturbing a woman's life or scaring her? Nora, who is impassive, a bit stubborn, and satisfied with being a wife or a perverse accomplice does not seem to have any reaction to this. On the other hand, whatever the biological causes of her ill-being may be, Lucia's madness reveals that the father's undefined identifications come at a cost, for they cannot be welcomed by another still-forming identity. The reader, who feels threatened himself, if not terrified, finds a way out of this through catharsis and through a dissociation between the real and the imaginary: After all, Joyce is not someone's dad, but a name, a text that is, in fact, wonderful.

Joyce considered naming his hero Orpheus instead of Dedalus. He was undoubtedly right in choosing a name that would not only suggest the mazelike complexity of discourse and psychic life, but that would also evoke the technical aura of our modern world. Yet, although modern man is more akin to the engineer than to the poet, it would seem that an *Orpheus complex*—or rather an Orpheus without a complex—is the driving force behind that enigmatic economy that we oppose to repression and refer to as sublimation. Neither Oedipus nor Orestes, neither a mere lover nor a mere murderer of his mother or father: Orpheus, that is, Stephen-Bloom, agape-eros, defies Apollo-Shakespeare and assimilates Eurydice-Molly. This serves to liquidate and liquefy the "female" and the "male" into a flowing style. He never latches on to any identity, whether a personal, sexual, or ideological one. He knows them all—might he be a Judeo-Christian Orpheus?

Was Joyce sick, esoteric, postmodern? Such questions are still being asked today. Nevertheless, his symptom and his obscurity, along with their deepest twists and turns, have the virtue of positing the crucial issues of postmodernism: identification and representation. *Ulysses,* which does not eliminate these issues as do the dizzying acceleration of *Finnegans Wake* and the later avant-garde poetic experiments, confronts us with the very space in which an image about to topple over into flesh *and* meaning is coagulated within language. The themes of *Ulysses* are a perfect illustration of this incandescence of imaginary space, whose two-sided nature (body *and* signification) and "transcorporality" cause it to challenge the place of the sacred. Was this not Joyce's ultimate ambition, which so much "literature" sometimes makes us forget?

.

13. THE SECRETS OF AN ANALYST: ON HELENE DEUTSCH'S AUTOBIOGRAPHY

Three Sources of Psychoanalytic Desire

You have before you an autobiography—Helene Deutsch's *Confrontations with Myself*[1]—that resists the two dramatic imperatives that are often inherent in this genre: the cry of distress and the call to glory. The restraint of its serious and scientific style, its fleeting and curbed emotion, and its faithful yet sometimes incomplete recollection of the "confrontations" that a great lady of psychoanalysis engaged in with herself leave the reader with the impression that the text has the implacable exigency of a *memento mori* along with the freshness of an adolescent reverie.

One might wonder if the psychoanalyst's function is compatible with the rest of our passions, which is what make up an autobiography. Do analysts not freely implicate themselves, as well as their biographies, when they listen to each of their patients? Do they not compose an autobiography, secretive because it is transformed, at the core of each of their interpretations? It is likely that some of these "remnants" have an effect on the mysteriously absorbing process of analytic work. Yet it seems logical that these digressions sustain a literary fiction or a theoretical construction, rather than a

189

desire to ascertain the ultimate truth of the matter. Are we analysts not always caught between at least two discourses? How can we claim to capture our own part of our story if not through a new analysis, or self-analysis, that inevitably casts some doubt on the truth of the preceding ones?

However this may be, I have a very positive reaction to Helene Deutsch's autobiography. Deutsch, who was one of Freud's colleagues, read Freud beginning in 1908 and was analyzed by him in 1918. She was also the director of the Vienna Psycho-Analytic Institute and one of the major figures of the American analytic movement from 1934 until her death. At the end of her journey, she wanted to inquire into the fate of her analytic practice, on the one hand, and into the primary sources that gave birth to and secretly maintained her desire to be an analyst, on the other. She was curious about the basis (which some would consider to be unanalyzed or even impossible to analyze) of her interpretive language and her organizational abilities. This brings up a question: what is the "other" of psychoanalysis from which she clearly freed herself, but which made her what she was, accompanied her throughout her career, and thus provided the deepest inspiration for her discourse and the precondition for her "internal ear" and sense of truth?

According to Deutsch's autobiography, three paths guided her through her adventure. I believe that their significance exceeds the frame of one individual life, for they may also have repercussions for the evolution of psychoanalytic discourse as a whole. These three paths were the *Russian Revolution, women,* and *art.*

Let us first consider the Revolution. Hala Rosenbach, who was born in 1884 in Przemysl, in Galcia, Poland, came from a liberal and well-assimilated Jewish family, especially on her father's side. Her father, Wilhelm Rosenbach, enjoyed a degree of fame and a "national responsibility" that were rarely entrusted to a Jewish person in those days. According to Deutsch, "I usually identified more with the romantic 'suffering, enslaved Poland' than with my Jewish background."[2] Her first lover, who mirrored this idealized father, was Herman Lieberman. A married man sixteen years her senior and a militant socialist leader, Lieberman was inspired by the ideals of the French Revolution and shaken by what was going on in Russia. Deutsch shared his political fervor and accompanied him to the International Socialist Congress in Stockholm in 1910, where she met Rosa Luxembourg.

Deutsch saw her discovery of Freud as a perpetuation of this spirit of revolution and liberation. In a Europe torn apart by social, religious, and racial hatreds and rejuvenated by the ideas of the bourgeois revolution and of socialism, a Jewish woman who had broken off her ties with tradition had little difficulty joining the psychoanalytic movement. Deutsch believed that this movement would be able to internalize this secular, libertarian, and revolutionary spirit: "Psychoanalysis was my last and most deeply experienced revolution; and Freud, who was rightly considered a conservative on social and political issues, became for me the greatest revolutionary of the century."[3]

In this context, psychoanalysis emerges as the culmination of progressive rationality, not only within the history of ideas, but also through the life stories of its founding members (Helene Deutsch was a paroxysmal, though not unique, member of this group). What is more, psychoanalysis emerges as an ethical basis for this rationality. Hala discovered her feminine freedom and professional success by renouncing the political zeal to which her youthful love had bound her.

Although numerous references to "virile revolutionary women" in the *Psychology of Women* bear witness to Helene Deutsch's understanding of this behavior, they also show that she distanced herself from it. In such texts as "The Impostor," she goes on to say that false personalities, that is, *"as-if"* personalities, might have been able to avoid (or conceal?) their psychopathology if they had discovered the "favorable circumstances" of political action: "under more favorable circumstances, [the impostor], like so many other heroes of wars and revolutions, might have made his pathology serve a glorious career."[4] This means that psychoanalysis stakes out a different path, one that makes the impostor vanish and offers a chance to build up a viable relationship of desire and love with another person. This is what seems to be the implicit message of Helene Deutsch's relentless examination of the omnipresence of the impostor, whom she claimed to see everywhere, even in herself: "Ever since I became interested in the impostor, he pursues me everywhere. I find him among my friends and acquaintances, as well as in myself."

The end of Deutsch's militant political activities, which instilled her with a permanent gift for organization, was immediately followed by another proclamation. This one was also inscribed in the political conflicts of this century, although psychoanalysis hoped to assuage it of its harsh light: she proclaimed to be a woman. We are indebted to Helene Deutsch for two volumes of a *Psychology of Women,* and her autobiography shows how this psychology was rooted in her own experience.

Hala, the youngest of three sisters, felt estranged from her mother, whom she believed did not love her very much and whom she consequently rejected. Let us note, however, that she had a very close relationship with her father. During puberty, this idealization broke out, as might be expected, into a sexual liberation. Those who read these autobiographical memoirs will be reminded of the remarkably dispassionate pages of the *Psychology of Women* in which Deutsch promotes this situation to the rank of a psychological generalization without leaving any trace of its autobiographical origin:

> *Interestingly enough, such a relation very often obtains with the third daughter, especially if she is also the youngest. It is as though the father's relation to the daughter had got rid of its dangers and freed itself from the fear of incest with the two older daughters. The third one—Cinderella—seems to be particularly suitable for her father's love choice because of her helplessness and apparent innocuousness. The need to save the little girl from the aggressions of the mother and the older sisters certainly plays a great part here.*[6]

And later, under the authorship of the delicate and devoted Mrs. Felix Deutsch, the autobiography of the former Miss Rosenbach, who still gave her loyal support to her father and to his double, Herman Lieberman, contains a poignant description of a daughter's love for her father:

[*At first, the daughter sees her father as*] *a great man who deserves a better fate, a victim of the prosaic mother who has tied him to the gray business of earning a living. She, the little daughter, would be a more suitable object for him, though he must painfully renounce it. In a large number of instances, a psychologically sound woman may have as her first love object—an object to which she often remains attached for life—an unfree man, often a married man, who fans her love and responds to it, but who cannot break his old tie. Such a man reproduces the situation described above. The fantasy of his painful love yearning and the woman's own suffering, shared with him, often prove stronger motives for faithfulness than the fulfillment of love.*[7]

Helene Deutsch believed that the first revolution of her life consisted of her liberation from her tyrannical mother. She emphasized relentlessly what she saw as the two essential and elemental components of feminine psychology: masochism and narcissism. Her affinities with the feminist movement of her day did not prevent her from steadfastly maintaining her belief that masochism and narcissism were determinants of femininity. It is important to note, however, that Deutsch sought to derive the term "masochism" from pathology, and more specifically, from perversion. First she showed that masochism stems from a natural inhibition of female psychic development, an inhibition that is reinforced by the father's love *and* rejection of his little girl. Deutsch saw that this tendency is manifested by the organization of the feminine libido, not into an actual passivity, but into an "interior activity"—inside the house, the body, or the self. This position led her to transform the concept of a *masochistic symptom* into a *masochistic organization* of the personality. She explained that such an organization results from biological restrictions (an inaccessible and passive vagina, the physical pain of intercourse and childbirth) as well as social constraints. It is easy enough to see what might be gained through this neutralization or "naturalization" of the concept of masochism. Yet by completely ignoring the perverse pleasure of this notion of personality organization, we lose the essential dynamics of female sexuality. Moreover, Deutsch's point of view seems to neglect the symbolic determinations of female jouissance.

In this paradigm, narcissism would be the element that counterbalances masochistic tendencies, and even ensures that masochism will be overcome. A woman would thus be an ambivalent, if not divided, structure, for she enacts the ambiguous human fate of being an *individual* who is at the same time a member of the *species*. The woman-individual seeks pleasure. The procreative woman—who ensures the survival of the species—endures pain, which she can only tolerate if it becomes the source of a certain sort of pleasure. In Helene Deutsch's eyes, the unconscious willingness to suffer renders women particularly adaptable and sociable. When reading these texts (both biographical and theoretical), one does not sense a hymn to feminine surrender, as has often been suggested. Instead, one becomes aware of a commanding lucidity that speaks the truth for so many women of this century. Indeed, Deutsch's autobiography convincingly shows how a woman inevitably confronts the subtle alchemy of masochism-narcissism by tackling both a professional career and maternity—which are the themes of the entire second volume of the *Psychology of Women*. Helene Deutsch had already predicted that new techniques of procreation and childbirth would alter this feminine psychic reality.

There is one last source that served to maintain Deutsch's desire to analyze: art. Her autobiography is strewn with references to Proust, Flaubert, Gide, Italian art, and ancient Greece.

Freud's fascination with artists who may have preceded him in discovering the unconscious does not fully explain this constant partnership with art, which is more pronounced in old age, once analytic practice has come to an end. Does art prevent us from dying of the very truth in which we engulf the pain caused by the words addressed to us? I would prefer to think that Helene Deutsch did not see beauty as a mere means of escape, as a disavowal of or an antidote for abjection. She drew one of her possible discourses from beauty; she thus was able to express our unbearable situation as speaking beings who can "go to the end of night" while referring to it with pleasure, and who can forget the meaning of life while appealing to the desire of other people. Helene Deutsch found strength in the dangerous well of narcissism and sublimation, and she was also one of the first people to delve into it.

As-If

In my opinion, Deutsch's exploration of narcissistic affections was one of her most valuable contributions to analytic thought. Beginning in 1934, that is, long before the sophisticated analyses of "borderline states" or "false selves" were carried out, Helene Deutsch was already referring to "as-if personalities." Without doubt, the emphasis she placed on female narcissism allowed her to modify the conventional notion of "schizophrenia" and to use this refurbishing to propose her own, broader notion of "as-if personalities." The affective difficulties of "as-if" personalities resemble schizophrenic symptoms, although these are two distinct disorders:

> Psychoanalysis discloses that in the "as-if" individual it is no longer an act of repression but a real loss of object cathexis. The apparently normal relationship to the world corresponds to the child's imitativeness and is the expression of identification with the environment, a mimicry which results in an ostensibly good adaptation to the world of reality despite the absence of object cathexis.[8]

Although the objects of hysterical identification are heavily invested with libido, even if repression affects this investment and leads to the absence of anxiety that can solve conflicts,

> in "as-if" patients, an early deficiency in the development of affect reduces the inner conflict, the effect of which is an impoverishment of the total personality, which does not occur in hysteria. . . . In

"as-if" patients, the objects are kept external and all conflicts are acted out in relation to them. Conflict with the superego is thus avoided because in every gesture and in every act the "as-if" ego subordinates itself through identification to the wishes and commands of an authority which has never been introjected.[9]

With great finesse, Helene Deutsch analyzed those men and women who give the impression of being empty, absent, and cold, regardless of their apparent devotion to their activities or love life. These pages, which we cannot help reading in counterpoint to many other autobiographical confessions, brilliantly prefigure Winnicott's notion of the "false self."[10]

Frigidity: The Language of Depression

Following her analysis with Freud, about which she unfortunately said very little (besides recalling such matters as bringing some milk with her for her analyst's wife and family), and which she said ended "abruptly," Helene Deutsch became Karl Abraham's analysand in Berlin, in 1924. At that time, she met Melanie Klein, who was also one of Abraham's analysands. Deutsch cautiously acknowledged Klein's originality, but she preferred a different "father's daughter"—Miss Anna Freud. With acute perceptiveness and a little irony, Helene Deutsch scrutinized her identifications with the women of the revolutionary movement (Rosa Luxembourg, Angelica Balabanoff) as well as the analytic circle (Anna Freud, along with Marie Bonaparte, Jeanne Lampl-de Groot, and others). At the same time, she remained quite discreet about her aggressions, jealousies, and incompatibilities with her "rival sisters" (Lou Andreas-Salomé, Melanie Klein, Karen Horney).

Apparently, it was later in Deutsch's life that this half-loving, half-warlike quadrille of Freud's female colleagues obtained a truly personal meaning for her. As a grandmother, Deutsch spoke again of her adoration for her older sisters, who had replaced a rejecting and rejected mother. Finally, she analyzed the bonds she had formed with her half-daughter and half-granddaughter. In a narcissistic fashion, the three women of the latter configuration were bent over the son or grandson—the ultimate object of love and anxiety, the germ of their masochism-narcissism. And then Helene Deutsch, this time as the eldest mother, claimed to have faded away—not without some humor—in order to make room for the youngest one, who she no longer was.

Helene Deutsch, who analyzed Victor Tausk, who was intrigued by Ferenczi, and who was the admiring analysand of Abraham (one of the first people to study depression), became aware of the melancholic undercurrent of many neuroses, especially in women. Her work in feminine psychology led her to inquire (through the language of anatomy and physiology) into feminine suffering and sadness as a possible source of pleasure, or conversely, as a fundamental inhibition of female jouissance. Going beyond masochism, she incessantly stressed what truly seems to be a fundamental female depression, a depression that she primarily analyzed through the psychic events of maternity (pregnancy, childbirth, and nursing). Finally, she seems to have associated feminine depression with frigidity by declaring that they both stemmed from the vagina's biological fate of being the receptacle of death anxiety: "The original sexual organ of the woman, the clitoris, is the receiver of castration fears. The vagina is the receiver of the deepest anxiety, i.e., of death, which accompanies motherhood and is mobilized in pregnancy and delivery. It is this anxiety which seems to prevent sexual responses in the vaginal part of the female organ."[11]

Were it possible to place Helene Deutsch's statement in another theoretical frame, I would say that regardless of the anatomical bases for this process, a woman uses the *fantasy* to enclose an inaccessible object inside her body. In a phantasmatic sense, this interior ends up being the vagina or, as Lou Salomé would say, the "vagina is 'rented' to the anus." The object in question is the "bad mother" whom the woman imprisons to prevent losing her, to dominate her, to put her to death, or even to kill herself inside this melancholic embrace between two women. This phantasmatic of the frigid woman with a bad mother espouses the dynamics of depression, in which the depressed subject incorporates the man or woman she hates in order to keep from losing him (or her). And, by killing him (or her), she kills herself.

For a woman who is in a sexual relationship, two forms of jouissance may be possible. On the one hand, phallic jouissance— competition or identification with her partner's symbolic partner— mobilizes the clitoris. On the other hand, there is *another* jouissance that the fantasy imagines and puts into action by focusing on the core of psychic and corporeal space. This other jouissance requires that someone literally "dissolve" the melancholic object that blocks psychic and corporeal interiority. Who might be able to do this? A partner who is believed to be capable of being a more-than-mother, who could dissolve the mother imprisoned inside me, by giving me what she was or was not able to give me. Although this partner would remain in a separate place from my own, he would be the one to provide me with the most important gift that she was never able to give me—a new life. Such a partner would be neither the father who ideally gratifies his daughter, nor the symbolic standard that the woman tries to achieve through a virile competition. Through the help of this partner, feminine interiority (psychic space, and, on the corporeal level, the association between vagina and anus) might cease to be the tomb that shelters the dead woman and prepares for frigidity.

By putting to death the deadly mother within me, my sexual partner acquires the charms of a giver of life, of a veritable "more-than-mother." Without being a phallic mother, he compensates for the mother by way of a phallic violence that destroys what is bad, but that also gives and gratifies. The "vaginal" jouissance that follows, then, is contingent upon a relationship with the Other that is no longer conceived within a phallic overstatement, but as support for the narcissistic object and as capable of ensuring its displacement *somewhere else*. The man incites ecstasy by giving me a child and by becoming the link between the mother-child bond and symbolic power.

We cannot assume that this other jouissance is absolutely essential for a woman's psychic fulfillment. Quite often, in fact, either professional or maternal phallic compensation or clitoral pleasure can veil frigidity in a reasonably efficient manner. Nevertheless, if men and women assign a quasi-sacred value to this other jouissance, it is perhaps because the language of a female body is what has temporarily triumphed over depression—a triumph over death. Of course, this is not the ultimate fate of the individual. It is, rather, an imaginary death to which premature human beings are subject if they are abandoned, neglected, or misunderstood by their mother. In the female fantasy, this other jouissance presupposes a triumph over the deadly mother, so that interiority might become not only a source of biological life, but also a source of gratification and psychic life. The pages that Helene Deutsch consecrates to maternity, as well as her discreet autobiographical traces of her disputes with her mother and of her own experiences as a wife and mother might constitute one of the possible manifestations of this theoretical conjecture.

An "Open Structure": The Adolescent

At the end of her journey, the elderly lady saw herself as an eternal adolescent: "Yet I feel that my Sturm und Drang period, which continued long into my years of maturity, is still alive within me and refuses to come to an end. I find that there are still ecstasies and loves in me, and that these feelings are rooted in my adolescence."[12] Helene Deutsch, who treated many adolescents, knew that the Sturm und Drang of adolescence is less a matter of age than of a structure that I have called an "open structure."[13] Although this term has been used to describe a living organism whose sole purpose is to renew itself by opening itself up to its environment or another structure, there are also some speaking beings who possess this property within the boundaries of their psychic realm. Through a massive freeing-up of the superego—which occurs for most of us during adolescence—such subjects are exposed to a rotation of representations between the various psychic registers (for instance, drives—primary inscriptions—secondary inscriptions). This experience gives us a greater capacity to engage in frequent and creative transferences onto other people, objects, or symbolic systems. This transferential opening-up and restructuring of psychic dynamics make such subjects particularly suited for "love and ecstasy," as Helene Deutsch said.

Women are undoubtedly capable of this transferential plasticity and these adolescent dynamics. What is more, certain subjects attain the symbolic elaboration and the creative transmission of this particularity—I am referring to artists. A "domestication" of perversion follows, which focuses on an ideal father and enables us to adapt to other people by giving our utmost effort within an optimal jouissance.

I am convinced that this sort of specificity is necessary if one wishes to become an analyst. Helene Deutsch's autobiography enables us to discover the way in which a woman was able to develop, preserve, and maintain this "open structure," which she adorned with a discourse that was appropriate for the dramatic events of our century, on the one hand, and through the trying hazards of her calm, nomadic existence, on the other.

Helene Deutsch was almost one hundred years old when she died in 1982.

14. WOMEN'S TIME

National and European Women

The nation, which was the dream and the reality of the nineteenth century, seems to have reached both its peak and its limit with the 1929 crash and the National Socialist apocalypse. We have witnessed the destruction of its very foundation—economic homogeneity, historical tradition, and linguistic unity. World War II, which was fought in the name of national values, brought an end to the reality of the nation, which it turned into a mere illusion that has been preserved for ideological or strictly political purposes ever since. Even if the resurgence of nations and nationalists may warrant hope or fear, the social and philosophical coherence of the nation has already reached its limit.

The search for economic *homogeneity* has given way to *interdependence* when it has not yielded to the economic superpowers of the world. In like manner, *historical* tradition and *linguistic* unity have been molded into a broader and deeper denominator that we might call a *symbolic denominator:* a cultural and religious memory shaped by a combination of historical and geographical influences. This memory generates national territories determined by the ever-diminishing but still widespread conflicts between political parties. At the same time, this common "symbolic denominator" is a means not only to globalization and economic standardization, but also to entities that are greater than any one nation, and that *sometimes* embrace the boundaries of an entire continent.

In this way, a "common symbolic denominator" can lead to a new social grouping that is greater than the nation, though it enables the nation to retain and build upon its characteristics instead of losing them. This transformation occurs, however, within a paradoxical temporal structure, a sort of "future perfect" in which the most deeply repressed and transnational past gives a distinctive character to programmed uniformity. For the memory in question (the common symbolic denominator) is linked to the solution that spatially and temporally united human groupings have offered less for the problems of the *production* of material goods (which is the domain of economics, human relations, and politics) than of *reproduction*—the survival of the species, life and death, the body, sex, and the symbol. If it is true, for instance, that Europe represents this sort of sociocultural grouping, its existence stems more from its "symbolic denominator" of art, philosophy, and religion than from its economic profile. Of course, economics is a function of collective memory, but its characteristics are easily modified by pressures from one's partners in the world.

Therefore, we see that this sort of social grouping is endowed with a *solidity* rooted in the various modes of reproduction and its representations by which the biological species is placed within a temporally determined humanity. Yet, it is also tainted with a certain *fragility,* for the symbolic denominator can no longer aspire to universality and endure the influences and assaults inflicted by other sociocultural memories. Hence, Europe, which is still fairly inconstant, is obliged to identify with the cultural, artistic, philo-sophical, and religious manifestations of other supranational groupings. Such identifications are of no surprise when the entities in question share a historical connection, like Europe and North America, or Europe and Latin America. They also occur, how-ever, when the universality of this symbolic denominator juxtaposes two modes of production and reproduction that may seem incongruous, like those of Europe and the Arab world, Europe and India, Europe and China, and so forth.

In short, when dealing with the sociocultural groupings of the "European" type, we are forever faced with two major issues: first, that of *identity*, which is brought about by historical sedimentation, and second, the *loss of identity*, which is caused by memory links that bypass history in favor of anthropology. In other words, we are confronted with two temporal dimensions: the time of linear, *cursive* history, and the time of another history, that is, another time, a *monumental* time (the nomenclature comes from Nietzsche) that incorporates these supranational sociocultural groupings within even larger entities.

I would like to draw attention to certain formations that seem to embody the dynamics of this sort of sociocultural organism. I am speaking of groups we call "sociocultural" because they are defined by their role in production, but also (and especially) because of their role in the mode of reproduction and its representations. Although these groups share all the traits of the sociocultural formation in question, they *transcend* it and link it to other sociocultural formations. I am thinking specifically of sociocultural groups that we summarily define according to age categories (for instance, "European youth"), or gender divisions (for instance, "European women"), and so forth. Clearly, European youth and European women have a particularity of their own, and it is no less obvious that what defines them as "youth" or "women" is concomitant with their "European" origin and shared by their counterparts in North America and China, among others. Insofar as they participate in "monumental history," they are not merely European "youth" or "women." In a most specific way, they will mirror the universal features of their structural position with regard to reproduction and its representations.

In the pages that follow, I would like to place the problematics of European women in the context of an inquiry into time, that is, the time that the feminist movement has not only inherited but altered. Then, I shall delimit two phases or two generations of women, whose respective demands cause them to be directly universalist or cosmopolitan, though they still can be distinguished from each other. The first generation is particularly linked to national concerns, and the second, which tends to be determined by the "symbolic denominator," is European and trans-European. Finally, I shall attempt to use the problems I am addressing and the type of analysis I am proposing to show that against the backdrop of what has become a global generality, a European stance (or at least a stance taken by a European woman) has emerged.

Which Time?

Joyce said "Father's time, mother's species," and it seems indeed that the evocation of women's name and fate privileges the *space* that *generates* the human species more than it does *time,* destiny, or history. Modern studies of subjectivity—of its genealogy or its accidents—have reaffirmed this separation, which may result from sociohistorical circumstances. After listening to his patients' dreams and fantasies, Freud grew to believe that "hysteria was linked to place."[1] Subsequent studies on children's acquisition of the symbolic function have shown that the permanency and quality of maternal love pave the way for the earliest spatial references, which give rise to childhood laughter and then prepare the whole array of symbolic manifestations that permit sign and syntax.[2]

Before endowing the patient with a capacity for transference and communication, do not both anti-psychiatry and applied psychoanalysis (when applied to the treatment of psychoses) purport to mark out new places that serve as gratifying and healing substitutes for long-standing deficiencies of maternal space? The examples of this are many, but they all converge upon the problematics of space, which so many religions with a matriarchal bent attribute to "the woman," and which Plato, who echoed the atomists of antiquity within his own system, referred to as the aporia of the *chora,* a matrixlike space that is nourishing, unnameable, prior to the One and to God, and that thus defies metaphysics.[3]

As for time, female subjectivity seems to offer it a specific concept of measurement that essentially retains *repetition* and *eternity* out of the many modalities that appear throughout the history of civilization. On the one hand, this measure preserves cycles, gestation, and the eternal return of biological rhythm that is similar to the rhythm of nature. Its predictability can be shocking, but its simultaneity with what is experienced as extra-subjective and cosmic time is a source of resplendent visions and unnameable jouissance. On the other hand, it preserves a solid temporality that is faultless and impenetrable, one that has so little to do with linear time that the very term "temporality" seems inappropriate. All-encompassing and infinite, like imaginary space, it reminds us of Hesiod's Kronos, the incestuous son who smothered Gaea with his entire being in order to take her away from Ouranos the father. It also recalls the myths of resurrection in the various traditions that have perpetuated the trace of a maternal cult through its most recent manifestation within Christianity. In Christianity, the body of the Virgin Mother does not die, but travels from one space to another within the same time frame, whether by dormition (according to the Orthodox faith) or assumption (according to Catholicism).[4]

These two types of temporality—cyclical and monumental—are traditionally associated with female subjectivity, when female subjectivity is considered to be innately maternal. We must not forget, however, that repetition and eternity serve as fundamental conceptions of time in numerous experiences, notably mystical ones.[5] That the modern feminist movement has identified with these experiences suggests that it is not intrinsically incompatible with "masculine" values.

On the other hand, female subjectivity poses a problem only with respect to a certain conception of time, that of time as planning, as teleology, as linear and prospective development—the time of departure, of transport and arrival, that is, the time of history. It has been amply demonstrated that this sort of temporality is inherent in the logical and ontological values of any given civilization. We can assume that it explains a rupture, a waiting period, or an anxiety that other temporalities hide from our view. This sort of time is that of language, of the enunciation of sentences (noun phrase and verb phrase, linguistic topic and comment, beginning and end), and it is maintained through its outer limit—death. A psychoanalyst would call it obsessional time, for the very structure of the slave can be found within the mastery of this time. A male or female hysteric (who suffers from reminiscences, according to Freud) would identify, rather, with prior temporal modalities—the cyclical, the monumental.

Within the bounds of a given civilization, however, this antinomy of psychic structures becomes an antinomy among social groups and ideologies. Indeed, the radical viewpoints of certain feminists are akin to the discourse of marginal spiritual or mystic groups, as well as, interestingly enough, to the concerns of modern science. Is it not true that the problematics of a time indissociable from space—of a space-time placed in an infinite expansion or articulated by accidents and catastrophes—are of great interest to space science as well as genetics? And in a different way, is it not true that the media revolution that has manifested itself as the information age suggests that time is frozen or exploded according to the fortuity of demand? Is it a time that returns to its source but cannot be mastered, that inexorably overwhelms its subject and restricts those who assimilate it to only two concerns: who will wield power over the origin (its programming) and the end (its use)?

The reader may be struck by these fluctuating points of reference—mother, woman, hysteric. Although the seemingly coherent use of the word "woman" in current ideology may have a "popular" or "shock" effect, it eradicates the differences among the various functions and structures that operate beneath this word. The time may have come, in fact, to celebrate the *multiplicity* of female perspectives and preoccupations. In a more accurate, honest, and less self-serving way, we must guarantee that the *fundamental difference* between the sexes arises out of the network of these differences. Feminism has accomplished a formidable task by making this difference a *painful* one, which means it is able to generate contingency and symbolic life in a civilization that has nothing to do besides playing the stock market and waging war.

We cannot speak about Europe or about "women in Europe" without defining the history that encompasses this sociocultural reality. It is true that a feminine sensibility has been in existence for more than a century now, but it is likely that by introducing its notion of time, it clashes with the idea of an "Eternal Europe," or perhaps even a "Modern Europe." Feminine sensibility, rather, would look for its own trans-European temporality by way of the European past and present as well as the European "ensemble," defined as the storehouse of memory. We can contend, however, that European feminist movements have displayed three attitudes toward this conception of linear temporality—a temporality that we readily deem to be masculine, and that is as "civilizational" as it is obsessional.

Two Generations

When the women's movement began as the struggle of suffragists and existential feminists, it sought to stake out its place in the linear time of planning and history. As a result, although the movement was universalist from the start, it was deeply rooted in the sociopolitical life of nations. The political demands of women, their struggles for equal pay for equal work and for the right to the same opportunities as men have, as well as the rejection of feminine or maternal traits considered incompatible with participation in such a history all stem from the *logic of identification* with values that are not ideological (such values have been rightly criticized as too reactionary) but logical and ontological with regard to the dominant rationality of the nation and the state.

It is unnecessary to enumerate all the benefits that this logic of identification and spirited protest have offered and still offer to women (abortion rights, contraception, equal pay, professional recognition, and others). These benefits have had or will soon prove to have even more significant effects than those of the Industrial Revolution. This current of feminism, which is universalist in

scope, *globalizes* the problems of women of various social categories, ages, civilizations, or simply psychic structures under the
banner of Universal Woman. In this world, a reflection about
generations of women could only be conceived of as a succession, a
progression that sought to implement the program set out by its
founding members.

A second phase is associated with women who have come to
feminism since May 1968 and who have brought their aesthetic or
psychoanalytic experiences with them. This phase is characterized
by a quasi-universal rejection of linear temporality and by a highly
pronounced mistrust of political life. Although it is true that this
current of feminism still has an allegiance to its founding members
and still focuses (by necessity) on the struggle for the sociocultural
recognition of women, in a *qualitative* sense, it sees itself in a
different light than did the prior generation of feminists.

The "second phase" women, who are primarily interested in
the specificity of feminine psychology and its symbolic manifestations, seek a language for their corporeal and intersubjective experiences, which have been silenced by the cultures of the past. As
artists or writers, they have undertaken a veritable exploration of
the *dynamics of signs*. At least on the level of its intentions, their
exploration is comparable to the most ambitious projects for religious and artistic upheaval. Attributing this experience to a new
generation does not merely imply that new concerns have been
added to the earlier demands of sociopolitical identity, for it also
means that by requiring that we recognize an irreducible and self-
sufficient singularity that is multifaceted, flowing, and in some
ways nonidentical, feminism is currently situated outside the linear
time of identities that communicate through projections and demands. Today, feminism is returning to an archaic (mythic) memory as well as to the cyclical or monumental temporality of marginal movements. It is clearly not by chance that the European
and trans-European problem has manifested itself at the same time
as this new phase of feminism.

What sociopolitical processes or events have led to this mutation? What are its problems, its contributions, its limits?

Socialism and Freudianism

It could be maintained that this new generation of women has a more pronounced presence in Western Europe than in the United States, which may be attributed to the *rupture* in social relations and attitudes that has been caused by socialism and Freudianism. Although *socialism* as an egalitarian doctrine is presently experiencing a profound crisis, it still requires that governments and political parties of all persuasions expand solidarity by redistributing wealth and allowing free access to culture. *Freudianism,* which serves as an internal mechanism of the social realm, challenges egalitarianism by exploring sexual difference as well as the singularity of subjects who preserve their individuality.

Western socialism, shaken from its beginnings by the egalitarian or differential demands made by its women (Flora Tristan, for instance), has not hesitated to rid itself of those women who want us to recognize the specificity of the female role in culture and society. In the spirit of the egalitarian and universalist context of Enlightenment humanism, the only idea that socialism has held to is the notion that identity between the sexes is the only way to liberate the "second sex." For the moment, I shall refrain from pursuing the fact that this "ideal of equality" has not really been adopted by the actual movements and political parties that lay claims to socialism, and that since May 1968, the new generation of Western European women has been inspired, to some extent, by a revolt against the reality of the situation. Let me simply note that in theory (and in practice, in the case of Eastern Europe), socialist ideology, which is founded on the idea that human beings are determined by their relation to *production,* has ignored the role of the human being in *reproduction* and the *symbolic order.* As a result, socialist ideology has been compelled, in its totalizing, if not totalitarian, spirit,[6] to believe that the specific nature of women is unimportant, if not nonexistent. We have begun to realize, moreover, that Enlightenment humanism and even socialism have imposed this same egalitarian and censuring treatment onto individual religious groups, especially Jewish ones.[7]

Nevertheless, the effects of this attitude are of paramount importance for women. Let us take the example of the evolution of women's destiny in the socialist countries of Eastern Europe. It would only be a slight exaggeration to say that in these countries, the demands of the suffragists and existential feminists have been met, at least to a large degree. What is more, in Eastern Europe, various blunders and vacillations have not prevented three of the most important demands of the early feminist movement from being answered to: the demands of economic, political, and professional equality. The fourth demand, sexual equality, which would require permissiveness in sexual relationships as well as abortion and contraceptive rights, remains inhibited by a certain Marxist ethics as well as by the reason of state. Thus, it is the fourth equal right that poses a problem and seems *vital* to the struggle of the new generation. This may be true, but because of the successful socialist agenda (which has been quite disappointing, in reality), this struggle will no longer aim specifically for equality. At this point in its journey, the new generation is coming up against what I have called the *symbolic* question.

Sexual, biological, physiological, and reproductive difference reflects a difference in the relation between subjects and the symbolic contract—that is, the social contract. It is a matter of clarifying the difference between men and women as concerns their respective relationships to power, language, and meaning. The most subtle aspects of the new generation's feminist subversion will be directed toward this issue in the future. This focus will combine the sexual with the symbolic in order to discover first the specificity of the feminine [*le féminin*] and then the specificity of each woman.

The saturation of socialist ideology and the exhaustion of its plan in favor of a new social contract has made way for Freudianism. I am not unaware, however, that militant women have seen Freud as an annoying male chauvinist from a Vienna that was at once puritanical and decadent, as someone who believed women were submen, castrated men.

Castrated or Subject to Language

Before we bypass Freud in order to propose a more accurate vision of women, let us first attempt to understand his notion of castration. The founder of psychoanalysis posited a castration *anxiety* or *fear* and a correlative penis *envy,* both of which are *imaginary* constructs peculiar to the *discourse* of neurotic *men as well as women.* A close reading of Freud that goes beyond the biological and mechanical models of his day enables us to delve into these issues more deeply.

First, the castration fantasy and its correlative penis envy are like the "primal scene" in that they are all *hypotheses, a priori* judgments intrinsic to psychoanalytic theory itself. These notions represent logical necessities that are relegated to the "origin" in order to explain that which never fails to function in neurotic discourse. In other words, neurotic discourse (in men as well as women) can only be understood in terms of its own logic if we acknowledge its fundamental sources—the primal scene and castration fantasy—even if these are never present in reality itself. The reality of castration is as real as the supposed "big bang" at the origin of the universe, yet we are much less shocked when this sort of intellectual process concerns inanimate matter than when it is applied to our own subjectivity and to the fundamental mechanism of our epistemic thought.

Furthermore, certain Freudian texts (like *The Interpretation of Dreams,* but especially those of the second topology, in particular the *Metapsychology*) as well as their recent elaborations (notably by Jacques Lacan), suggest that castration is an imaginary construction stemming from a psychic mechanism that constitutes the symbolic field as well as anyone who enters it. Castration, then, would be the advent of sign and of syntax, that is, of language as a *separation* from a fusion state of pleasure. In this way, the institution of an *articulated network* of *differences,* which refers to objects separated from a subject, forms *meaning.* This logical operation of separation, which has been described by child psychology and psycholinguistics, anticipates the syntactic links of language for boys as well as girls. Freud offers a new approach to this notion by postulating that certain biological or familial conditions prompt some women (notably hysterics) to deny this logical operation of separation and the language that ensues, whereas some men (notably obsessional neurotics) glorify this separation and language while trying, petrified as they are, to master them.

Analytic practice has shown that in fantasies, the penis becomes the primary referent of this operation of separation and gives full meaning to the *lack* or *desire* that constitutes subjects when they join the order of language. In order for this operation, which constitutes the symbolic and social orders, to reveal its truth and be accepted by both sexes, it would be wise to add to it the entire series of deprivations and exclusion that accompany the fear of losing one's penis, and impose the loss of wholeness and completeness. Castration, then, would be the ensemble of "cuts" that are indispensable to the advent of the symbolic.

Living the Sacrifice

Whether or not women are aware of the mutations that have generated or accompanied their awakening, the question they are asking themselves today could be formulated as follows: *what is our place in the social contract?* If this contract, whose terms do not treat everyone in an equal fashion, bases itself upon an ultimately sacrificial relationship of separation and articulation of differences that serves to create a meaning that can be communicated, what is our place in the order of sacrifice and/or language? Since we no longer wish to be excluded from this order, and we are no longer satisfied with our perpetually assigned role of maintaining, developing, and preserving this sociosymbolic contract as mothers, wives, nurses, doctors, teachers, and so forth, how might we appropriate our own space, a space that is passed down through tradition and that we would like to modify?

It is difficult to enumerate with certainty the aspects of the current relationship between women and the symbolic that stem from sociohistorical circumstances (including patriarchal, Christian, humanist, and socialist ideologies, among others), or from a structure. We can only speak of a structure observed in a sociohistorical context, that of Western Christian civilization and its secular ramifications. At the interior of this psychosymbolic structure, women feel rejected from language and the social bond, in which they discover neither the affects nor the meanings of the relationships they enjoy with nature, their bodies, their children's bodies, another woman, or a man. The accompanying frustration, which is also experienced by some men, is the quintessence of the new feminist ideology. Consequently, it is difficult, if not impossible, for women to adhere to the sacrificial logic of separation and syntactic links upon which language and the social code are based, and this can eventually lead to a rejection of the symbolic that is experienced as a rejection of the paternal function and may result in psychosis.

Faced with this situation, some women have sought to develop a new perspective—through new objects and new analyses—for anthropology, psychoanalysis, linguistics, and other disciplines that explore the symbolic dimension.[8] Other, more subjective women, who have come forth in the wake of contemporary art, have attempted to modify language and other codes of expression through a style that remains closer to the body and to emotion. I am not referring here to "female language,"[9] whose existence as a particular syntactic style is problematic, and whose apparent lexical specificity may be less a product of sexual difference that of social marginality. I am also not speaking of the aesthetic value of creations by women, most of which mirror a more or less euphoric and depressed romanticism, on the one hand, and stage an explosion of an ego that lacks narcissistic gratification, on the other. This leads me to believe that the primary focus of the new generation of women has become the sociosymbolic contract as a sacrificial contract.

For more than a century, anthropologists and sociologists have attracted our attention to the society-sacrifice that works behind "savage thought," wars, dream discourse, or great writers. In so doing, these scholars have reformulated and analyzed the metaphysical question of evil. If society is truly founded on a communal murder, the realization that castration provides the basis for the sociosymbolic is what will enable human beings to postpone murder. We symbolize murder (and ourselves), and thus have an opportunity to transform baleful chaos into an optimal sociosymbolic order.

Today's women have proclaimed that this sacrificial contract imposes itself against their will, which has compelled them to attempt a revolt that they perceive to be a resurrection. Society as a whole, however, considers this revolt to be a refusal and it can result in violence between the sexes (a murderous hatred, the break-up of the couple and the family) or in cultural innovation. In fact, it probably leads to them both. In any event, that is where the stakes are, and they are of enormous consequence. By fighting against evil, we reproduce it, this time at the core of the social bond—the bond between men and women.

The Terror of Power or the Power of Terrorism

First in the former socialist countries (such as the former Soviet Union and China) and later, increasingly, in Western democracies, feminist movements have enabled women to attain positions of leadership in the worlds of business, industry, and culture. Even if various forms of unfair discrimination and persecution continue to hold sway, the struggle against these is a struggle against the ways of the past. Even if the cause has been made known and the principles accepted, there still are obstacles that need to be overcome. Thus, although the ensuing struggle remains one of the major *preoccupations* of the new generation, in a strict sense of the word, it is no longer its primary *problem*. With respect to *power,* however, its problem could be stated as follows: What occurs when women attain power and identify with it? What occurs when they reject power but create an analogous society, a counterpower that ranges from a coterie of ideas to terrorist commandos?

That women have assumed commercial, industrial, and cultural power has not changed the nature of this power, which can be clearly seen in the case of Eastern Europe. The women who have been promoted to positions of leadership and who have suddenly obtained economic (as well as narcissistic) advantages that had been refused to them for thousands of years are the same women who become the strongest supporters of the current regimes, the guardians of the status quo, and the most fervent protectors of the established order.[10] This identification between women and a power that they once found frustrating, oppressive, or unattainable has often been used to the advantage of such totalitarian regimes as the German National Socialists or the Chilean junta.[11] One possible explanation of this troubling phenomenon might be that it results from a paranoid counterinvestment (in the psychoanalytic sense) of an initially denied symbolic order. Even so, this does not prevent its massive propagation around the world, sometimes in more subtle forms than the totalitarian ones I have mentioned. In any event, all these forms share an interest in equalization, stability, and conformity, though this comes at a cost: the eradication of each individual's uniqueness, of personal experiences, and of the vagaries of life.

Some may regret that the rise of a libertarian movement such as feminism may wind up reinforcing conformity, and others will celebrate this consequence and use it to their advantage. Electoral campaigns and political life never fail to bet on the latter alternative. Experience has shown that even the antiestablishment or innovative initiatives led by women dragged in by power (when they do not readily submit to it) are quickly attributed to "the system." The self-proclaimed democratization of institutions that pride themselves on accepting women most often means that they simply add a few female "bosses" to their ranks.

The various feminist currents, which tend to be more radical in approach, reject the powers that be and make the second sex into a *countersociety,* a sort of alter ego of official society that harbors hopes for pleasure. This female society can be opposed to the sacrificial and frustrating sociosymbolic contract: a countersociety imagined to be harmonious, permissive, free, and blissful. In our modern societies, which do not acknowledge an afterlife, the countersociety is the only refuge for jouissance, for it is precisely an anti-utopia, a place outside the law, yet a path to utopia.

Like all societies, the countersociety bases itself upon the expulsion of an already excluded element. The scapegoat deemed responsible for evil thus keeps it away from the established community,[12] which is thereby exonerated of any responsibility for it. Modern protest movements have often reproduced this model by designating a guilty party that shields them from criticism, whether it be the foreigner, money, another religion, or the other sex. If we take this logic at face value, does feminism not become a sort of reverse sexism?

In our world, the various marginal groups of sex, age, religion, ethnic origin, and ideology represent a refuge of hope, that is, a secular transcendence. All the same, insofar as the number of women affected by these problems has increased (albeit in a less dramatic way than was the case a few years ago), the problem of the countersociety is becoming an enormous one, no more and no less important than "half the sky."

It is not the case that protest movements, including feminism, are "libertarian at first" and then dogmatic only later. They do not fall into the abyss of defeated models through the fault of some internal deviation or external maneuver. The particular structure of the logic of counterpower and countersociety is what lies behind its essence as an image of defeated society or power. In such a perspective, which is most likely too Hegelian, modern feminism would be a single moment in an ongoing process—the process of becoming aware of the implacable violence (of separation and castration) that underlies *any* symbolic contract.

The large number of women participating in terrorist groups like the Palestinian commandos, the Baader-Meinhoff Gang, and the Red Brigades, has been noted. Exploitation of women is still far too frequent, and the traditional prejudices against women are so fierce that we cannot evaluate this phenomenon in an objective manner, though we may rightfully claim that it stems from a negation of the sociosymbolic contract as well as its counterinvestment. This paranoid mechanism is at the base of all forms of

political commitment and it can generate various humanizing attitudes. Yet when a woman feels ruthlessly isolated and becomes
aware of her affective experience as a woman or her status as a
social being who remains unknown to the discourse and the powers that be (everything from her own family to the social institutions of the world), she can make herself into a "possessed" agent
through the counterinvestment of the violence she encounters. She
fights against her frustration, then, with weapons that may appear
extreme at first glance, but that are justifiable and understandable
once the narcissistic suffering that elicits their use is recognized.

This terrorist violence, which is inevitably directed against the
regimes of current bourgeois democracies, assigns itself a program
of liberation that consists of an order even more repressive and
sacrificial than the one it is fighting. Indeed, the object of female
terrorists groups' aggression is not the various totalitarian regimes,
but the liberal regimes that are becoming increasingly democratic.
Their mobilization comes about in the name of a nation, an oppressed group, or what is believed to be a good and sound human
essence, that is, the fantasy of an archaic fulfillment that would be
disturbed by an arbitrary, abstract, and thus undesirable order.
Although this order has been accused of being oppressive, is our
primary criticism not that it is weak? That it does not stand up to
a substance believed to be pure and good but that is lost forever, a
substance that the marginalized woman hopes to recover?

Anthropologists have affirmed that the social order is a sacrificial one, yet sacrifice stops violence and develops into its own
order (through prayer or social well-being). If we reject it, we
subject ourselves to the explosion of the so-called good substance
that uncontrollably erupts outside the bounds of law and rights,
like an absolute arbitrariness.

As a result of the crisis of monotheism, two centuries of revolutions (most recently materialized as Fascism and Stalinism) have
staged the tragedy of the logic of oppressed goodwill that winds
up as a massacre. Are women more able than other social groups
to invest in the implacable terrorist mechanism? Perhaps one
might merely note that ever since the dawn of feminism (and even

before), women who fall outside the norm have often gained power through murder, conspiracy, or assassination. Eternal debt toward the mother has made her more vulnerable to the symbolic order, more fragile when she suffers from it, and more virulent when she protects herself. If the archetypal belief in a good and sound chimerical substance is essentially a belief in the omnipotence of an archaic, fulfilled, complete, all-encompassing mother who is not frustrated, not separated, and who lacks the "cut" that permits symbolism (that is, who lacks castration), the ensuing violence would be impossible to defuse without challenging the very myth of the archaic mother. It has been noted that feminist movements have been invaded by paranoia,[13] and we may remember Lacan's scandalous pronouncement that "There is no such thing as Woman." Indeed, she does not exist with a capital "W," as a holder of a mythical plenitude, a supreme power upon which the terror of power as well as terrorism as the desire for power base themselves. All the same, talk about a forceful subversion! Talk about playing with fire!

Creators: Male and Female

The desire to be a mother, which the previous generation of feminists held to be alienating or reactionary, has not become a standard for the current generation. Nevertheless, there is a growing number of women who find maternity to be compatible with their professional careers (this is also due to such improvements in living conditions as the increase of daycare centers and nursery schools, the more active participation of men in domestic life, and so forth). Furthermore, women are finding that maternity is vital to the richness of female experience, with its many joys and sorrows. This trend is illustrated to its fullest extent in lesbian mothers or in certain single mothers who reject the paternal function. The latter cases exemplify one of the most dramatic examples of the rejection of the symbolic order to which I referred earlier on, and they also exhibit an ardent deification of maternal power.

Hegel distinguishes between female right (familial and religious) and male law (civil and political). Although our societies are very well acquainted with the uses and abuses of this male law, we must admit that for the moment, female right appears to be a void. If these practices of fatherless maternity were to become the norm, it would become absolutely necessary to develop appropriate laws that could diminish the violence that might be inflicted on the child and the father. Are women equipped for this psychological and legal responsibility? That is one of the most profound questions that the members of this new generation of women are coming up against, especially when they refuse to confront such questions because they are gripped with a rage against the order and its law that victimizes them.

Faced with this situation, feminist groups are becoming increasingly aware (especially when they try to broaden their audience) that refusing maternity cannot be their primary political approach. The majority of women today feel that they have a mission to put a child into the world. This brings up a question for the new generation that the preceding one repudiated: what lies behind this desire to be a mother? Unable to answer this question, feminist ideology opens the door to a return of religion, which may serve to pacify anxiety, suffering, and maternal expectations. Although we can only offer a partial adherence to Freud's belief that the desire to have a child is the desire to have a penis, and is thus a replacement for phallic and symbolic power, we still must pay close attention to what today's women have to say about this experience. Pregnancy is a dramatic ordeal: a splitting of the body, the division and coexistence of self and other, of nature and awareness, of physiology and speech. This fundamental challenge to identity is accompanied by a fantasy of wholeness of narcissistic self-containment. Pregnancy is a sort of institutionalized, socialized, and natural psychosis. The arrival of the child, on the other hand, guides the mother through a labyrinth of a rare experience: the love for another person, as opposed to love for herself, for a mirror image, or especially for another person with which the "I" becomes merged (through amorous or sexual passion). It is rather a slow, difficult, and delightful process of becoming attentive, tender, and self-effacing. If maternity if to be guilt-free, this journey needs to be undertaken without masochism and without annihilating one's affective, intellectual, and professional personality, either. In this way, maternity becomes a true *creative act*, something that we have not yet been able to imagine.

At the same time, women's desire for affirmation has emerged as a longing for artistic and especially literary creation. Why the emphasis on literature? Is it because when literature is in conflict with social norms, it diffuses knowledge and occasionally the truth about a repressed, secret, and unconscious universe? Is it because literature intensifies the social contract by exposing the uncanny nature of that which remains unsaid? Is it because it plays with the abstract and frustrating order of social signs, of the words of everyday communication, and thus creates a place for fantasy and pleasure?

Flaubert said, *"Madame Bovary, c'est moi."* These days, some women think, *"Flaubert, c'est moi."* This claim points not only to an identification with the power of the imaginary, but also to women's desire to lift the sacrificial weight of the social contract and to furnish our societies with a freer and more flexible discourse that is able to give a name to that which has not yet been an object of widespread circulation: the mysteries of the body, secret joys, shames, hate displayed toward the second sex.

For this reason, women's writing has recently attracted a great deal of attention from "specialists" as well as the media. Nevertheless, the stumbling blocks that it must overcome are not inconsequential. Does women's writing not consist of a morose rejection of the very "male literature" that serves as a model for so much of women's writing? Thanks to the stamp of feminism, do we not sell many books whose naïve whining or commercialized romanticism would normally be scoffed at? Do female writers not make phantasmatic attacks against Language and the Sign, which are accused of being the ultimate mainstays of male chauvinist power, in the name of a body deprived of meaning and whose truth would only be "gestural" or "musical?"

Nevertheless, however questionable the results of women's artistic productions may be, the symptom has been made clear: women *are* writing. And we are eagerly awaiting to find out what *new material* they will offer us.

In the Name of the Father, the Son— and the Woman?

These few characteristic features of the new generation of women in Europe show that these women are placed within the same framework as the religious crisis of contemporary civilization. In my view, religion is our phantasmatic necessity to procure a *representation* (which could be animal, feminine, masculine, or parental, among others) that replaces the element that makes us what we are—our capacity to form symbols. Feminism today seems to constitute exactly this sort of *representation,* one that complements the frustration that women feel when faced with the Christian tradition and its variation—secular humanism. That this new ideology has some affinities with so-called matriarchal beliefs does not obliterate its radical innovation, for it participates in the anti-sacrificial trend that drives our culture. Although this ideology contests these constraints, it still remains vulnerable to the hazards of violence and terrorism. When radicalism goes this far, it challenges the very notion of social exchange.

Some contemporary thinkers maintain that modernity is the first era in human history in which human beings have attempted to live without religion. As it stands today, is feminism not about to become a sort of religion? Or will it manage to rid itself of its belief in Woman, Her power, and Her writing and support instead the singularity of each woman, her complexities, her many languages, at the cost of a single horizon, of a single perspective, of faith?

Is it a matter of ultimate solidarity, or a matter of analysis?

Is it an imaginary support in a technocratic era that frustrates narcissistic personalities, or a measurement of the time in which the cosmos, atoms, and cells—our true contemporaries—call for the formation of a free and flowing subjectivity?

Another Generation Is Another Space

It is now becoming possible to have a more objective perspective on the two preceding generations of women. I am suggesting, then, that a *third one* is taking shape, at least in Europe. I am thinking neither of a new age group (although its importance is far from negligible) nor of a new "mass feminist movement" that would follow in the footsteps of the second generation. The meaning I am attributing to the word "generation" suggests less a chronology than a *signifying* space, a mental space that is at once corporeal and desirous.

For this third generation, which I strongly support (which I am imagining?), the dichotomy between man and women as an opposition of two rival entities is *a problem for metaphysics*. What does "identity" and even "sexual identity" mean in a theoretical and scientific space in which the notion of "identity" itself is challenged?[14] I am not simply alluding to bisexuality, which most often reveals a desire for totality, a desire for the eradication of difference. I am thinking more specifically of subduing the "fight to the finish" between rival groups, not in hopes of reconciliation—since at the very least, feminism can be lauded for bringing to light that which is irreducible and even lethal in the social contract—but in the hopes that the violence occurs with the utmost mobility within individual and sexual identity, and not through a rejection of the other.

As a result, both individual equilibrium and social equilibrium (which emerges through the homeostasis of aggressive forces typical of social, national, and religious groups) are made vulnerable. All the same, does not the unbearable tension that underlies this "equilibrium" lead those who suffer from it to avoid it, to seek another way of regulating *difference?*

Despite the apparent indifference that has been shown toward the militancy of the first and second generations of women, I have generally found sexism to be less pronounced than before.

With the exception of the proclaimed rights of male and female homosexuals, sex has an evershrinking hold on subjective interest.

This "desexualization" goes as far as challenging not only humanism, but also the anthropomorphism that serves as a basis for our society. For this reason, "the man and the woman" are less of a fulcrum for social interest than they once were. The paroxysmal narcissism and egoism of our contemporaries only seem to contradict the retreat from anthropomorphism, for when anthropomorphism does not fall into technological supremacy or a general state of automation, it is forced to look to spirituality. Could the sexual revolution and feminism have merely been transitions into spiritualism?

That spiritualism turns to evasion or to conformist repression should not obscure the radical nature of the process, which comes forth as an *interiorization of the fundamental separation of the sociosymbolic contract.* From that point on, the other is neither an evil being foreign to me nor a scapegoat from the outside, that is, of another sex, class, race, or nation. I am *at once the attacker and the victim,* the same *and* the other, identical *and* foreign. I simply have to analyze incessantly the fundamental separation of my own untenable identity.

Religion is willing to accept this European awareness of *intrinsic evil,* which emerges from the ideological accomplishments and impasses of the feminist experience. Is any other discourse able to support it? Along with psychoanalysis, the role of aesthetic practices needs to be augmented, not only to counterbalance the mass-production and uniformity of the information age, but also to demystify the idea that the community of language is a universal, all-inclusive, and equalizing tool. Each artistic experience can also highlight the diversity of our identifications and the relativity of our symbolic and biological existence.

Understood as such, aesthetics takes on the question of morality. The imaginary helps to outline an ethics that remains invisible, as the outbreak of the imposture and of hatred wreaks havoc on societies freed from dogmas and laws. As restriction and as play, the imaginary enables us to envision an ethics aware of its own sacrificial order and that thus retains part of the burden for each of its adherents, whom the imaginary pronounces guilty and responsible, though it offers them the direct possibility of jouissance, of various aesthetic productions, of having a life filled with trials and differences. This would be a utopian ethics, but is any other kind possible?

In this sense, we might return to Spinoza's question: are women subject to ethics? Women are probably not subject to the ethics laid out by classical philosophy, with which generations of feminists have had a dangerously precarious relationship. Nevertheless, do women not participate in the upheaval that our society is experiencing on several levels (war, drugs, artificial insemination), an upheaval that will require a new ethics? If we consider feminism to be a *moment* in the thought pertaining to the anthropomorphic identity that has diminished the freedom of our species, we will only be able to answer this question in the affirmative once this moment has come to a close. And what is the meaning of the current "politically correct" movement that has swept across the United States? European consciousness has surpassed such concerns, thanks, in some respects, to the dissatisfaction and creativity of its women.

NOTES

1. The Soul and the Image

1. Jackie Pigeaud's excellent book *La Maladie de l'âme: Étude sur la relation de l'âme et du corps dans la tradition medico-philosophique antique* (Paris: Les Belles Lettres, 1989) retraces the history of these issues and draws some epistemological and moral conclusions that are relevant to the contemporary human sciences. This book has greatly influenced my own thoughts on the subject.

2. See Michel Foucault, *The Birth of the Clinic: An Archaeology of Medical Perception*, A. M. Sheridan Smith, tr. (New York: Pantheon Books, 1973); and his *Madness and Civilization: A History of Insanity in the Age of Reason*, Richard Howard, tr. (New York: Pantheon Books, 1965).

3. See Philippe Pinel, *Treatise on Insanity*, D. D. Davis, tr. (Birmingham, Ala: Classics of Medicine, 1983); and his *Nosographie philosophique* (Paris, 1813).

4. See Pigeaud, *La Maladie de l'âme*, p. 534.

5. The dualist point of view is sustained throughout Freud's writings. It is most clearly exemplified by his opposition of the life drive and the death drive. "Our views have from the very first been dualistic and today more than ever more definitely dualistic than before—now that we describe the opposition as being not between ego instincts and sexual instincts, but between life instincts and death instincts." *Beyond the Pleasure Principle* (1920), in *The Standard Edition of the Complete Psychological Works of Sigmund Freud*, James Strachey, ed. (London: Hogarth Press, 1953–1974), 18:53.

6. From *Project for a Scientific Psychology* (1895) to *The Interpretation of Dreams* (1900) and *Metapsychology* (1915), this "psychic apparatus" adopts the

form of two well-known topographical models (Conscious, Preconscious, Unconscious; and Superego, Ego, and Id). Freud's notion has not ceased to influence the work of his followers (Lacan and Bion have proposed their own variants of the psychic apparatus).

7. Jacques Hochmann and Marc Jeannerot, *Esprit où es-tu? Psychanalyse et neuroscience* (Paris: Odile Jacob, 1991), p. 71.

8. Z. Pylyszyn, "Computation and cognition: Issues in the foundation of cognitive science," *Behavioural Brain Sciences* (1980): 111–69. Cited by Hotchmann and Jeannerot, *Esprit où es-tu?*, p. 81.

9. Hochmann and Jannerot, *Esprit où es-tu?*, p. 129.

10. Hochmann and Jannerot, *Esprit où es-tu?*, p. 53.

11. I indicate here some of the best-known nosographical contributions:

—Helene Deutsch, "Some forms of emotional disturbances and their relationship to schizophrenia" (1942), *Neurosis and Character Types*. New York: International Universities Press, 1965.

—D. W. Winnicott, "Distortion of the ego as a function of the true and false self," *The Maturational Processes and the Facilitating Environment*. London: Hogarth Press, 1965.

—P. Marty, *L'Ordre psychosomatique*. Paris: Payot, 1980.

—Otto Kernberg, *Borderline Conditions and Pathological Narcissism*. New York: Jeffery Aronson, 1976.

—André Green, *Narcissisme de vie, narcissisme de mort*. Paris: Éditions de Minuit, 1983.

12. Masud Khan and other analysts have described two characteristics of the pervert: first, his predilection for a strong and secretive emotional "closeness," and second, his tendency to "command" (in the dictatorial sense) that his partner strictly obey his rules. See Masud Khan, *Figures de la perversion* (Paris: Gallimard, 1981), p. 31.

13. "Experiences of these cases that are considered abnormal have shown us that in them the sexual instinct and the sexual object are soldered together—a fact which we have been in danger of overlooking in consequence of the uniformity of the normal picture, where the object seems to form part and parcel of the instinct." And later: "It is perhaps in connection with the most repulsive perversions that the mental factor must be regarded as playing its largest part in the transformation of the sexual instinct. It is impossible to deny that in their case a piece of mental work has been performed which, in spite of its horrifying result, is the equivalent of the idealization of the instinct." *Three Essays on Sexuality*, in *Standard Edition* 7:148, 161.

14. See P. Marty and M. de m'Uzan, "La pensée opératoire," *Revue française de psychanalyse* 27 (1963): 345–46. See also P. Marty, *L'Ordre psychomatique* (Paris: Payot, 1980).

15. I am using this term in a way that does not completely conceal its psychoso-

matic connotations, though it sheds light on Didier's complex psychological organization, which was centered on an affective investment withdrawal of speech. Indeed, this patient held back his affects and produced a technical, academic, and cold discourse that was not only an obsessional isolation, but also verged on somatization. In my interpretation, the word "operative" conveys the semiologies of Didier's perversion, somatic symptoms, "false self," and obsessive nature.

16. W. H. Gillepsie, "Notes on the analysis of sexual perversions," *International Journal of Psychoanalysis* 33 (1952).

17. Edward Glover, "The relation of perversion-formation to the development of reality sense," *On the Early Development Mind* (London: Imago, 1956).

18. D. W. Winnicott, *The Maturational Process and the Facilitating Environment* (London: Hogarth Press, 1965).

19. While reflecting upon "psychological causality in relation to premature libidinal drives," Joyce McDougall discovered that preoedipal conflicts are a factor in perversion—see her *Plea for a Measure of Abnormality* (New York: International Universities Press, 1980)—and postulated a primitive sadistic fusional sexuality that might be at the origins of psychosomatic regressions. Such regressions seem to be defenses against mortifying experiences that are susceptible to perverse actings-out—see her *Theaters of the Mind: Illusion and Truth of the Psychoanalytic Stage* (New York: Bunner/Mazel, 1991). Though she develops Melanie Klein's and Margaret Mahler's notion of perversion as an avoidance of the depressive position, Joyce McDougall believes that the pervert's behavior can maintain a *sexual* identity that nevertheless conceals a threat to *subjective* identity. See Joyce McDougall, "Identifications, Neoneeds and Neosexualities," *International Journal of Psychoanalysis* 67, no. 19 (1968): 19–31. See also Margaret Mahler, *On Human Symbiosis and the Vicissitudes of Identifications,* vol. 1 (New York: International University Press, 1968).

20. In order to propose the clinic of a "*blank* series," André Green has postulated a "death narcissism" that he calls "negative narcissism." The blank series is defined as the "negative hallucination, blank psychosis, and blank mourning that result from a massive, radical, and temporary investment withdrawal that leaves traces of itself in the unconscious through 'psychic holes' that are subsequently filled with new investments. Such a weakening of libidinal, erotic investment gives a freer expression to destructiveness. Manifestations of hatred, as well as the processes of rectification that they make necessary, are secondary to this central investment withdrawal of the primary maternal object." *Narcissisme de vie, narcissisme de mort,* pp. 226–27. André Green defines "negative narcissism" as that which "aspires to psychic death" (p. 278). Didier was not the child of a "dead mother," as Green uses the term. Didier's analysis revealed, however, that during his sexual identification, he experienced an investment withdrawal of *his gender* as well as his *entire subjectivity.*

21. The dissociation I observed between language, phantasmatic representation, and drives seems implicit in Lacan's belief that within the perverse structure,

the symbolic, the imaginary, and the real are not "broken off," but "distinct." A certain persistence of the paternal function ensures this distinct connection, which links the pervert to the "sinthome" [*saint homme*-saint man] as well as to the "symptom." As an idealized longing for an ideal father, "perversion simply means *version* toward the *père*—it challenges the law and then holds it up to ridicule so as to get more pleasure out of it." See *Ornicar? "Le Sinthome"* 6 (November 11, 1975). In the course of Didier's treatment, the modification of the relationship between language, fantasy, and drive relation led to the acknowledgment of castration as the paternal function. After the analysis of the somatic symptom, the father, who is disavowed as a "sinthome" (idealized and/or disregarded) would attain the consistency of an oedipal father, in the patient's eyes. See Jacques Lacan "The Subversion of the subject and the dialect of desire in the Freudian unconscious," *Ecrits: A Selection,* Alan Sheridan, tr. (New York: Norton, 1977), pp. 320–22.

22. "If we believe what Freud says, all human sexuality is perverse." *Ornicar?* 11 (March 11, 1976).

23. Janine Chasseguet-Smirgel has shown that "anal-sadistic regression brings about the erosion of all differences." By replacing the fantasy, the pervert's regression "is able to restore desire, its source, its aim, and the representations associated with it to the anal-sadistic realm—a process that enables him not only to avoid the postponement of satisfaction, but also to disregard the notion of postponement itself, in the same way that the genital dimension of psychosexuality disappears." *Éthique et esthétique de la perversion* (Paris: Champ Vallon, 1984), p. 186. Using a different approach, the analysis that I propose results in similar constructs. For instance, my interest in Didier's divested discourse can be read as a counterpart to the problematic of "falsehood" (the paranoid person's substituting of anality for phallic characteristics) that Chasseguet-Smirgel has addressed most directly in "Le rossignol et l'empereur de Chine: Essai psychanalytique sur le "faux," *Revue française de psychanalyse* (1969): 115–41. Nevertheless, since Didier lacked a paranoid counterinvestment (he is neither Sade nor "Marienbad"), he invalidated, personalized, and impaired everything around him, including his anal defenses and his artwork.

24. Philip Greenacre, "On focal symbiosis," *Dynamic Psychopathology in Childhood,* L. Jessner and E. Ravensteld, eds. (New York: Grune and Stratton, 1969).

25. Masud Khan has referred to an "internal object-collage" in the formation of perversion—see his *Figures de la perversion.* Didier fabricated actual collages, as if to confirm the hypothesis of an intrapsychic "object-collage." I felt I was discovering Didier's *acting-out* of the "internal object-collage," which is not the same thing, but perhaps at one level higher . . . in perversion or in art? It is most likely in idealization, itself an integral part of sublimation. "It is impossible to deny that in their case a piece of mental work has been performed which, in spite of its horrifying result, is the equivalent of the idealization of the instinct." Sigmund Freud, "Three Essays on Sexuality" (1905), in *Standard Edition* 7:220.

26. This plasticity of the different logical structures of the fantasy, like the logical structures of the dream, is akin to Michel Neyraut's work on the plurality

of the logical structures of the unconscious. See his *Les Logiques de l'inconscient* (Paris: Hachette, 1978).

27. I distinguish the semiotic (pre-sign and pre-language) from the symbolic (signs and syntax). The semiotic and the symbolic are two modalities of the process of *significance*. I define the semiotic as prior to the mirror stage and to the phallic position—see my *Revolution in Poetic Language*, Margaret Waller, tr. (New York: Columbia University Press, 1984). By relying on the symbolic, the technique of collage-making might be seen as a facsimile of primary processes (as Michel Neyraut has suggested to me).

28. "The neurosis is, at it were, the negative of perversion." Sigmund Freud, *Three Essays on Sexuality*, in *Standard Edition* 7:231.

2. In Times Like These, Who Needs Psychoanalysts?

1. Marcel Proust, "Les Plaisirs et les jours," *Jean Santeuil* (Paris: Bibliothèque de La Pléiade, 1971), p. 6.

2. Marcel Proust, *Swann's Way*, in *Remembrance of Things Past*, vol. 1, C. K. Scott Moncrieff and Terence Kilmartin, trs. (New York: Random House, 1981), p. 93.

3. André Green, *Narcissisme de vie, narcissisme de mort*.

4. Julia Kristeva, *Black Sun: Depression and Melancholia*, Léon S. Roudiez, tr. (New York: Columbia University Press, 1989).

5. A more detailed interpretation of this analysis can be found in the first chapter of the present book.

3. The Obsessional Neurotic and His Mother

1. See Julia Kristeva, "L'impossibilité de perdre," *Cahiers de l'IPPC*, Université de Paris VII, no. 8 (November 1988): 29–40.

2. The references come from research reported during the Psychopathology and Semiology Seminar (Université de Paris VI and Paris VII) on Obsessional Neurosis, which was directed by D. Widlöcher, P. Fédida, and J. Kristeva in 1987–88.

3. John R. Anderson, *Language, Memory, and Thought* (New York: Wiley, 1976).

4. See also Daniel Widlöcher, *Métapsychologie du sens* (Paris: Presses Universitaires Françaises, 1986).

5. Trans. note: The abbreviation RM ("Rat Man") indicates "Notes upon a Case of Obsessional Neurosis," in *Standard Edition*, vol. 10.

6. See also Pierre Fédida, *Corps du vide et espace de séance* (Paris: Editions universitaires, 1977).

7. Trans. note: The French edition of this record, which is more complete than the English one, is entitled "L'homme aux rats," *Journal d'une analyse* (Paris: Presses Universitaires Françaises, 1974). The author quotes the information given

on page 27 of this text. The English version of this record ("Original Record of the Case") is included as an addendum to the published version in volume X of the *Standard Edition.* I shall refer to this original record as OR.

8. *Journal d'une analyse,* p. 231.

9. *Journal d'une analyse,* note 505.

10. Trans. note: the *Standard Edition* gives "whole series of ideas."

11. André Green, "La mére morte" in *Narcissisme de vie, narcissisme de mort,* pp. 222–54.

12. See Julia Kristeva, *Black Sun: Depression and Melancholia,* Léon S. Roudiez, tr. (New York: Columbia University Press, 1989).

4. Countertransference: A Revived Hysteria

1. Pierre Janet, *The Mental State of Hystericals,* Caroline Rollin Corson, tr. (Washington D.C.: University Publications of America: 1977), p. 486.

2. See "Observations on Transference-Love" (1915), in *Standard Edition.* 12:157–172.

3. Aldo Carotenuto, *A Secret Symmetry: Sabina Spielrein Between Jung and Freud,* Arno Pomerans, tr. (New York: Pantheon Books, 1982).

4. Carotenuto, *A Secret Symmetry,* p. 190.

5. Carotenuto, *A Secret Symmetry,* p. 120. Letter from Freud to Spielrein, August 28, 1913.

6. Pierre Janet, *The Mental State of Hystericals,* p. 486.

7. See Jean-François Allilaire, "Modélisation des mécanismes psychopathologiques de l'anxiété: Mode d'action des thérapeutiques." Paper presented at the DRAPS Seminar at the Université de Paris VI–VII, 1991.

8. "Hysterics suffer mainly from reminiscences." Sigmund Freud, *Studies on Hysteria* (1893–1895), in *Standard Edition* 2:7.

9. See the final pages of the present chapter.

10. See Sigmund Freud, "On the Psychical Mechanism of Hysterical Phenomenon: Preliminary Communication," *Studies on Hysteria,* in *Standard Edition* 2:1–18.

11. See Sigmund Freud and Josef Breuer, *Studies on Hysteria* (1893–95) as well as Sigmund Freud, *Fragments of an Analysis of a Case of Hysteria* (1905). To trace the shift from "trauma" to "fantasy," see Sigmund Freud, *Five Lectures on Psychoanalysis* (1909) and *On the History of the Psychoanalytic Movement* (1914).

12. See Sigmund Freud, *The Ego and the Id* (1923), *An Outline of Psychoanalysis* (1928), and *Analysis Terminable and Interminable* (1937).

13. See "Observations on Transference-Love" (1915), in *Standard Edition* 12:157–72.

14. "On Countertransference," *International Journal of Psychoanalysis* 32 (1951): 26.

15. M. A. Silberman, "Countertransference and the Myth of the Perfectly Analyzed Analyst," *The Psychoanalytic Quarterly* 4 (1985): 175–97. See also "Countertransference in Theory and Practice: A Panel at the Annual Meeting of the American Psychoanalytic Association," *Journal of the American Psychoanalytic Association* 34, no. 3 (1986): 699–708.

16. Paula Heimann, "On Countertransference," *The International Journal of Psychoanalysis* 31, no. 1–2 (1950): 81–84; "Further Observations of the Analyst's Cognitive Process," *Journal of the American Psychoanalytic Association* 25 (1977): 313–33.

17. Jacques Lacan, *Séminaire sur le transfert* (Paris: Editions du Seuil, 1991), p. 227. Trans. note: The author has slightly altered the original wording of Lacan's text, which reads: "C'est seulement si l'analyste ne comprend pas, qu'il est affecté et qu'il se produit une déviation du contre-transfert normal."

18. Lacan, *Séminaire,* p. 230.

19. Lacan, *Séminaire,* p. 221.

20. Jacob A. Arlow, "Some Technical Problems of Countertransference," *The Psychoanalytic Quarterly* 54, no. 2 (1985): 164–174.

21. Arlow, p. 167.

5. Symbolic Castration: A Question

1. That is how some linguists of yesteryear expressed it, linguists that still remain among the most reflective of them all. See Damourette and Pichon, *Des mots à la pensée,* 4:1383.

2. Trans. note: The term *retranchment* refers here to Lacan's original translation of the German term for *forclusion* or repudiation.

3. Julia Kristeva, *Black Sun: Depression and Melancholia,* Léon S. Roudiez, tr. (New York: Columbia University Press, 1989).

4. I have presented parts of this analysis in another setting, at the Conference on Affect and Thought sponsored by the Université de Paris VII on November 24, 1989.

5. Sigmund Freud, *An Outline of Psychoanalysis* (1938), *Standard Edition,* 23:177.

6. Julia Kristeva, *Revolution in Poetic Language,* Margaret Waller, tr. (New York: Columbia University Press, 1984).

6. The Inexpressible Child

1. Sigmund Freud, "The Ego and the Id," in *Standard Edition* 19:31.

2. See the first part of Julia Kristeva, *Revolution in Poetic Language,* Margaret Waller, tr. (New York: Columbia University Press, 1984).

3. See the first two chapters of Julia Kristeva, *Black Sun: Depression and Melancholia,* Leon S. Roudiez, tr. (New York: Columbia University Press, 1989).

7. Reading the Bible

1. Jacob Neusner, *The Idea of Purity in Ancient Judaism* (Leiden: E. J. Brill, 1973).

2. See Mary Douglas, *Purity and Danger: An Analysis of Concepts of Pollution and Taboo* (London: Routledge and Kegan Paul, 1978).

3. J. Soler, "Sémiotique de la nourriture dans la Bible," *Annales* (July/August 1973): 93.

4. E. M. Zuesse, "Taboo and the Divine Order," *Journal of the American Academy of Religion* 42, no. 3 (1974): 482–501.

5. Julia Kristeva, *Powers of Horror: Essay on Abjection*, Léon S. Roudiez, tr. (New York: Columbia University Press, 1982).

6. Sigmund Freud, *The Ego and the Id*, in *Standard Edition* 19:31.

8. From Signs to the Subject

1. See Raymond E. Brown, *The Community of the Beloved Disciple* (New York: Paulist Press, 1979). Xavier Léon-Dufour has made an excellent study of recent work on the Gospel According to St. John in his "L'Évangile de Jean," *Bulletin d'exégèse du Nouveau Testament in Recherche des sciences religieuses* 2 (April/June 1985): 245–80.

2. *Sphragiô*, denominative verb; *sphragis*, seal. The etymology of these words is unclear. Some authors have detected shades of meaning like "to shatter," "to puncture," "to break," (the seal thus shatters the clay or the polish when one affixes it), or rather "to heat" and "to sizzle." As a noun, this term may imply a "crack" or a "fissure." The semantic field of this term would thus encompass violence, break-ins, and a sort of formation through deformation, all of which suggest the theme of "passion." All the same, "since the usage of the seal was pre-Hellenic in the Aegean world," one cannot exclude that it may be a borrowed term. See Pierre Chantraine, *Dictionnaire étymologique de la langue grecque* (Paris: Klincksieck, 1980).

The Latin version gives *"signavit"* for this sentence taken from the Gospel According to St. John, and opts for the value of "meaning" in "to seal," thereby disregarding its other possible meanings.

Gregory of Nazianzus used this same term in the sense of "baptism." One might compare this to Paul, "[. . .] and having believed in him, were sealed with the promised Holy Spirit." (Eph. 1:13). Trans. note: The French gives *marked* for *sealed*.

The *Thesaurus Graecae Linguae* indicates that *sphragis* has been used to designate the circumcision of the Jews as a sign of a pact with the God of Abraham.

3. Note the *spatial* character of John's revelation: Jesus *"proceeds and comes forth from God," "comes down from heaven," "comes into the world,"* and *"departs out of this world to the Father."* See Virgilio Pasquetto, *Incarnazione e Communione con Dio* (Rome: Edizioni del Teresianum, 1982). Cited in Léon-Dufour, "L'Évangile

de Jean," p. 257. Absolute signification is presented as a spatial process, an unfolding path whose limits and mode of transport must be defined.

9. The Adolescent Novel

1. Segal, "Notes on Symbol Formation," *International Journal of Psychoanalysis* 37, no. 6 (1957).

2. See Julia Kristeva, *Le Texte du roman* (The Hague: Mouton, 1970).

3. See Jean Rousset, *L'Intérieur et l'Extérieur, essai sur la poésie et sur le théâtre au XVIIè siècle* (Paris: José Corti, 1968).

4. The following remarks were inspired to some degree by the doctoral dissertation of Sylvie Lougarre-Bonniau, "Sexe, genre, et filiation: étude sur le roman et le théâtre au XVIIIè siècle," Université de Paris VII, 1985.

5. Jean-Jacques Rousseau, *Emile; or, On Education,* Allan Bloom, tr. (New York: Basic Books, 1979), p. 211.

6. Rousseau, *Emile,* p. 393.

7. Rousseau, *Emile,* p. 212.

8. Fyodor Dostoevsky, *The Adolescent,* Andrew R. MacAndrew, tr. (New York: Doubleday, 1971), p. 91.

9. Dostoevsky, *The Adolescent,* p. 93.

10. "Dostoevsky and Parricide" (1928), in *Standard Edition* 21:173–194. See also Philippe Sollers' discussion of Freud's thesis in his "Dostoevsky, Freud et la roulette," in *Théories des exceptions* (Paris: Gallimard, 1986), pp. 57–74.

11. Witold Gombrowicz, *Journal 1953–1956* (Paris: Bourgois, 1981), p. 171.

12. Gombrowicz, *Journal,* p. 259.

13. Gombrowicz, *Journal,* p. 260.

14. See the opening chapter of Julia Kristeva, *Revolution in Poetic Language,* Margaret Waller, tr. (New York: Columbia University Press, 1984).

10. The Wheel of Smiles

1. In his study on Leonardo da Vinci, Freud quotes the artist's *Notebooks:* "It seems I was always destined to be so deeply concerned with vultures; for I recall as one of my very earliest memories that while I was in my cradle a vulture came down to me and opened my mouth with its tail, and struck me many times with its tail against my lips." Cited in "Leonardo da Vinci and a Memory of His Childhood" (1910), in *Standard Edition* 13:82. Freud perceived the form of this vulture within the drapes of the Virgin, who leans toward the Child. He analyzed what he believed to be less a memory than a fantasy, in an effort to account for Leonardo da Vinci's childhood relationship with his mother as well as his subsequent homosexuality.

11. Glory, Grief, and Writing

1. *A Treatise on the Influence of the Passions Upon the Happiness of Individuals and of Nations* (London, 1798), p. 72.

2. *Influence of Passions*, p. 45. Trans. note: Some translations of Mme de Staël's works have been slightly modified in the name of clarity and accuracy.

3. *Influence of Passions*, p. 45.

4. *Influence of Passions*, p. 46.

5. *Influence of Passions*, p. 48.

6. *Influence of Passions*, p. 50.

7. *Influence of Passions*, p. 51–52.

8. *Influence of Passions*, p. 56.

9. *Influence of Passions*, p. 57.

10. *Influence of Passions*, p. 66.

11. "Réflexions sur le procès de la Reine," in *Oeuvres complètes de Mme La Baronne de Staël* (Strasbourg, 1820), 2:27.

12. "Réflexions," 2:33.

13. "Quelques réflexions sur le but moral de Delphine, in *Oeuvres complètes*, 5:10–12.

14. "Quelques réflexions," p. 14.

15. *Corinne, ou de l'Italie*, chapter 5.

16. *The Influence of Literature Upon Society* (Hartford: S. Andrus, 1845), p. 11.

17. *Influence of Literature Upon Society*, p. 54.

18. *Influence of Literature Upon Society*, p. 90–91. Italics mine.

19. *Influence of Literature Upon Society*, p. 80.

20. *Influence of Literature Upon Society*, p. 98.

12. Joyce "The Gracehoper" or Orpheus' Return

1. See Robert Boyle, S. J., *James Joyce's Pauline Vision: A Catholic Exposition* (Carbondale: Southern Illinois University Press, 1978); and J. L. Houdebine, "Joyce, littérature et religion," *Excès de langage* (Paris: Denoël, 1984), pp. 211–50.

2. See Anders Nygren, *Agape and Eros*, Philip S. Water, tr. (Chicago: University of Chicago Press, 1982); as well as the analytic interpretation of this distinction offered in my *Tales of Love*, Léon S. Roudiez, tr. (New York: Columbia University Press, 1983).

3. *Ornicar?* 7 (1976): 3–18; and *Ornicar?* 9 (1977): 32–40.

4. Joyce's letters allude to this, but we have not found Nora's. See Brenda Maddox, *Nora: The Real Life of Molly Bloom* (Boston: Houghton Mifflin, 1988).

5. ". . . a man capable of writing a woman this well from the inside out upsets the annals of psychology." Philippe Sollers, "La Voix de Joyce," in *Théorie des exceptions* (Paris: Folio Essais, 1986), p. 103.

6. Pietro Redondi, *Galileo Eretico*, Raymond Rosenthal, tr. (Princeton, N.J.: Princeton University Press, 1987).

7. James Joyce, *Ulysses* (London: Penguin, 1983), p. 27.

8. *Ulysses*, p. 43–44.

9. *Ulysses*, p. 207.

10. *Ulysses*, p. 188–189.

11. *Ulysses*, p. 517.

12. *Ulysses*, p. 273.

13. *Ulysses*, p. 331–332.

14. *Ulysses*, p. 244.

15. Richard Ellmann, *James Joyce* (New York: Oxford University Press 1982), p. 437.

13. The Secrets of an Analyst: On Helene Deutsch's Autobiography

1. Helene Deutsch, *Confrontations with Myself: An Epilogue* (New York: Norton, 1973).

2. *Confrontations*, p. 30.

3. *Confrontations*, p. 131.

4. "The Impostor: Contribution to Ego Psychology of a Type of Psychopath," *Neuroses and Character Types: Clinical Psychoanalytic Studies* (New York: International Universities Press, 1965), p. 326.

5. *Neuroses and Character Types*, p. 337.

6. *Psychology of Women* (2 vols.; Philadelphia: Saunders, 1945), p. 249. Italics mine.

7. *Psychology of Women*, p. 201.

8. "Some Forms of Emotional Disturbance and Their Relationship to Schizophrenia," *Neuroses and Character Types*, p. 265.

9. *Neuroses and Character Types*, pp. 277–78.

10. D. W. Winnicott, "Distortion of the Ego as a Function of the True and False Self," *The Maturational Processes and the Facilitating Environment* (London: Hogarth Press, 1965). Helene Deutsch's ideas can be linked to Heinz Hartmann's, whose theory of the Ego defines the Self as a magnet of narcissistic investment. See Heinz Hartmann, "Comments on the Psychoanalytic Theory of the Ego," *Essays on Ego Psychology* (1964).

11. "Frigidity in Women," *Neuroses and Character Types*, p. 361.

12. *Confrontations*, p. 216.

13. See chapter 9, "The Adolescent Novel."

14. Women's Time

1. See *The Freud/Jung Letters*, Ralph Manheim and R. F. C. Hull, tr. (Princeton, N.J.: Princeton University Press, 1974).

2. See René Spitz, *The First Year of Life: A Psychoanalytic Study of Normal and*

Deviant Development of Object Relations (New York: International Universities Press, 1966); D. W. Winnicott, *Playing and Reality* (New York: Basic Books, 1971); Julia Kristeva, "Place Names," *Desire in Language: A Semiotic Approach to Literature and Art,* Thomas Gora, Alice Jardine, Léon S. Roudiez, tr. (New York: Columbia University Press, 1980), pp. 271–95.

3. See Plato, *Timaeus,* Francis M. Cornford, tr. (New York: Harcourt, Brace 1937): "Space, which is everlasting, not admitting destruction; providing a situation for all things that come into being but itself apprehended without the senses by a sort of bastard reasoning, and hardly an object of belief. This, indeed, is that which we look upon as in a dream and say that anything that is must needs be in some place and occupy some room" (52a–52b). See my remarks on the chora in *Revolution in Poetic Language,* Margaret Waller, tr. (New York: Columbia University Press, 1984).

4. See Julia Kristeva, "Stabat Mater," in *Tales of Love,* Léon S. Roudiez, tr. (New York: Columbia University Press, 1983).

5. See H. C. Puech, *La Gnose et le temps* (Paris: Gallimard, 1977).

6. See D. Desanti, "L'autre sexe des bolcheviks," *Tel Quel* 76 (1978); and Julia Kristeva, *On Chinese Women,* Anita Barrows, tr. (London: Marion Boyars, 1977).

7. See Arthur Hertzberg, *The French Enlightenment and the Jews* (New York: Columbia University Press, 1968); and *Les Juifs et la révolution française,* B. Blumenkranz and A. Soboul, ed. (Paris: Editions Privat, 1976).

8. From time to time, this work is published in various academic women's journals, one of the most prestigious being *Signs: Journal of Women in Culture and Society,* University of Chicago Press. Also of note are the special issue of the *Revue des sciences humaines* 4 (1977) entitled "Écriture, féminité, féminisme" and "Les femmes et la philosophie" in *Le Doctrinal de sapience* 3 (1977).

9. See the various linguistic studies on "female language," such as Robin Lakoff, *Language and Women's Place* (New York: Harper & Row, 1974); Mary R. Key, *Male/Female Language* (Metuchen, N.J.: Scarecrow Press, 1973); and A. M. Houdebine, "Les femmes et la langue," *Tel Quel* 74 (1977): 84–95.

10. See Julia Kristeva, *About Chinese Women.*

11. See M. A. Macciocchi, *Éléments pour une analyse du fascisme* (Paris: 10/18, 1976); Michèle Mattelart, "Le coup d'état au féminin," *Les Temps modernes* (January 1975).

12. The principles of a "sacrificial anthropology" have been laid out by René Girard in *Violence and the Sacred,* Patrick Gregory, tr. (Baltimore: Johns Hopkins University Press, 1977); and especially in *Things Hidden Since the Foundation of the World,* Stephen Bann and Michael Metteer, tr. (Palo Alto: Stanford University Press, 1987).

13. See Micheline Enriquez, "Fantasmes paranoïaques: différences de sexes, homosexualité, loi du père," *Topiques* 13 (1974).

14. See Claude Lévi-Strauss et al., *L'Identité: séminaire interdisciplinaire* (Paris: Grasset & Fasquelle, 1977).

INDEX OF SELECTED CONCEPTS

Index of Selected Concepts

Index of Selected Concepts

Designer: Teresa Bonner
Text: Monticello
Compositor: Maple-Vail Book Manufacturing Group
Printer: Maple-Vail Book Manufacturing Group
Binder: Maple-Vail Book Manufacturing Group